Freud Revisited

Also by Roger Horrocks

AN INTRODUCTION TO THE STUDY OF SEXUALITY

MALE MYTHS AND ICONS

MASCULINITY IN CRISIS

Freud Revisited

Psychoanalytic Themes in the Postmodern Age

Roger Horrocks
Psychotherapist

Consultant Editor: Jo Campling

palgrave

First published 2001 by
PALGRAVE
Houndmills, Basingstoke, Hampshire RG21 6XS and
175 Fifth Avenue, New York, N. Y. 10010
Companies and representatives throughout the world

PALGRAVE is the new global academic imprint of St. Martin's Press LLC Scholarly and Reference Division and Palgrave Publishers Ltd (formerly Macmillan Press Ltd).

ISBN 0–333–74647–3

This book is printed on paper suitable for recycling and made from fully managed and sustained forest sources.

A catalogue record for this book is available from the British Library.

Library of Congress Cataloging-in-Publication Data
Horrocks, Roger, 1946–
Freud revisited : psychoanalytic themes in the postmodern age / Roger Horrocks.
p. cm.
Includes bibliographical references and index.
ISBN 0–333–74647–3 (alk. paper)
1. Psychoanalysis. 2. Freud, Sigmund, 1856–1939. I. Title.
BF173 .H7635 2000
150.19'52'092—dc21

00–033350

10 9 8 7 6 5 4 3 2 1
10 09 08 07 06 05 04 03 02 01

Printed and bound in Great Britain by
Antony Rowe Ltd, Chippenham, Wiltshire

In memory of my mother,
Margaret Horrocks,
1925–96

Contents

Acknowledgements

Many thanks go to Jo Campling who helped me formulate the plan of this book in the first place and helped me throughout. Thanks also go to my editor Annabelle Buckley and her successor Karen Brazier. I am very grateful to the assessor who gave me many useful comments and suggestions.

One never writes a book like this in isolation: I am indebted to a number of friends, colleagues and clients who have given me many ideas, insights, images – in short, inspiration – while I was writing it. Particular thanks to go Victoria Zinovieff, Alan Danks, Sybilla Madigan and Simon Jackson.

Thanks and love to Rachel Floater.

Roger Horrocks

1
Introduction

Freud revolutionized modern thought with his conception and development of depth psychology. The word 'depth' is critical here, for Freud postulated a fundamental incoherence in the human being, a division between the surface and what lies underneath – the unconscious.

The notion of the unconscious is perhaps one of the most important concepts of the modern age, for it introduces into the human self-image a fundamental gap, or what Lacan calls a 'heteronomy'.[1] Just as Darwin shattered human complacency through the historicization of the human being itself – found to have an origin in animal evolution, not in heaven – so Freud shattered any idea that human beings are homogeneous and rational. Whereas Christianity had conceived of a fundamental flaw introduced into humanity through the fall from grace, Freud showed us a fundamental split at the heart of the individual that is derived from our conception of ourselves as selves. That is, the fundamental conflict between ego and id – between the conscious and the unconscious, between the repressing force and the repressed – is said to lie at the heart of being a human self. We can no more remove this conflict than we can, in the Christian ethic, will our own state of grace. What we can do, however, in the Freudian schema, is to become more aware of our inner conflicts.

But this is only the beginning. The unconscious is the apex of Freud's achievements: underneath it lies an Everest of discoveries, postulates, theoretical schemes, empirical observations. Furthermore, Freud carried on reworking his ideas until his death. This partly makes his work difficult to summarize, since it never ceased to evolve – but also gives it an intellectual density that is unique.

I have not written this book as a technical introduction to psychoanalysis, nor as a popularized account of Freud's ideas. In fact, I feel that such books, which dutifully present us with the Oedipus complex, the unconscious, dream interpretation, and so on, give a rather one-dimensional picture of Freud. He was a remarkably fertile thinker and writer, who developed some ideas at length, but left others in a rather undeveloped state. For example, Freud points out that the unconscious seems to be a timeless zone of the psyche, but he does not elaborate on this fascinating idea, which seems to have many reverberations and connections with his ideas about time, memory and repetition.[2] There are many such contributions in Freud's writings, and it is often striking how later developments in psychoanalysis and psychotherapy were anticipated by him. In this book, I have tried to provide a representative overview of some of these topics.

Freud also invented psychoanalysis as a practical form of psychotherapy. This has massive importance, for Freud's theoretical work – impressive as it is in its own right – fuels the ongoing development of techniques used in the treatment of patients. In other words, Freud was a practical researcher. He did not have his head in the clouds, but was constantly immersed in the concrete work with people's psyches. His theories about dreams are used in dream interpretation; the postulate of the Oedipus complex becomes of vital importance in the analysis of neuroses; the notion of infantile sexuality is linked to the essentially determinist approach of psychoanalysis: that the past is repeated in the present, even if in a garbled form. To put it more dramatically: those who do not remember the past are compelled to repeat it. Consequently, the only way out of this trap is to 'remember', that is, to trace one's present feelings and actions to their infantile roots.

It is fashionable to cite Freud's intellectual ancestry. Other figures had discussed the unconscious, infantile sexuality, Oedipal jealousy, and so on.[3] But this is a trivial observation, surely there is no researcher in any field who does not stand on the shoulders of many others. But Freud was a brilliant synthesizer: he brought together ideas from disparate fields, such as neurology, hypnosis, cathartic therapy, sexology, psychiatry, and amalgamated them into a theoretically coherent whole. But there was a fundamental restlessness about the man – he continually worked over his ideas, changed them, recast them, introduced completely new theoretical concepts. Thus in the posthumously published *Outline of Psycho-analysis*, written at the age of 82, we find Freud calmly discussing the 'splitting of the ego', found not only in fetishism, but in many other psychological mechanisms.[4] This concept is generally associated with later analysts such as Melanie Klein, but it is characteristic of Freud that he was able, shortly before his death, to introduce radical new ideas.

It would be negligent to carry out a kind of empiricist review of Freud – that is, merely listing his ideas or carrying out a taxonomy of them – for Freud was an anti-empiricist, who spurned the superficial and the apparent, and strove to penetrate to the murky depths, where a deeper reality and truth might lie. Freud said that we are 'lived by unknown and uncontrollable forces',[5] and this is a deeply shocking idea, which conflicts with all notions of human will, dignity and rationality. Freud dethroned reason and showed us the irrational depths that lie within us all, and yet, curiously, provided a kind of road to freedom. If I can borrow Marx's dictum 'Freedom is the recognition of necessity', it can be applied to the Freudian project of the integration of the unknown into the known, for the 'unknown' – by which I mean the unconscious – is an objective fact (a kind of 'necessity') that must be recognized as such if we are to achieve inner stability and a relative freedom. This is a paradoxical project, for one can never become free from the psyche itself, just as one cannot become free from the body. Similarly, we cannot become free from inner conflicts, but we can achieve a certain freedom in the acceptance of them.

Modernism and postmodernism

Freud is one of a handful of thinkers whose ideas dominated the twentieth century. Darwin, Marx, Einstein – one characteristic of these figures is that their ideas have not only been important in their own disciplines, but have spread far and wide, both among the intelligentsia and among the population at large.

One example of this in relation to Freud can be found in Hollywood, which for a period in the 1940s and 1950s produced many films which referred to psychoanalysis, and some which have it as their central theme – Hitchcock's *Spellbound*, for example. Similarly, certain psychoanalytic ideas, albeit in a popularized or vulgarized form, have become common currency – for example, the 'Freudian slip'.

But these are rather superficial manifestations of Freud's influence: it is possible to argue that Freudianism has been an important part of both modernity and modernism. By this I mean that psychoanalysis represents a culmination of the Enlightenment ideals of rationality and progress; yet at the same time, Freud's ideas are part of the twentieth-century modernist movement which began to break up the stable forms found in art, music, literature, and so on. Freud presents us with a fragmented picture of the individual, divided into warring factions – ego, id and super-ego – and this image seems commensurate with those artistic movements such as Cubism which also broke up traditional stable forms into disparate images.

One can also point to an interesting relationship between psychoanalytic ideas and postmodernism – that while postmodern critics have tended to attack psychoanalysis as a 'grand narrative' which in the guise of liberating the individual produced yet another form of coercion, at the same time there seem to be connections between depth psychology and certain postmodern ideas. For example, Freud invents the psychoanalytic space in which two people have a dialogue – in a sense, Freud invents a discursive space, and later analysts such as Lacan, who have been influential in the postmodern movement, have argued that psychoanalysis is a thoroughly linguistic event. There is also a sense of fragmentation and dissimulation in Freud's model of the psyche which seems sympathetic to postmodernism: the hypothesis of the unconscious suggests that we can never be sure about our motives. Freud also lays stress on the irrational and fantastic nature of our mental life: and this seems to match the postmodern emphasis on the representation of things rather than things themselves.

Also relevant here is the way in which psychoanalytic ideas have fertilized many other disciplines, such as literary criticism, film criticism, feminism, anthropology, and so on. In this book I have therefore attempted to map out some of the interesting ways in which Freud's thought represents a climax in modernity; is also part of the modernist movement; and can be said to anticipate certain postmodern ideas whilst at the same time falling foul of a fundamental postmodern critique.

Against Freud

The 1980s and 1990s have seen another, more complex testament to Freud's influence. A number of journalists, writers and academics have launched a series of fierce assaults on Freud, in terms of both his personal morality and his scientific credentials.[6] They have argued that his ideas are a *pot pourri* of unverifiable fantasies, and that Freud himself manipulated his patients and colleagues shamelessly and corruptly. However, this extensive spate of 'Freud-bashing' is a kind of ironic testament to his enduring influence, for who would bother to make such ferocious attacks on a figure who was unimportant or to whom we felt indifferent? None the less, these attacks have sharpened the debates over the value of psychotherapy and Freud's own contribution, and I certainly do not intend to idealize Freud's work in this book.

I frequently find myself disagreeing with Freud's conclusions, but also find that the routes he took to get there – the tools he used – are very productive. In fact, the psychoanalytic method offers one of the most complex, dialectical and sophisticated means of analysis and interpretation available in Western knowledge. Its only rival is Marxism, with which it bears some surprising similarities, for example, a stress on contradictions making up wholes.

There is also an excitement in discovering Freud – for example, I remember the first time I read his statement that criminals do not feel guilt because they are criminal, but become criminal because they already feel guilty.[7] With such ideas, Freud took commonplace associations, turned them upside down, or showed how if one thing is true, this does not prevent its opposite being true also. In this sense, Freud overturned many liberal and Christian shibboleths. There is almost a kind of rage in him towards such 'ethical' systems – see, for example, his discussion of the Christian commandment 'Love thy neighbour', which he describes with characteristic irony as: 'a commandment which is really justified by the fact that nothing else runs so strongly counter to the original nature of man'.[8]

It would be difficult to arrive at an overall estimate of Freud's influence in the twentieth century simply from a perusal of his writings, the growth of psychoanalysis, its influence on other disciplines, important as these factors are. For what is left out of this account is the prophet-like status which Freud acquired. In other words, Freud has become a kind of mythical figure. What does this mean? That he has become one of those figures who acquire a transpersonal significance for us, seen as imparting truths that are beyond the ordinary and conventional. It is interesting that Jung has also become such a figure, although probably within a narrower circle. But Freud is known very widely, and Freud's ideas, albeit in a popularized form, have been disseminated in all kinds of areas – they have influenced painting, cinema, literature and other cultural forms.

I think this partly explains the great hostility to Freud that is found amongst some writers, academics and others. For such mythical figures tend to arouse adulation and obloquy in equal amounts. If some want to put Freud on a pedestal or a throne, then others will strive to pull him off. The prophet is unconsciously seen as close to God, and granting to human beings certain truths which are God-given, rather as Moses brought down the tablets from the mountain.

It is, of course, extremely ironic that Freud, that most vehement of polemicists against religion, should himself be seen as a prophet or a seer. Yet the irony conceals a paradoxical truth, which Jung grasped –

that Freud's driving passion has a quasi-religious side to it, and the foundation and development of psychoanalysis have more than a passing resemblance to a religious cult. Of course, some critics have seized on these parallels and argued that they invalidate psychoanalysis.[9] I find this argument bizarre, just as the analogous argument that Marxism, which became, in some of its forms at least, another quasi-religious cult, is thereby discredited, also strikes me as illegitimate. Indeed, one might argue that there is an inherent tendency for all human groupings to move towards such semi-religious characteristics. Why this should be so is beyond the scope of this book to ponder – although I might mention that Jung discussed this phenomenon frequently.[10]

I have been a psychotherapist for twenty years, and I am sure that my debt to Freud's ideas outstrips any others. I mean this in a practical sense – I value Freud above all as a practical thinker, whose ideas have an immediate impact on our understanding of people. Take, for example, Freud's ideas about guilt, which were never developed at length or in a particularly coherent manner, yet which none the less offer many brilliant insights and are of great practical value in helping people who suffer from guilt – and in Western culture, I am sure that there are many such people!

Freud describes how afraid of success many people are; how they are determined to sabotage themselves; how they may commit crimes in a desperate wish to be punished; how the progress of therapy itself can be ruined by their fear and hatred of success. These ideas provide us with a very fertile base from which contemporary theories of human guilt can be developed.[11]

Let me cite one more example: Freud's brief description of mourning, part of which, he claims, involves the incorporation of the mourned person into the self.[12] Again, this idea has spurred much research not only into mourning itself, but into the complex and rich phenomena of identification, projection, introjection, and so on. But there are many such insights in Freud, some of which he developed at length, or which he turned into core concepts at the heart of psychoanalysis; others of which seem to be peripheral issues for Freud, but which have been developed later. In this sense, I am sure there is much more that remains to be discovered in his writings.

Organization of the book

This book has four chief aims: first, to provide a brief commentary on Freud's relationship with modernity, modernism and postmodernism;

second, to examine in greater detail some of the key ideas in psychoanalysis, especially those which have been influential outside the world of psychotherapy; third, to show how psychoanalysis has been employed in a variety of other disciplines as both a descriptive and explanatory tool; and fourth, to present some of the criticisms that have been made of Freud's fundamental ideas and procedures.

Chapters 2–4 consider the intellectual background to psychoanalysis. Chapter 2 considers the relationship between Freud's work and modernism, and the interaction it has had with postmodernism. Chapter 3 considers the revolutionary implications of Freud's work for our understanding of human knowledge and how knowledge is obtained. Chapter 4 examines the central concept of the unconscious.

I have selected five key topics in Freud's work, which give some idea of the driving forces in his work. Chapters 5 and 6 look at the notions of forgetting, remembering and repeating, and the way in which psychotherapy can be seen as a form of story-telling. Chapter 7 considers the important issue of the role of the instincts as against the environment, and chapter 8 the dialectical structure of Freud's model of the psyche. Chapter 9 examines the revolutionary aspects of Freud's theory of human sexuality.

Chapters 10 and 11 examine two areas of 'applied' psychoanalysis: in chapter 10, the way in which feminism has made a rapprochement with Freud's ideas. In chapter 11, I have demonstrated briefly how analytic ideas throw light on cultural fields such as film.

Finally, chapter 12 looks at some of the revisions and criticisms that have been made of Freud's work.

2
Freud, Modernism and Postmodernism

The huge influence of Freudian thought in the twentieth century cannot simply be ascribed to Freud's technical contributions to psychoanalysis. Rather, one must take a wider perspective and consider the historical context in which Freud's ideas were being developed. In the first place, along with Marxism and Darwinism, Freudianism has represented one of the climactic movements in modernity, that is, post-Renaissance thought. This has been characterized by the development of rationality and scientific methodology, and what might be called 'objectivism': the separation of the thinking subject from the object of enquiry. T. S. Eliot, in a famous remark, refers to this as a 'dissociation of sensibility', whereby thought and feeling become split from each other.[1] This can be placed within the historical development of Cartesian thought – Descartes' separation of mind and body separates feelings from the mind, since feelings often seem to be experienced as physical sensations.[2]

There is an enormous paradox in psychoanalytic thought, since a rational system of enquiry is brought to bear on the irrational – on the impulses stemming from the unconscious, whose expression is found in dreams, neurotic symptoms and in many life-events. Thus, Freud can be said to have made sense of nonsense, or to have imposed a rational method of interpretation upon the fragmented and mutilated messages from the unconscious.

At all times, Freud claimed that psychoanalysis could be ranked as part of modern science and was annoyed that its scientific credentials should be questioned: 'I have always felt it as a gross injustice that people have refused to treat psychoanalysis like any other science.'[3] What has continued to trouble Freud's critics is the idea that one can construct a scientific description of mental events, which are not observable but must be inferred. This is clearly not 'scientific' in the sense in which the 'hard' sciences such as physics and chemistry are scientific. Perhaps Freud was unwilling to see that psychoanalysis is not 'like any other science' at all, and that if it is a science, it sets out new parameters for our understanding of science. However, at the end of the twentieth century, we find that challenges to the 'hardness' and objectivity of science were being mounted within science itself, and linear, cause-and-effect models have given ground to field theory and chaos models.[4] In this sense, psychoanalysis does not seem as anomalous as formerly.

Second, Freud's ideas contributed to 'modernism', that is, the movement from the late nineteenth to the early twentieth centuries which involved an artistic and philosophical revolution. This movement was characterized by a tremendous restlessness, a fragmentation of traditional forms, a favouring of the irrational and the subjective. Some of the tendencies in modern art – particularly Surrealism – were directly influenced by Freud but many movements were haunted by what Peter Nicholls, in his book *Modernisms*, describes as 'a deeper recognition of some fissure in the self which Freud would later formulate in terms of the conscious and unconscious'.[5]

Third, the movement known as 'postmodernism' has certain features which can be found in Freud – for example, the 'deconstruction' of the stable human subject and the dethroning of rationality. At the same time, many postmodern thinkers have criticized psychoanalysis for its tendency to globalization – Freud employed a number of transhistorical categories such as the Oedipus complex. There is also the criticism that psychoanalysis is too rationalistic, too influenced by the medical model of the human being, and that ultimately it does not lead to personal liberation, but only to a further kind of imprisonment within the psychoanalytic 'power-trip'. In a discussion of Freud and Marx, the literary critic Patricia Waugh argues that:

> The focus of much postmodern writing has been to dismantle the basic assumptions of their writing to lay bare an epistemology and methodology which, it is argued, is at one with an oppressive and authoritarian rationalism which has produced terror in place of emancipation and disguised its will to power as a disinterested 'scientific' desire for truth.[6]

Clearly, the position of the Freudian project in the history of ideas in the West is a complex and controversial one. In this chapter I would like to highlight some of the key philosophical tendencies in psychoanalysis which seem to link it with, and at times separate it from, modernity, modernism and postmodernism.

Freud and modern thought

1. Against theism

First, one must allude to the 'modern' abandonment of theistic assumptions and the placing of the human being at the centre of enquiry. For the last 500 years, there has been a gradual – and sometimes not so gradual – erosion of religious ideas and an acceptance that we live in a materialist universe and that human beings are as much a part of that universe as stars, rocks, trees or other animals. Freud himself cited the figures of Copernicus and Darwin as intellectual giants with whom he would like to be compared.[7] The choice is significant: Copernicus demolished the view that the earth was the centre of the universe; and Darwin argued that human beings are part of a continually developing evolutionary chain. In other words, as against the claims of many religions, there is nothing special about human beings within the whole context of matter and life. One does not need the hypothesis of God to explain our existence.

Freud argues that these scientific discoveries produced shattering blows to 'human megalomania', and that psychoanalysis can be ranked with them, since it 'seeks to prove to the ego that it is not even master in its own house'.[8]

Freud's anti-religious views are patently clear throughout his writings, but the principles of psychoanalysis are relevant here. In Freud we find an appeal not to supernatural forces, but to human understanding, a belief in psychic determinism and the possibility of alleviating suffering without recourse to divine help. Indeed, Freud describes religion as an 'enemy', which provides false explanations of reality and offers false comforts to those who are suffering.[9]

2. Self and Other

Second, as a corollary to the abandonment of God or the 'death of God', post-Renaissance human culture has become obsessed with the self and what has been called 'self-experience'.[10] Previously in Western culture, and in most other cultures, culture had been dominated by the relationship with some kind of mystical Other, whether spirit, fetish or God. But modernity is predicated on the human self in isolation from God, and sometimes in isolation from other selves.

Psychoanalysis offers a view of the human being as containing its own demons and angels in the unconscious. All the projected contents of the psyche are withdrawn from heaven and hell: one no longer grapples with the angel of God or with the devil, but with one's own desires, fears and hatreds.

Freud's work, therefore, can be said to continue the study of the individual which was begun during and after the Renaissance by those thinkers who enquired into the nature of the self – figures such as Montaigne, Descartes and Rousseau. The analyst Masud Khan places Freud's work in a direct line of descent from them:

> If Montaigne was his own witness, Descartes his own creator, Rousseau the apostle of his own feelings, and the Romantics the exorcists of their sensibility, then Freud's genius and courage lay in becoming his own patient.[11]

Yet Khan points out that Freud's 'self-analysis' involved a very close intimacy with his friend Wilhelm Fliess, and that this relationship in many ways foreshadowed the strange intimacy of psychoanalysis itself: 'It is only with Freud that self-experience finds its true instrumentality through the other for reflective introspection and discovery.'[12]

One can suggest, then, that the modern (post-Renaissance) individual, deprived of its relationship with the mystic or transcendent other, experiences great loneliness or even anguish at its apparent isolation in the universe. Different cultural forms – for example, romantic love, art and music, the use of alcohol and recreational drugs – arise to fill this huge abyss, so that the need for the other is to some extent satisfied outside of religious experience – yet these forms perhaps also have a quasi-religious quality to them. Psychoanalysis fills the gap in another way, by bringing the self into contact with a mysterious Other – the analyst – who remains an almost anonymous figure, yet who, like the priest, promises attention and some kind of absolution.

Is this a cynical view of psychoanalysis? I would say it was not at all cynical, but places the growth of psychotherapy as a whole within an historical context in which human beings have suffered a massive loss in the decay of religion, and have had to search for compensations for that loss. If God was once my witness, now my witness is my therapist.

3. Rationality and irrationality

I have already commented on Freud's highly paradoxical attitude to rationality: on the one hand, he prides himself on demonstrating how the apparently bizarre productions of the unconscious, for example in dreams, have a sense which can be deciphered. In this, Freudianism is a highly rational theory of the mind. In particular, Freud pins his colours to the mast of strict determinism and claims that psychic events, no less than physical ones, are never due to chance. In a discussion of 'parapraxes', that is, slips of the tongue, forgetting of names and other mistakes, Freud imagines a critic who argues that these are indeed coincidental:

> What does the fellow mean by this? Is he maintaining that there are occurrences, however small, which drop out of the universal concatenation of events – occurrences which might just as well not happen as happen? If anyone makes a breach of this kind in the determinism of natural events at a single point, it means that he has thrown overboard the whole *Weltanschauung* of science.[13]

Of course, Freud also argues that the causes of parapraxes and other psychic revelations are often unconscious, as for example with many slips of the tongue, which may reveal hidden feelings of hostility, and so on.

The principle of determinism is perhaps not as controversial as the use made of it by Freud and later psychoanalysts. Here the interaction between the objective and the subjective becomes highly contentious, in that the analyst claims to be able to detect the determining factors in the patient's dreams, behaviour, symptoms, speech, and so on. Here is the crux, not just for psychoanalysis, but for psychotherapy as a whole: does the analyst/therapist have special access to the 'determinism of natural events' in relation to the psyche? Can the patient acquire a proficiency in these matters?

As against this pronounced rationalist emphasis in Freud's work, his theory of the unconscious, and his insistence that the ego is not master in its own house, give us a decidedly post-Enlightenment portrait of human beings, who are beset by 'unknown and uncontrollable forces'. It is not surprising that Freud has been criticized for being too rationalistic but also for being too irrational, since arguably he subverts reason whilst giving it a high priority.

Freud's turn to the irrational is best illustrated by his emphasis on the dream as the 'royal road to a knowledge of the activities of the unconscious mind'.[14] Western science has tended to disparage dreaming as a means of acquiring knowledge. It seemed symptomatic of more 'primitive' cultures which interpreted dreams much as they might consult the witch-doctor or looked for premonitions in chickens' entrails. Freud comments that 'to concern oneself with dreams is not merely unpractical and uncalled-for, it is positively disgraceful. It brings with it the odium of being unscientific and rouses the suspicion of a personal inclination to mysticism.'[15]

In fact, in my experience it is this area of psychotherapy which causes most concern to new patients, especially those who are strongly intellectual. With such patients, any talk of dreams, or symbols, or the unconscious itself causes suspicion and fear. Such a way of looking at human life is quite alien to them, used as they are to thinking rationally. None the less, they have often come to therapy because a split-off, irrational part of their personality is beginning to make trouble.

One might see this as a paradigm of the Western individual: trapped inside the prison of the intellect, yet beset on all sides by desires, fears, needs and hatreds which have been kept at bay during a life-time, yet which also threaten to erupt into daily life. Freud uses a very powerful metaphor to describe this process:

> These wishes in our unconscious, ever on the alert, and so to say, immortal, remind one of the legendary Titans, weighed down since primaeval ages by the massive bulk of the mountains which were once hurled upon them by the victorious gods and which are still shaken from time to time by the convulsions of their limbs.[16]

This is a rather awesome image, and conveys some of Freud's attitude to the unconscious. Yet the Titans must be encouraged to speak, or at least the communications which emanate from them must be deciphered if the individual is to find some relief from the 'convulsions' which beset him or her.

4. Subjectivity

Psychoanalysis and the psychotherapies that it has spawned are subjective methods of work. How does analysis work as a technique? Through an intense and self-reflexive relationship. How does psychotherapy ascertain what is best for a particular patient? By helping the patient to decide what he or she wants.

Freud also focuses on desire itself, on what people want, or rather what they want without knowing it. Again, this marks a shift from the principles of reason, which emphasize what we know. Thus Freudianism is part of an epistemological break from the Enlightenment landmarks of reason and knowledge, towards a metapsychology of desire and hatred, or Eros and death. To put it extremely, Freudianism argues that much philosophy is a neurotic sublimation of depression, and that the answers to the questions found in philosophy cannot be discovered philosophically, but only through the concrete examination of one's motives, wishes and prohibitions.

Freud's pessimism is expressed in his opposition between the wishes of the individual and the demands of the culture, which enforces the repression of those wishes: 'on the one hand, love comes into opposition to the interests of civilization; on the other, civilization threatens love with substantial restrictions'.[17] Psychoanalysis steps in, therefore, to help the individual, if not to enact the wishes that still lurk in the repressed unconscious, then at least to permit them conscious expression. Hence it can be linked with Romanticism in its rescue of the alienated individual from the imprisoning coils of a repressive culture.

5. Fragmentation

Freud's model of the mind is characterized by its decentring and fragmentation. The central concept of repression introduces the basic split between the repressing force and the repressed forces. Lacan was to point out the inherent incoherence which this produces: 'this ego, whose strength our theorists now define by its capacity to bear frustration, is frustration in its essence.'[18] I feel that Lacan takes a more extreme and pessimistic view of human frustration and the impossibility of fulfilment than Freud, but one cannot deny that Lacan is not turning Freud upside down, but merely drawing out some of the logical conclusions from the Freudian schema.

According to Freud, many of our most intense desires must be repressed if we are to live in a civilized culture, yet they still exist in the unconscious, from where they exert a powerful influence. Thus at the same time they are part of our identity, yet not part of it. Freud expresses this very starkly in relation to his theory of dreams: 'the dreamer *does* know what his dream means: *only he does not know that he knows it, and for that reason thinks he does not know it*' (original emphasis).[19]

This perception of deep fissures in the self can be related to developments in the whole of Western culture. For example, we see in twentieth-century painting the abandonment of figurative art and the turn to abstraction, Cubism, Surrealism, and so on. Modern painters begin to pull reality to pieces and demonstrate the subjectivity of experience, for example in the Impressionist school.

This huge shift in art has been described as follows, in relation to Cubism:

> Cubism stood out as the most revolutionary movement to appear in figurative painting since the 15th century. In fact, it broke away from all the conventions of optic realism and completely discarded 'traditional' perspective, modelling and versimilitude of light effects, not because it was indifferent to objects, but because it wanted to analyze them more closely and try to give a more total representation of them. The cubists were the first to realize fully that by choosing a single viewpoint, the Renaissance had introduced a certain order in the picture, but at the same time it had condemned itself to giving only a partial view of things, that seen by a motionless observer.[20]

Pre-Freudian psychology can be compared with 'figurative painting', in the sense that it gave an essentially empiricist view of the human being, which conveys the appearances of things. For example, Freud's crucial shift in relation to hysteria lay in his belief that the symptoms of hysterics were not simply a bizarre set of behaviours, but were meaningful and could be decoded. Freud makes a distinction between his work and that of others, such as the French psychologist Janet:

> According to Janet's view a hysterical woman was a wretched creature who, on account of a constitutional weakness, was unable to hold her mental acts together, and it was for that reason that she fell victim to a splitting of her mind, and to a restriction of the field of her consciousness. The outcome of psychoanalytic investigations, on the other hand, showed that these phenomena were the result of dynamic factors – of mental conflict and repression.[21]

Thus while Janet had seen hysteria as the outcome of a 'splitting' in the mind, this was seen as caused by non-mental factors ('a constitutional weakness'), whereas psychoanalysis proposed that the conflict was properly a psychological one, should be treated accordingly and eventually could be understood.

Going back to the remarks cited above about Cubism, the comment about the 'single viewpoint' can be compared with Freud's dismantling of the individual into various components: ego, id and superego in his 1920s formulations.[22] Each of these components has its own 'viewpoint', which is often quite antithetical to the others. As against this multiple view, the pre-Freudian view of human personality could be described as giving a 'partial view of things'.

It is clear that psychoanalysis has a very complex and paradoxical role within both modern thought and modernism. It seems simultaneously to assert and negate rationality, notions of the self, ideas of progress, and so on. Freud could be said to be one of the last great figures of post-Enlightenment rationalism, yet he also subverts any rational basis for understanding human motivation; he places great emphasis on the individual, yet also deconstructs the self into warring factions; he holds out the promise of a kind of 'remission of sins' yet also takes a rather pessimistic attitude towards therapeutic success – 'I am not a therapeutic enthusiast,' he stated in 1932. And added with characteristic irony: 'I do not think our cures can compete with those of Lourdes.'[23]

Psychoanalysis seems to be full of contradictions – along with Marxism, it is one of the last great flourishes of modern thought, yet also anticipates postmodern scepticism and the sense of disintegration and unease that characterized the twentieth century. Freud believed fervently in the scientific status of his work, yet affirmed the crucial role of subjectivity and irrationality in human self-knowledge. He believed that a partial self-knowledge could be won, but also showed how often it is illusory and fragmented. His sense of irony and absurdity seem very contemporary.

Psychoanalysis is a critical voice within modernity – it is in fact a *voice of crisis*. It articulates a fracture in human awareness – that what I think I am may turn out to be only part of the truth, or even the opposite of the truth. As against the lucid Cartesian assertion, 'I think, therefore I am', and the Romantic aphorism of Rousseau, 'I feel, therefore I am', it seems to propose a more uncertain truth: 'I dream, therefore I am not what I thought.'

Postmodernism

If the position of Freud within modernity is an ambivalent one, since he both emphasizes reason while pointing out how much of human existence is not governed by it, this seems to anticipate some postmodernist ideas. Again, Freud's ideas are Janus-faced: part of the movement towards the postmodern, whilst also falling foul of some of its judgements.

Postmodernist thought can certainly be seen as antithetical to psychoanalysis, since it offers a resistance to notions of 'truth', 'depth' or any kind of discourse being privileged. In other words, postmodernism offers us a kind of relativism – there are no absolute truths, there are no 'grand narratives', but rather a number of 'little stories':

> The mutation of culture into postmodernity spells serious trouble for traditional psychoanalytic notions, for a thorough postmodernist will

> distrust metaphors of depth. There is no self or internal experience to be recovered from the patient's past; there is no past to be taken forward for self-understanding, and there is no narrative, scientific or otherwise, that could be privileged over any other.[24]

However, psychoanalysis has also proved amenable to postmodernist deconstruction – figures such as Lacan have noted that analysis itself is a totally linguistic series of events, especially if the unconscious itself is construed as a kind of linguistic organ.[25] Psychotherapy can therefore be understood, not as a search for a mythical 'self' or 'truth', but as a set of discourses which overlap and interpenetrate, and continually refer to themselves. Psychoanalysis has the merit of being sensitive to its own discourses and their interrelations: in other words, the analyst and the patient are able in the end to ask the compelling question: 'Why are we talking about this?', and even the question: 'Who is talking?' Analysis has a meta-discursive element at its heart.

But are these ideas absolutely *post*-Freudian? I would suggest that Freud has a more sophisticated and relativist view of 'truth', 'depth', and so on, than he is sometimes given credit for. For example, Freud is very hesitant about claiming that analysis discovers a single unambiguous sense of a dream or a symptom. His use of the term 'overdetermined' – meaning that a neurotic symptom has several causative factors – can be found in his early collaborative work with Breuer in the 1890s.[26]

Granted, Freud's use of archaeological metaphors suggests that the past lies buried in the psyche, intact and awaiting discovery. But Freud's account of what 'remembering' is, and how the process of reconstruction goes on in analysis, is complex and sophisticated. For example, in his discussion of how patients fall in love with their analysts, Freud states at first that 'the outbreak of a passionate demand for love is largely the work of resistance' – in other words, the patient falls in love in order to 'hinder the continuation of the treatment'. But later in the same discussion, Freud points out that this does not mean that the patient's love is unreal: 'the resistance did not, after all, *create* this love; it finds it ready to hand, makes use of it, and aggravates its manifestations.'[27] Freud is therefore making a complex and dialectical statement here: that 'transference love' is both real and unreal, both of the present and of the past, both authentic and also a device intended to obfuscate the analysis.

Furthermore, Freud definitely does not claim that the unconscious or the id contains an absolute truth lying hidden beneath the inauthentic repressions wrought by the ego. If this were correct, then the task of therapy would be to liberate the unconscious in action! But this is never stated to be the analytic task: rather, therapist and patient set out to become more aware of the desires hidden in the unconscious, not necessarily with the aim of fulfilling them, but to restore choice to the individual. In fact, Freud talks about replacing repression with condemnation – by which he means that in the majority of cases, one will choose not to act on a desire in the id.[28] But of course, one has the choice, whereas previously repression ensured that there was none. But in terms of 'truth', one cannot simply say that the unconscious contains a kind of sublime or distilled truth, since the individual has to balance between those forces in the unconscious and the forces which exist in the culture, which are antithetical to the repressed desires. The 'truth' therefore consists of the management of conflicts in the individual.

Features of postmodernism

In the Introduction to the anthology *From Modernism to Postmodernism*, the philosopher Lawrence Cahoone argues that postmodernism is centrally interested in the representation of things rather than things themselves, or even denies that 'things' exist; that it denies the possibility of returning to the origin of something; it breaks down the unity of something into a plurality; it denies that there are transcendent norms, such as 'justice' or 'truth', removed from the social processes involved; and is interested in the margins or the peripheries of things.[29]

If psychoanalysis is examined against this background of ideas, a variegated picture emerges. Psychoanalysis also attempts to break down phenomena into opposites or fragments – so the psyche itself is broken into id, ego, superego, and the unconscious itself is seen as consisting of an aggregate of unrelated fragments. In this sense, Freud's model is a pluralist one. Freud is also concerned to take apparently transcendent categories such as love and describe them in terms of the instinctual processes going on within the individual. One might also argue that the 'representational' motif is found in psychoanalysis in Freud's assertion that fantasies about events are as important as events themselves, or even more interestingly, that in the unconscious, there is no distinction between such categories.

On the other hand, one might conclude that psychoanalysis is not postmodern in spirit, in that it does pursue origins, in the sense of tracking down the infantile events or fantasies which are being repeated in adult life; it does postulate certain primitive entities such as instincts;

it does hypothesize about universal tendencies in human motivation and behaviour; and in some of its manifestations, it seems to adopt an ethos of 'expertise' that goes distinctly against the grain of the post-modern.

In short, one can conclude that certain aspects of Freud's thought lend themselves to postmodern deconstructionism; while other aspects seem quite antithetical to it. It is striking how those contemporary disciplines which incorporate psychoanalytic insights tend to reject certain areas of Freudian psychology, while embracing others. For example, it is possible for a contemporary feminist to reject Freud's 'phallocentric' views on women and female sexuality while at the same time claiming the right to employ Freudian notions of the unconscious, repression, infantile sexuality, and so on. In such a case we can see the Janus-faced character of Freudianism vis-à-vis modernism and postmodernism. Psychoanalysis is attacked by postmodernism as one of the key 'foundational' disciplines of the twentieth century; yet analytical insights and techniques may also be used by postmodernism writers. Here the role of Lacan seems crucial, for in his emphasis on language, desire and 'lack', Lacan arguably transformed psychoanalysis from a modernist to a post-modernist discipline.

Lacan famously denies the possibility of our desires ever being fulfilled, for they are created by lack, in fact by a lack which has no possible object as its fruition.[30] If one relates this very radical notion to Freud's own thinking, one can argue that it both carries on the logic of Freud, while at the same time transforming it into a claim which Freud would himself have rejected. For Freud also speaks about the hallucinatory quality of our desires and the impossibility of satisfying them. But at the same time, he grants that some people are able to make compromises in life, which while not bringing them absolute happiness, give them a sense of well-being.[31]

This tension no doubt stems in part from the historical context in which Freud lived, straddling as he does both the great philosophical outpouring of German thought in the nineteenth century – Hegel, Marx, Nietzsche – and the disintegration of German society in the 1930s. Freud came at the end of the Enlightenment, but was sufficiently part of it to partake of its trumpeting of rationalism and its hope of human progress, while at the same time he was part of the post-Enlightenment movements which came to prize incoherence, irrationality and rejected all thoughts of progress. Freud contains both strands of thought: at times, this makes his thought seem contradictory; but at its best, the tension produces a great richness and dialectical insight.

Freud's sense of humour is relevant here, for he delighted in describing some of the absurdities of human thought – the ways in which we fool ourselves about our motives, for example – in a way which seems more relevant to postmodernism than the high seriousness of the nineteenth century. For example, Freud delighted in pointing out the contradictions to be found in the great religions, especially Christianity, which, he claimed, espoused universal love, but did not practise it:

> When once the Apostle Paul had posited universal love between men as the foundation of his Christian community, extreme intolerance on the part of Christendom towards those who remained outside it became the inevitable consequence.[32]

Postmodernism may also be of great benefit to psychoanalysis, in the sense that it can be brought out of the blinkered closet into which it had retreated – it can form part of a multiplicity of discourses concerning the human self. We can see this enlargement of psychoanalysis in writers such as Adam Phillips, Christopher Bollas and Stephen Frosch, where we find that psychoanalysis is not seen as a monolithic set of truths which stand alone, but is connected to other disciplines. In other words, there is a kind of cultural leavening and broadening out so that the suffocating atmosphere of some narrow versions of psychoanalysis is removed. One can also see this in the rapprochements that are being made between formerly hostile psychological camps: it no longer seems shocking or exceptional that Freudians should refer to Jung, and vice versa.

The turn to Freud

The 1980s and 1990s saw some remarkable shifts in opinion towards Freud. There has been a barrage of fierce attacks on him, and on psychoanalysis. Freud was called an intellectual and scientific fraud, an emotional coward, a purveyor of mumbo-jumbo dressed up in scientific clothes, and so on. This attack mainly emanated from America. But other developments have gone on in relation to the status of Freud's ideas. A number of disciplines have turned more and more to Freud as a source of fertile and innovative ideas. For example, in place of the rather crude psychobiography which often used to go on under the name of 'psychoanalytic literary criticism', a number of critics have pointed out the importance of the text in psychoanalysis, and have suggested that psychoanalysis is a 'narratology' like literary criticism. That is, analysis or therapy is very much concerned with the story told by the patient, and the therapist is concerned to help the patient tell that story, sometimes providing links where are gaps. In effect, there are several stories going on – the patient's, the therapist's, and perhaps a jointly constructed one. This transforms the relationship between psychoanalysis and criticism. Whereas formerly the analyst attempted to decode the underlying meaning of literary texts, now critics are able to point out the textual structures in analysis.[33]

Other critics have made some brilliant observations on literature using psychoanalytic ideas. For example, feminist critics have been able to indicate how the repressed nature of women and femininity in literature has some unexpected expressions. For example, in relation to Charlotte Brontë's *Jane Eyre* a number of critics have suggested that the 'madwoman in the attic' may represent the unconscious feelings of Jane Eyre herself, particular feelings of rage and sexuality. Bertha (Rochester's mad wife) appears whenever Jane has an emotional crisis – she tries to burn Rochester in his bed, her cries are often heard by Jane as she wanders through the house, finally, of course, she burns down the house and is killed.[34]

Another example of the repressed feminine finding an underground expression can be found in Jane Austen's *Emma*, in which the heroine denies her own emotional and sexual needs, and tries to organize other people's amorous affairs. Thus the novel begins as Emma is fantasizing that she arranged the marriage of her friend and governess, Mrs Weston. Then she begins to look for a suitable suitor for her protégée Harriet Smith, and begins to fantasize about other characters, such as Frank Churchill and Jane Fairfax. This projected sexuality is comical to the reader, who is aware that Emma is destined to be Mr Knightley's wife – but Emma is unaware of this, or at least denies it. Instead, her denied sexuality is projected onto others with disastrous and comic effects.

One can also point to the use of psychoanalytic ideas in film criticism – particularly with regard to the voyeuristic aspect of cinema and the role of women as 'images of castration'.[35] Feminism itself, after showing considerable hostility to Freud in the 1960s, began to find his ideas indispensable in the attempt to theorize about gender and sexuality.

One can also talk of a 'turn to Freud' within the world of psychotherapy itself. In the 1960s and 1970s the so-called 'New Therapies' began to arise in opposition to the perceived intellectuality and aridity of psychoanalysis. The cry was 'Against Freud' and there was much talk of 'emotional catharsis', turning to the neglected body, the spiritual dimension of therapy, and so on.

But the last decade has seen the reverse movement: many of these non-analytical therapies, such as gestalt, humanistic therapy, bodywork, and so on, have begun to look to psychoanalysis for certain important ideas. Many non-analytical training courses now demand considerable study by their students of Freudian and post-Freudian themes. One could argue that the anti-intellectual revolution ran out of steam, as people began to realize that one cannot simply throw Freud out of the window, since it was Freud who invented the window!

It is remarkable, therefore, that Freud's writings, which he began over a century ago, still arouse strong feelings of admiration and antipathy, and that his ideas are seen as indispensable by so many different disciplines. Some unexpected reconciliations have taken place – particularly that between feminism and psychoanalysis, and between Humanistic therapy and analysis.

Indeed, without being hagiographical, it is possible to make the claim that Freud is the most important thinker and the most important writer of the twentieth century. I have separated out these two aspects of Freud, for it strikes me that while Freud's ideas have been hugely influential, one also has to grapple with Freud the writer, who poured out a constant stream of theoretical schemata and revisions, clinical observations, cultural analyses, and so on. This written *oeuvre* was unique in the twentieth century. The only figures from the nineteenth century who are comparable in influence are Marx and Darwin, both of whose ideas also still arouse considerable passion. Freud would have been pleased and proud to be linked with Darwin, perhaps less so with Marx. Yet perhaps it is Marx who is the only comparable figure: both men invented systems of thought which have changed the way we think, and who continue to inspire some and appal others with their ideas.

3
Truth, Knowledge and Subjectivity

There is a deep paradox in Freud's attitude to psychological reality. On the one hand, he puts forward a very rationalist, positivist approach – that there is a reality 'out there', or in the patient, waiting to be uncovered by psychoanalysis. Thus he was fond of archaeological metaphors: an unconscious idea exists in the patient like buried ruins, which can be excavated and laid bare. In the case history of the 'Rat Man', Freud explains this carefully to his patient:

> I then made some short observations upon the differences between the conscious and the unconscious, and upon the fact that everything conscious was subject to a process of wearing-away, while what was unconscious was relatively unchangeable; and I illustrated my remarks by pointing to the antiques standing about in my room. They were, in fact, I said, only objects found in a tomb, and their burial was their preservation: the destruction of Pompeii was only beginning now that it had been dug up.[1]

This is a traditional view of reality as fixed and 'objective', distinct from the observing subject, and characterizes both nineteenth- and twentieth-century conceptions of scientific methodology. It gives psychoanalysis a very hard-edged character: the task is to 'dig up' those unconscious contents which are troublesome. Of course, one of the great problems with this approach is that it tends to turn the analyst or psychotherapist into something of an expert who dispenses his knowledge to the untutored patient, and this is in part the tone adopted by Freud in the 'Rat Man' case.

This approach is often distinguished from other disciplines such as literary criticism, in which the whole point is the subjective response of the critic, and where objectivity cannot be attained, and is indeed not desirable. Freud was particularly insistent on the irreproachable scientific nature of psychoanalysis, and was keen to dispel any notions that it smacked of the 'occult' or any other fringe discipline. By contrast, Jung was fascinated by disciplines such as astrology and alchemy, and wrote about topics such as Marian visions, flying saucers, and so on – all of this anathema to Freud.

But there is another methodology at work in psychoanalysis, which is quite subversive of this positivist approach. For example, Freud's rejection of the seduction hypothesis in the 1890s – the view that his patients had been sexually abused – has revolutionary implications. It was a rejection of 'naive realism': instead of there being an 'objective' historical truth which awaits discovery, truth is subjective or intra-psychic. The sexual stories told his patients told him were, he claimed, fantasies in the patient's unconscious, experienced as very real and confused with external reality.[2] Incidentally, Freud is not suggesting – *contra* Jeffrey Masson – that his patients were 'lying'.[3] That would be to confuse a conscious act of suppression (lying) with an unconscious fantasy.

This turn inwards continues to shock many critics of psychoanalysis, for it seems to fly in the face of the empiricist view that neurosis or psychosis are caused by external 'traumatic incidents' in a person's life. Freud suggested instead that the roots of neurosis lay in part in the internecine conflicts in the patients' psyches, which often paralyse them: 'neurosis is the result of a conflict between the ego and the id.' Of course, matters are more complicated than that – the ego sides with the super-ego, and ultimately with those influences in the external world which are hostile to the 'instinctual impulses' in the unconscious.[4]

Neurotic conflicts therefore point us in two directions: they have intimate connections with events in the past, from whence most people have probably derived some influences hostile to their own instinctual desires, and the 'reconstruction' of the past is of great importance in psychotherapy. At the same time, it is vital that the structure of the inner world is elaborated, for although this has a connection with the past, it remains an autonomous world. To put it rather crudely, people who have been abused invariably abuse themselves, since the abuse is now internalized. They also tend to seek out people who will abuse them, in a desperate repetition of the past – yet this repetition may provide a turning point, since it enables us to reconstruct both the past and the inner world. But the recall of past abuse does *not* of itself prevent the present self-abuse.

In fact, it is quite likely that Freud went too far away from an environmental view of neurosis and began to suggest that psychic conflicts were entirely self-determined. For example, in the case of Dora, he seems to suggest that Dora is simply paralysed by an internal block on her sexual desire:

> The behaviour of this child of fourteen was already entirely and completely hysterical. I should without question consider a person hysterical in whom an occasion for sexual excitement elicited feelings that were preponderantly or exclusively unpleasurable.[5]

However, Freud provides enough information about Dora's background to indicate that this 'hysteria' is closely connected with Dora's position in the complex machinations going on between her parents and the K. couple. In other words, Dora is being exploited by the adults around her, and her rejection of Herr K. is completely intelligible. Freud seems unconsciously to provide ample material for us to work this out, but fails to make the theoretical connection between Dora's sexual repugnance and her relations with others. At the time that this case-study was written (1901), this inference did not fit in with Freud's hypotheses.

None the less, the rejection of 'seduction' as an explanation of neurosis is crucial to the foundations of psychoanalysis, and indeed of all depth psychology and psychotherapy. It represents the rejection of a crude external view of trauma and psychic conflict, which is indeed adopted by Jeffrey Masson, and other militant anti-Freudians: children are abused and therefore grow up with psychological problems; the solution is to discover or remember what the abuse was. If only that were true! In fact, it proves extremely difficult to get people to give up their self-abuse, as can be seen in the treatment of drug addicts, alcoholics, and so on. I have had patients who knew all about the sexual, emotional or physical abuse they had suffered as children, and could describe it in great detail. But this did not overcome the great difficulties they had in forming intimate relationships, nor their own crippling guilt and self-punishment.

The shift away from positivism in psychoanalysis was underlined by the discovery of transference. For, from having been seen at first as an obstacle to treatment, transference came to be seen as one of its key tools. The fantasies and feelings that the patient has about the therapist are very revealing of the patient's past relationships and the patient's inner world – and when counter-transference was recognized at a later date, the therapist's fantasies and feelings about the patient could be seen as adding a further rich texture.

But this enrichment and complication of the therapeutic process begins radically to change the conceptions of 'truth', 'reality', 'knowledge' and 'cure' under which psychotherapy operates. To put it crudely, the relationship between therapist and patient – which is often emotionally intense – itself forms the prime revelation of the patient's conflicts. So far from the 'truth' being discovered in some 'objective' or 'neutral' way, it is found in the love and hate – and the barriers to love and hate – that exist between two people deeply involved with each other.

Furthermore, this approach takes us away from the notion that there is a single, definitive truth about a person that is waiting to be discovered. All we can say is that a particular relationship between therapist and patient brings up certain issues; but that a relationship between the same patient and a different therapist could well bring up different issues. If therapy is seen in part as the revelation of the unconscious, then this is not a one-off, absolute revelation, for the unconscious is fantastically complex, is always shifting its focus and the facets that it reflects back to us, partly depending on the context. Let me give a personal example: I have undergone three separate periods of psychotherapy with therapists of different schools. These three relationships were quite different from each other, brought up different issues and were equally valuable.

No doubt Freud would have drawn back from such a radical interpretation of his views, yet at the same time, there is a sense in which the development of psychoanalysis leads us inexorably away from any empiricist psychology and towards a greater emphasis on the covert and the subjective.

Such ideas concerning the 'subjective' means of acquiring knowledge are quite familiar today in social science – sometimes called 'new paradigm' methodology. Radical thinkers such as Foucault have in fact suggested that traditional science itself is not as 'objective' or 'neutral' as it would like to claim, but is often ideologically motivated.[6]

But Freud can be said to have anticipated such developments, for while in his public apologia he maintained an attitude of rationalism and positivism to the end of his life, his work led in a different direction – to a place where knowledge is as much emotional as rational, where insight is not simply gained intellectually but also through the developing ability of the patient to contain intense feelings and desires and to take part in a human relationship which is itself full of contradictory feelings.

Freud's stipulation that the unconscious is full of desires or wishes is therefore of great importance, for this suggests that any increase in 'self-knowledge' that we gain through therapy is not by means of some disinterested intellectual realization, but through the awakening of dormant desires in relation to the other person. As a patient, I begin to realize that I love and hate my therapist, and that she loves and hates me. *This is the truth I have painfully won*, and my journey towards an acceptance of such feelings will have taught me also about my own defences against them. In other words, frequently I resist having such feelings towards the therapist, or resist believing that she has feelings about me, but again such resistances themselves provide a kind of X-ray into my deep emotional make-up.

It strikes me that this conception of knowledge strikes a shattering blow to all forms of empiricism and objectivism. The goal of therapy is the experience of my own deepest subjectivity, my own intense desires and feelings for another. This is often very painful, because it involves letting go of taboos and self-denials that I have learned in childhood – for example, that I am not allowed to love passionately or hate passionately; that I am not allowed to have needs and make demands. For another person, it might be that they are not allowed to think or to speak. For another, that they are not allowed sexual desire; or they are not allowed to be alone. The 'boiling heat' of the therapist/patient relationship is the means whereby such ancient prohibitions are exhumed and hopefully dissolved, and as I have already mentioned, different relationships will bring up different prohibitions and different 'solutions'.

These procedures have considerable implications in various areas. First, in epistemology, we see that in psychoanalysis knowledge is arrived at subjectively, or rather 'inter-subjectively'. Furthermore, much of this exchange of knowledge is from unconscious to unconscious: it is only with great struggle and resistance that therapist and patient are able to become aware of some of this communication. Freud makes this illuminating comment: 'During the progress of a psychoanalysis it is not only the patient who plucks up courage, but his disease as well; it grows bold enough to speak more plainly than before.'[7] In other words, the unconscious begins to speak almost in spite of the conscious part of the personality.

Such an acquisition of knowledge shows that the traditional division between subject and object is transcended, for the object of knowledge for the patient is him- or herself as subject. Furthermore, this knowledge is arrived at via relationship, not in a state of detached abstraction or introspection. We see also how important fantasy is in this process.

Psychoanalysis seeks the recovery of lost desires, and these desires are often imaged forth in the form of various fantasies for both therapist and patient. The imagination itself is shown to be a crucial knowledge-gathering organ. This is shown graphically in the Rat Man case, for this patient is tormented by a series of horrific images of torture, yet Freud proceeds with the case on the basis that these images are 'speaking' or telling a story.

One can see why Freud's ideas have often been seen as scandalous, and the vehement criticism which his ideas continue to attract surely stems in part from opposition to this anticipation of postmodernism. Reason, detachment and objectivity, so beloved in Western society since the Enlightenment, are overthrown. The human being gazes in the mirror of another person, and sees, not a rational temperate 'man of reason', but a creature who is torn by conflicting passions, many of which are unknown to itself. Furthermore, the morbid individualism fostered by capitalism is shattered in psychoanalysis, which propels the patient into an intense encounter with another. Identity is seen to be closely linked with relationship; indeed one might say that identity stems from relationship, is born in it and takes its character from it, just as knowledge is acquired via relationship. Implicitly, therefore, psychoanalysis represents a severe critique of all forms of bourgeois thought which take the isolated individual as the base-line. One can compare Marx's comment that individualism itself is born out of social interrelations: 'the human essence is no abstraction inherent in each single individual. In its reality it is the ensemble of the social relations.'[8]

In this respect, Freud exhibits yet another profound contradiction: in his metapsychological writings, he does suggest that the individual can be studied in isolation from others, but in his practical work as a psychoanalyst he was compelled to develop methods of work that are intrinsically dyadic. The Freudian individual may be seen theoretically as an isolate, but in practical terms, can be understood only within and via relationship.

Anti-empiricism

Without doubt, Freud shrank from some of the implications of his own ideas. For example, his attitude towards the unconscious is quite ambivalent. On the one hand, he argues that it is a 'seething cauldron', without organization, a kind of aggregate of primitive desires, which jostle together in a rather ramshackle manner.[9] This seems to represent a kind of positivist or empiricist view of the unconscious.

On the other hand, he says that the unconscious has a will of its own, is dynamic, almost 'decides' to take a certain course of action. One can cite, for example, the famous simile comparing the ego/id relationship to that between horse and rider:

> In its [the ego's] relation to the id it is like a man on horse-back, who has to hold in check the superior strength of the horse; with this difference, that the rider tries to do so with his own strength, while the ego uses borrowed forces. The analogy may be carried a little further. Often a rider, if he is not to be parted from his horse, is obliged to guide it where it wants to go; so in the same way, *the ego is in the habit of transforming the id's will into action as if it were its own.* (added emphasis)[10]

Freud leaves no doubt here that the unconscious has its own will, and that the ego frequently cannot supersede this will, but has to carry it out. He also argues that in the super-ego, the unconscious sets up a force to which the ego is frequently subjected.[11] One must also cite the famous remark, borrowed from Groddeck, that 'we are lived by unknown and uncontrollable forces'.

These remarks about the unconscious have startling implications. For if the unconscious has a will of its own to which it can subject the ego, then what is this 'will'? If the ego represents our normal sense of identity – what I think I am, in simple terms – then what kind of identity is represented by the unconscious? Is there a different kind of I present here?

These ideas were to be developed further by Jung, who eventually argued that the chief archetype present in the unconscious was the Self, which represents the organizing and unifying principle of the whole psyche. Jung argued further that the Self is projected onto the figure of God, and that contact between ego and Self often has the characteristics of spiritual or religious experience – it is 'numinous', 'uncanny', and so on. In other words, while the Self always remains unconscious, it is possible for human beings to contact it by means of some image, for example the image of God.

Freud abhorred these aspect of Jung's ideas, and this was one of the things which led to their split. But, while Freud detested all talk of 'spiritual entities', it is clear that Jung's ideas about the Self represent only a further extension of Freud's ideas about the id's will. We see again how Freud developed so many ideas embryonically that the ensuing century saw the development of many of them into areas which he might have found uncomfortable. An example can be found in the analyst W. R. Bion, who developed the notion of the unconscious to include the notion of 'O', which is a kind of spiritual organ in the psyche, able to marshal the whole psyche and gives it value.[12]

Empiricism

Further confirmation of Freud's anti-empiricism can be found by examining some of the arguments of anti-Freudians. Many of them demonstrate a fierce adherence to empiricist modes of thought and enquiry, and remonstrate bitterly with Freud that with the notion of the unconscious and other components of the psyche, Freud had unwittingly dragged into psychology antiquated religious ideas.

Richard Webster's book *Why Freud Was Wrong* has a fascinating chapter entitled 'The Ghost in the Psychoanalytic Machine'. In this, he argues that Freud took over the Judaic-Christian notion of the soul, which he termed the psyche, the mind or the unconscious. In fact, as Webster points out, Freud frequently uses the German word *Seele* ('soul'), and the translation of this into English has presented many problems, not least that the English translators seemed to have been nervous about using the word 'soul' on the grounds that it seemed unscientific or unsufficiently technical. Some commentators have argued that the translation as 'psyche' represents a distortion of Freud's original text and meaning – in fact, there are many other examples of such technical translations: for example, the hideous and esoteric 'cathexis' translates the German *Besetzung*, which means something like 'interest' or 'occupation'. This whole debate about the translation of Freud is another indication of the apprehension felt by psychoanalysis about its own status as a respectable scientific discipline.[13]

The following remarks are indicative of Webster's own attitude to the mind:

> All these and many other terms were invented by Freud (or his translators) *not to describe any observable entities or behaviour*, but to postulate the existence of the spiritual entities and mental processes which he 'needed' in order to construct his theory of mind...
>
> What ordinary men and women do, what they believe, and *what they say that they feel* – which is to say the larger part of human behaviour and human history – is treated as though it constituted suspect evidence, or as though it belonged merely to some external, mechanical realm which bears no direct relationship to 'mental phenomena' and can therefore hold no interest for the psychologist...

> Secure in their faith in an invisible psychical reality, they have very little motivation to consider the merely visible . . .
>
> His theory failed because, too often, in his anxiety to construct an abstract and intellectually complex theory of mind, he missed *what simple men could see.*[14]

(I have emphasized those phrases which eloquently reveal Webster's philosophical predilection towards the surface of events, those things which 'simple men could see', those 'observable entities' which are apparent to us all, and those feelings which people 'say they feel'.)

This debate was a familiar one in the twentieth century. For example, in the field of linguistics a fierce battle raged in the postwar era between the proponents of 'mentalism', who argued that language has a psychological reality – if you like, a kind of 'internalized grammar', which consists of sets of rules – and those behaviourists who argued that language consists of 'verbal behaviour', that is observable chunks of speech. Exactly the same opposition is found: for example, between the 'invisible' and unconscious mental grammars which are postulated by the adherents of Noam Chomsky, and the 'visible' bits of verbal behaviour which were analysed by B. F. Skinner in his book *Verbal Behavior.* Behaviourism has been more or less routed within linguistics as within psychology itself, but it has acquired new adherents in the camp of Freud critics.[15]

Empiricists object, therefore, to the postulate that there are invisible components and operations at work in human mentation, which cannot be directly observed but must be inferred. They tend to argue that this is 'unscientific', since science must be based on the observable and verifiable aspects of the universe. Unfortunately, such a definition of science would seem to render 'unscientific' much of modern physics and cosmology, much of which seems to proceed by means of inference, since direct observation is impossible.

More relevant to the study of Freud, such a radical empiricism must in the end reject the notion of 'mind' altogether, for clearly we cannot 'observe' or 'measure' the human mind. We are able to infer its existence and its internal operations, and such a mode of inference seems appropriate as a scientific methodology. But of course we never 'see' it directly. Hence to a critic such as Webster, one must put the question: how then are we to construct a 'theory of mind' without inference? Or perhaps you are suggesting that such a theory is in itself impermissible? One might then wonder how psychology is going to deal with such issues as human motivation, cognition, indeed, any mental phenomena at all.

In fact, Webster suggests that the solution lies in the refinement in our understanding of the brain and human physiology. However, Freud struggled with these issues during the 1890s, and in his 1895 'Project for a Scientific Psychology' cut through the Gordian knot of Cartesian dualism by suggesting that 'thought' has an organic basis in the form of neuronal activity, which the subject has no direct experience of, but which is experienced as mental activity. This is a more sophisticated theory than Webster's, whose naive physicalism seems to take us back to nineteenth-century philosophy.

Webster discusses the 'Project' with derision, as a kind of leftover from nineteenth-century pre-scientific thinking – yet some philosophers have argued that Freud's attempted 'materialist theory of mind' in the 'Project' anticipates work in this area by over fifty years. Certainly, we can see Freud striving to overcome the many problems inherent in a dualist theory of mind and body, and feeling his way towards what would be called today an 'identity' theory of the mind/body relationship.[16]

Webster's comments about what people 'say they feel' is particularly interesting, for if taken seriously, it leads to a rather naive theory of human motivation, based on conscious intentions or avowals. But it will prove very difficult to base the treatment of neurosis and psychosis on such a foundation, for neurosis means *to be in conflict*. Frequently, the conflict is between conscious intentions and 'something else'. Thus, I 'intend' to be polite to my infuriating neighbour, but I find myself letting slip a rather insulting remark; or, I 'intend' to pay my therapist punctually every month, but somehow always forget. The empiricist critic of Freud, such as Webster, almost seems to suggest that it is impermissible to ask the question: 'Why did you forget to pay your therapist?' and that if I answer that I don't know why, that must be the end of it, and that if my therapist suggests that I am angry with her, or that I like to have an outstanding debt as a form of attachment to her, she has stepped outside the bounds of respectability or the bounds of 'the merely visible'.

Let me give a more detailed example. I had a patient who frequently brought small bottles of mineral water to the sessions, and would at times drink from them. If I asked him why he did this, he might answer, perfectly reasonably, that he got thirsty on the journey, as he travelled quite a long way to see me, and so on. But something else began to happen: not infrequently, he spilled some of the water on my carpet. These events reached a climax when he knocked over a whole bottle onto a rather beautiful Indian rug.

If we follow a Webster-type analysis of these events, they are uneventful. My patient is simply thirsty; perhaps he is also rather clumsy; at any rate, he feels apologetic about spilling the water, and very guilty about knocking over the bottle. This is, at any rate, the 'observable behaviour' going on in the room; my patient 'says' that he is sorry about spilling the water, and so forth.

But something else happened. My patient became quite obsessive about this water and began to suggest to me that something else was going on. In fact, he informed me that he wasn't normally clumsy at all; that he didn't really believe he was thirsty; that he didn't take water to other places. In the end, I put it to him that the whole water episode suggested two things: a reproach to me that I wasn't giving him enough, so he had to bring supplementary nourishment; and second, that spilling the water was a hostile act, akin to urinating on my carpet. Incidentally, I am not claiming that this is an exhaustive explanation – no doubt, there are other unconscious motivations at work – for example, such quasi-urination may also be an expression of love or eroticism.

My patient was greatly relieved when I made these comments, and began to express quite explicitly aggressive and hostile remarks to me – he told me I didn't give him enough, that I was useless as a therapist, and so on. The drinking and spilling of water then ceased. We can say that the unconscious communications ceased when the patient was enabled to make explicit communications about his intense need, his anger, his disappointment, his love, and so on.

Presumably Webster – and other empiricist critics of depth psychology – could argue here that I am being over-ingenious, that I am appealing quite illegitimately to 'invisible' motivations which are not observable, or perhaps that I am indoctrinating my patient, so that he is forced to agree with my bizarre interpretations, and so on.

But this example is not particularly bizarre. Nor is this approach applicable only to the therapy situation: such events take place all the time between people. How many domestic breakages – of ornaments, and so on – express covert aggression? How many car accidents stem from hidden murderous feelings? How many suicides express revenge?

But the empiricist is locked in a closed universe where things can only mean what people say they mean. This means that I only have to deny my hostility and it is abolished. I say that I am not hostile, therefore I am not hostile. This strikes me as very bizarre: we are in a kind of Alice in Wonderland world, where things are what I say they are, the notion of *covert mental operations* is ruled out of court, and where the idea of contradiction is presumably illicit.

These arguments demonstrate clearly how much hostility Freud's ideas arouse in the dominant Anglo-Saxon form of positivism or empiricism. The notion of 'invisible' entities, or of mental operations that cannot be directly observed, but must be inferred, seems to provoke great anxiety and hostility amongst such thinkers, for the world suddenly no longer seems to be as it looks. 'Appearance' and 'reality' cease to coincide – this is traumatic for all human beings no doubt, but this is not an excuse for saying that appearances are the only form of reality that is a legitimate object of study. Like Marx, Freud set a cat among the empiricist pigeons, and has never been forgiven for this. In particular, the notion of the unconscious as a dynamic component of the psyche has aroused enormous anxiety, revulsion and hostility. I have had many patients who were terrified by the idea of unconscious motives and some who actually begged me never to use the word 'unconscious' – but our anxiety about it does not mean it does not exist.

Fundamentally, Freud's ideas strike a massive blow at human omnipotence. The notion of the unconscious suggests that often I do not know why I am doing something; or even worse, that the reasons I tell myself I am doing something are mistaken or might even be the opposite of the truth. This is very upsetting to our dignity and our belief in ourselves as coherent beings. It may also strike even more deeply at our actual belief in our existence – again, I have had a number of patients who were terrified that they did not exist, and any mention of the unconscious increased this fear to unbearable heights.

Empiricism is therefore rather comforting. Appearances are not deceptive; my feelings are as I describe them; my motives are transparent; I am what I say I am. Freud lobbed a rather destructive grenade amongst such beliefs and has never been forgiven for it.

Psychoanalysis and science

This discussion is also important in a consideration of the scientific nature of psychoanalysis. The subjective and emotional nature of the therapeutic relationship, and the discoveries made within that relationship, fly against any view of science as a kind of 'objective' or 'neutral' process. Here is no disinterested observer/spectator.

But those critics who argue that psychoanalysis is therefore not 'scientific' are using a particularly narrow set of assumptions about what science is and how it operates, usually derived from the physical sciences. The arguments about science and psychoanalysis therefore tend to become circular and barren, since it is quite easy to set up a number of criteria against which psychoanalysis must fail – for example, its theories are not predictive in the way in which theories in physics or astronomy are. The psychologist Stephen Frosh argues in fact that certain theories of scientificity seem to be designed specifically to exclude Marxism and psychoanalysis – in other words, they are covertly politically biased.[17]

It is more interesting perhaps to consider if 'science' need inevitably be based on such narrow positivist lines as some would suggest. Can there be a 'social science' or a 'human science' which seeks to describe and explain the components of human subjectivity, and in which the role of the observer is not seen as a contamination to be minimized at all costs, but as an essential part of the research? Can we envisage a science of the emotions in which the scientists are themselves subject to emotions? Can scientific prediction be probabilistic rather than absolute? Can logic be fuzzy?

It is not the place of this book to go into this debate extensively. Suffice it to say that such a debate is going on, and that 'new paradigm' research is being considered by some as a valid means of scientific enquiry.[18] In addition, the relatively new discipline of 'cognitive science' is unashamedly interested in the internal operations of the mind.[19]

In short, the development of psychoanalysis and the fierce opposition to it should be set against the background of the 400-year-old obsession with objectivity in Western culture. This involved getting rid of the subject and subjective factors, in the hope of arriving at a neutral description and explanation of nature. In the postmodernist era, this seems perhaps a fanciful aim in itself, and philosophers such as Michel Foucault would argue that one cannot construct a value-free or apolitical system of enquiry, since, for example, the hypervaluation of rationality seen in modern science amounts to a fetishization and a covert political statement. Other researchers, for example in feminism, have shown how apparently 'neutral' scientific statements are loaded with many implicit assumptions which are not at all neutral.[20]

No doubt the turn to 'scientific' and 'objective' methods of enquiry was a revolutionary step in the Renaissance and post-Renaissance, for it cleared the way for a consensual scientific method – but at a very high price. The split between subject and object leads to feelings of alienation, a sense of anomie, a lack of meaning in people's lives and a lack of the self. Thus science and religion become sworn enemies, since affairs of the soul are considered by those enamoured of the scientific method to be beyond the pale.

But objectivism led to a counter-revolution in the shape of Romanticism, and later the cult of the irrational found in twentieth-century culture. In this historical context, we can argue that Freud attempted to return the subjective factor to science. Plainly, he was in a highly ambivalent position, since he tried to use positivist arguments to defend a method of enquiry which became less and less positivist!

In this sense, psychoanalysis is an offshoot of Romanticism – two people relate to each other very intensely yet non-sexually, and in this way attain profound knowledge. This procedure is definitely not objective, not empiricist. Thus many of the criticisms of psychoanalysis as unscientific describe the concept of the unconscious as unverifiable, smacking of the occult, non-consensual, and so on. On the other hand, it does not seem difficult to construct empirical procedures that test many of the Freudian hypotheses.[21]

There is also the suspicion that some of the critics of Freud are determined to prove him wrong at every turn. For example, Frederick Crews, one of the fiercest critics of psychoanalysis, paints a lurid portrait of

> a notably willful and opportunistic Freud who appears to have thrown together his magisterial-looking claims from various unacknowledged sources – some of them more folkloric than scientific – while passing them off as sober inferences from the data of his clinical practice. Once having arrived at those claims, we see, he adhered to them with a blind, combative stubbornness – though not without willingness to expand the system on an ad hoc basis to encompass newly perceived difficulties.[22]

This statement strikes me as very odd. First, the critique of Freud's method of theory construction is a red herring – one can construct a scientific hypothesis in any way you like, including dreaming, getting drunk or asking the bus driver what he thinks about it. The *source* of scientific theories is irrelevant to their value and efficacy. But then Crews argues both that Freud adhered to his theories stubbornly – not a trait unique to Freud one would have thought! – and also that he changed them to account for new problems. The last statement strikes me as a reasonable description of general scientific method. In other words, Freud is being criticized for assembling his hypotheses from a mixture of sources; then for being rigid; then for making adaptations to this theories.

For example, without doubt Freud began to perceive in the 1920s and 1930s that female sexuality could not be adequately explained in terms of the standard Oedipal theory, and he wrote a number of articles exploring these difficulties and possible solutions. This strikes me as a perfectly proper method of work: theories do get revised as new data emerge. In the same way, Freud changed his theory of the structure of the psyche as he began to realize that parts of the ego itself were unconscious: the distinction between ego and unconscious could not therefore be that of consciousness itself.[23]

Hence Crews' statement seems a reasonable defence of Freud's scientific credentials, but for Crews they amount to a demolition of them!

Freud's journey

Freud made an amazing journey from neurologist to founder of psychoanalysis. This is both a personal journey and a political journey, in the sense that it forms part of a cultural shift – what can be called the reclamation or redemption of subjectivity, the non-rational, the realm of desire and wishes. For 300 years scientists, philosophers and other thinkers had eulogized reason and objectivity and had excluded the imagination, intuition and other forms of non-reason. For example, in religion, the sacramentalism of Catholicism had been overthrown in favour of the stern rationality and lucidity of Protestantism – this is an overt root-and-branch rejection of symbolism and sensuality. Religion became *mindful* rather than sensual.

Hence Freudianism is part of a return of these repressed aspects of human life. For Freud, the human being is not simply a thinking animal, he/she is also full of desire and hate. Society may have its technological and productive drives, but the individual is rooted in the body with its emotions and primitive needs. Another expression of this 'return of the repressed' is the Romantic movement, which countered industrialism and capitalist production by means of the cult of the aesthetic, the emotive and the ardent.

No doubt Freud would cavil at being linked with Romanticism, yet it strikes me that psychotherapy is fundamentally a Romantic enterprise – an intense relationship between two people, who for periods of time (which may go on for many years) shut out the world completely and focus on their feelings, thoughts and fantasies. No wonder that those critical of long-term therapy sometimes argue that it is 'indulgent', a 'luxury', and so on. Yet therapy insists by its very practices that the individual is valuable, that relationship is valuable, and that these are indeed the key indices of value that we have. Surely this is one reason why therapy works – by giving attention to the patient regularly and reliably, and over a period of years, the therapist is implicitly stating that the patient is valuable, even if what is being talked about may often seem opaque, bizarre or tedious. The therapist's attention in itself is curative or healing.

One of the fascinating documents concerning Freud's own progression towards the formulation of psychoanalysis is the letters he wrote to Fliess, for Fliess was a kind of nineteenth-century biologist or behaviourist, who believed in the 'organic' or physiological roots of neurosis. We see Freud gradually and reluctantly moving away from this view towards a truly psychological one, until eventually a rift with Fliess is inevitable.

Looking at these developments at a distance, one can say that industrialism and the Enlightenment had led to an alienation of the individual from society, a split between mind and body, and that the nineteenth and twentieth centuries saw various attempts to heal these divisions, with Freudian thought part of this counter-movement.

At the same time, my comments about the individual being 'rooted in the body' can also be construed as a partial critique of psychoanalysis which seems to have found physicality and physical action a very problematic area. Far too often, it has been regarded as a 'flight into action' or a kind of 'acting out', seeming to demonstrate considerable fear about the role of the body in analysis. This was one of the factors leading to the break-away movement of 'New Therapies' in the 1960s and 1970s which attempted to integrate the body into therapy. Clearly psychoanalysis – and Freud – have an ambivalent attitude to the body, and what might be called an unconscious favouring of the mind.

4
The Unconscious

The unconscious is the crux of Freud's work: anyone who claims to employ psychoanalytic methods, either in therapy, art criticism, theorizing about gender and sexuality, and in other areas, must have a grasp of it; conversely, one finds that critics of Freud are usually critical of the unconscious. It is not difficult to see why it arouses fierce opposition, for it challenges many of our common-sense assumptions about the way life is and the way human beings operate.

In a kind of Hegelian logic, the unconscious is opposed to the conscious personality as an antithesis to a thesis. If one consciously believes that one is well-meaning, then we can expect the unconscious to contain malicious intentions; those we love we also unconsciously hate; my denials conceal their opposite. The theory of the unconscious makes a very pointed opposition between appearance and reality in human existence and motivation.

Of course, it is clear that the use made of the unconscious is open to abuse and can easily become a rather facile parlour-game. Whether or not this occurs in psychotherapy is open to question – it would generally lead to a swift termination by the patient! In other words, one cannot really play games with this kind of material, for one is dealing with people's deepest motives and wishes, and they will not take kindly to any manipulative or cerebral game-playing.

The unconscious refers to those things which I do not know about myself yet which also at times I seem to have some knowledge of. That is, the unconscious seems to lie hidden much of the time, but also pushes itself into our lives and our consciousness in surprising ways. Of course, people vary enormously in how much notice they take of the unconscious and how much credence they give to its existence. Those who steadfastly deny that there is such a thing will naturally tend to ignore its messages – for example, in dreams or slips of the tongue. There are also some people who are terrified of the whole concept, for it threatens their sense of self.

Arguably, the unconscious represents one of the key intellectual landmarks of modernity: one might compare it with Darwinian evolution or Einsteinian physics as a stepping stone in human knowledge. It has influenced many areas – art, cinema, photography, literature, linguistics, and so on. One might say that the twentieth century was the century of the unconscious.

Freud was the first to admit that he did not discover the unconscious – creative artists, particularly writers, had done that, and philosophers such as Nietzsche had commented on it extensively.[1] But Freud worked the notion of the unconscious into a systematic theory; he also described the characteristics of the unconscious, and showed how radically different it was from conscious thought – that it was primitive, disorganized, concerned with desires, did not admit negation, permitted the coexistence of contradictory impulses side by side, and so on. Crucially, the Freudian unconscious is also seen as intrinsically infantile, since it contains those impulses which were repressed in childhood. Freud goes so far as to say that 'all dreams are children's dreams'.[2]

Freud uses the term 'immortal' in relation to the wishes which exist in the unconscious: 'after the passage of decades they behave as though they had just occurred.' There is one important exception to this: analysis itself can reduce the force of these ancient childhood wishes by making them conscious.[3] The unconscious therefore has two chief means of egress: indirectly, through dreams, symptoms, life-events, which both reveal and conceal the true nature of the instinctual impulses involved, and also leaves them undiminished in intensity; and the 'working through' in analysis, which by making the impulses conscious, reduces their energy and reduces their power over us.

The unconscious marks a dislocation in human personality: what we are does not correspond to what we think we are. Our actions and words speak volumes which we are not consciously in touch with. Freud shows this very clearly in his analysis of everyday slips of the tongue and other 'parapraxes'. He states in relation to the meaning of a dream for the dreamer: 'he does not know that he knows it.'[4]

The theory of the unconscious therefore marks a fundamental shift in how human beings perceive themselves. Instead of an image of ourselves as coherent rational beings, we are forced to look in the mirror and appreciate our incoherence and our irrationality. We are all beset by inner conflicts; in particular, our moral and ethical stances are often betrayed by a more emotional and primitive side. In a sense, we could argue that the ten commandments exist precisely to forestall primitive human desires – but these desires form a bedrock in the human personality. Freud therefore exploded the Christian ethic, which he despised, that one should strive for the good and fight against the evil. This, for Freud, spells disaster: for the repressed 'evil' still speaks in us in a whole number of ways. It leaks out in our behaviour and our unconscious slips. One can cite the well-known phenomenon of the Christian group or Church circle which is beset by bitchiness. On a larger scale, Freud was fond of citing Christianity as a cultural movement that is consciously devoted to good, but that in reality has been one of the most murderous forces in human history![5]

As against the Christian ethic, therefore, Freud advocates the conscious acceptance of the evil wish, without having to act it out. Thus, if I can accept that I do desire my neighbour's wife, that sometimes I wish to harm people, that sometimes I hate my parents, I want to steal things from others, and so on, I will be more at peace and actually less likely to carry out such acts. There is some evidence, for example, that murderers are very impulsive people, who are unable to 'hold' their own feelings of rage and inadequacy, but are compelled into action to avoid the feelings.[6] I have found this in work with violent men. Many of them are terrified of feelings, not just angry feelings, but also feelings of need, tenderness, fear, and so on. Violence rises up as a blanket means of obliterating such terrifying emotions.

But the pacifist also denies his or her unconscious feelings of anger and destructiveness, and one would expect to find somewhere in the pacifist's life evidence for these feelings leaking out. For example, I am struck, in reading accounts of Bertrand Russell's life, how this noted pacifist and philosopher seems to have treated women abominably. This is one of the striking things about the 'Freud-bashing' that goes on: one senses those doing the bashing seem to be horrified that Freud was not a saint. But that is part of the thrust of Freudian psychology – that none of us are saints, and those who purport to be have dark secrets.

In a sense, therefore, Christianity and other religions discovered the unconscious thousands of years before Freud, but advocated a repressive attitude towards it. It became the property of Satan, the enemy of humanity, who constantly lurked round the borders of consciousness, trying to snare the unwary. Of course, Christianity can take on an heroic air, as one reads of those saints and martyrs who through their willpower refuse to submit to ordinary human weakness. But it is doubtful whether Christian heroism is really a serviceable philosophy for most people today.

The Freudian theory of the unconscious therefore marks a significant paradigm shift, away from moralistic attitudes about the personality, towards a more objective yet also compassionate attitude. Lust, rage and hatred are simply inevitable parts of human personality, Freud argued, particularly as they are found in young children. It is likely therefore that psychoanalytic ideas have affected the rearing of children towards a more permissive regime.

The notion of the unconscious implies that the psyche is not unified, and this has many interesting implications. Most importantly, it means that all human beings are involved in inner conflicts, for the unconscious contains much repressed material, which conflicts with the repressing forces. Of course, we handle these conflicts all the time, with varying degrees of success, but people who go to therapy have often found that the conflicts are beginning to break out into open warfare.

In fact, we can go so far as to claim that human beings who do not experience such conflicts are disturbed – for example, people without guilt or concern for others tend towards psychopathic personalities. People without apparent conflicts also tend to arouse conflict in others. When I used to run therapy groups, it became predictable that those people whose outer personality in the group tended towards a rather serene detachment would arouse rage in others, as if the deeply buried conflicts in the 'serene' person were expressed indirectly in the other group members. I remember that Buddhists in particular infuriated others! My feeling here was that repressed anger in one person was being expressed in another.

The notion of the 'divided psyche' has great importance in the understanding of dreams. There have been many critics of Freud's claim that dreams express covert wishes, but some of these criticisms clearly assume the notion of a coherent self. For example, sometimes it is claimed that a dream in which I am punished cannot represent a wish, for how can I wish to be punished? In fact, many people do wish to be punished out of an intense sense of guilt, but in any case we can argue that the inner critic or saboteur wishes to damage us, and that the dream represents that wish. In other words, we do not have to assume that the dream represents my best interests: it may represent an internal enemy. Similarly very frightening dreams – which superficially seem unlike wish-fulfilment – can represent the fear I feel about a reprehensible wish, or alternatively, the fear I feel when a hostile force wishes me harm. At its most extreme, a nightmare might depict my own death. Again, the sceptic might scoff that this cannot represent a wish. We can retort that it can indeed.

These examples show the powerful dynamism built into the Freudian notion of the psyche, split into different components, with their own striving, their own goals.

Justification for the unconscious

Freud's written work can be seen as a series of arguments in favour of the unconscious, especially in the early years of the twentieth century, when he published works on 'parapraxes', jokes, dreams and sexuality. He believed until the end of his life that this material provided convincing evidence for the existence of the unconscious, which could never be 'proved' or directly experienced, but had to be inferred. In particular, the notion of the unconscious rests on the existence of what Freud calls 'gaps': 'the data of consciousness have a very large number of gaps in them.' Freud goes on to adduce parapraxes, dreams, neurotic symptoms, obsessional behaviour as examples of experiences containing gaps; in addition, 'our most personal daily experience acquaints us with ideas that come into our head we do not know from where, and with intellectual conclusions arrived at we do not know how'.[7]

Freud's final step in this argument is a crucial one, which has caused much controversy and disagreement:

> all these conscious acts remain disconnected and unintelligible if we insist upon claiming that every mental act that occurs in us must also be necessarily be experienced through consciousness; on the other hand, they fall into a demonstrable connection if we interpolate between them the unconscious acts which we have inferred.[8]

Part of the problem with this argument has been that in his case studies, Freud demonstrates a zealous method of 'the interpolation of unconscious acts' towards his patients which has aroused disquiet and even revulsion in subsequent readers. For example, in the Rat Man case, when the patient expresses doubt that all of his 'evil impulses' stem from childhood experiences, Freud is unwavering: 'I promised to prove it to him in the course of the treatment.'[9] In other words, Freud seems to fill in the gaps somewhat imperiously and dogmatically. It is likely that many contemporary psychotherapists would shrink from 'proving' to their patients that their problems stem from some particular source – for one thing, it has become very clear that such dogmatic behaviour tends to provoke very negative reactions in patients, quite rightly, one might think. The classic case of this in Freud's work is 'Dora', who left the analysis, perhaps weary of his hectoring tone.

But the question of Freud's personal manner conceals a more fundamental issue: that evidence about the unconscious must always be inferred. For example, I referred in the previous chapter to a patient who brought bottles of water to the sessions and kept spilling the water on the carpet. This strikes me as a perfect example of behaviour which has 'gaps' in it: the gaps consisting of the motives for bringing the water and spilling it. Eventually, between us, we hypothesized that there were two main motives for this: first, that the patient was secretly reproachful of me – I didn't give him enough nourishment, so he had to bring his own. Second, spilling the water was a hostile act, akin to urination. The patient was not aware of these thoughts and feelings, and expressed them covertly or symbolically.

Following this discussion, and after he became able to express his hostility to me openly, the water spilling ceased. The logic of this whole episode can be paraphrased as follows: we assume that his behaviour has 'gaps' in it, in particular his feelings about me, which are probably being expressed covertly through the drinking and spilling of water; we then arrive at a series of hypotheses about his unconscious motives – when we discuss this openly, and as he becomes able to express these feelings openly, the behaviour ceases. Within the Freudian paradigm, we can say that the unconscious was made conscious, and therefore did not have to be manifest as a set of unintelligible acts. We have filled in the gaps.

But this process is open to attack by those who are worried about the process of inference as a valid procedure, and in addition, can argue that the patient is so open to suggestion from the therapist that the ceasing of the puzzling behaviour can equally be explained by patient compliance. Of course, I can never prove that our interpretation is correct, and the fact that the patient is satisfied with it can also be seen as the product of suggestibility.

We come down to this crux: if someone is determined not to be convinced by evidence for the unconscious, then they will never be convinced, since the evidence is always indirect. Granted, for many people, the sheer weight of evidence – from slips of the tongue, forgotten names, dream interpretation, neurotic symptoms, and so on – is convincing, but that is a subjective factor. I can never produce a piece of the unconscious for the sceptical critic, and say: 'There, now you have it, the thing itself.'

Freud was very impressed by the evidence taken from psychotic patients, for here it was assumed that such people are much less suggestible than neurotic patients, and Freud argued that psychotic material confirmed many psychoanalytic theories: 'so many things that in the neuroses have to be laboriously fetched up from the depths are found in the psychoses on the surface, visible to every eye.'[10] However, it is perhaps not so clear today that someone in the grip of a psychosis is less suggestible than anyone else, since such people often have a remarkable 'psychic' ability to read other people's thoughts and feelings.[11]

However, these arguments and counter-arguments pertain to many aspects of psychological research, which must necessarily proceed by means of inference. In fact, we can argue that all theories of the mind must rest on inference, since we can never produce the mind or a part of it as an observable three-dimensional object. But that type of requirement surely leads to an empiricist cul-de-sac – cognitive science as a whole, never mind theories of the unconscious, becomes impossible.

Identity

The Freudian notion of the unconscious has revolutionary implications for the issue of human identity. Put bluntly, the unconscious is like a grenade lobbed into any cosy humanist notion of identity. We are shown to be like icebergs: most of what we are lies hidden under the water, not only unknown to others, but unknown to ourselves.

Identity is therefore exploded by the irrationality of the unconscious. The post-Enlightenment view of identity is rational: the human being has certain goals, decides what he or she wants, sets out to obtain these things, lives a mainly orderly life. Of course, the twentieth century showed otherwise: human beings were seen at their worst, full of cruelty to others, engulfed in vast wars and revolutions, tidal waves of mass political energy.

We can also describe human identity as fragile. There is a veneer of rationality and consideration for others, but it may not take much to get further down to much more primitive feelings, such as envy, hatred, despair, and so on.

Such ideas have obviously been very important in the art of the twentieth century. If we look at the paintings of Picasso or Jackson Pollock, for example, there is a sense of affinity with Freudian thought. I am not suggesting, of course, that Freud caused these developments. Freudianism has been part of the eruption of the irrational into our conception of the human being; at the same time, it has probably influenced some writers and artists considerably.

Whether or not Freud consciously thought this, his ideas have been part of the revolution against the Enlightenment: notions of progress, rationality and order. Such figures as Foucault have openly scoffed at such notions – Freud was not really a scoffer, but his thought has been one of the major forces which have helped us to turn it upside down. We know now that we have to allow for the primitive and the irrational and the fragmented in the human being.

Another being?

Freud seems to teeter on the brink of the view that the unconscious is another being within the individual – the 'it' which actually controls a large part of our life. Freud draws back from a fully personalized view of the unconscious and stresses its chaotic qualities: each instinctual impulse is separate from the rest and functions in isolation. However, as we have seen, there is a kind of ambivalence in Freud about this: there is also the suggestion of the unconscious as an intelligent being within, with its own mind, its own will. For example, in relation to dreams, Freud makes the fascinating comment that 'the dreamer fighting against his own wishes is to be compared with a summation of two separate, though intimately connected, people'.[12]

Such ideas were to be developed more fully by Jung, with his notion of the Self, which is definitely not chaotic or incoherent. In fact, for Jung it is the Self which gives the whole psyche its unity. Freud cannot go as far as this, but some analysts have argued that this represents a failure of nerve on Freud's part, and that psychoanalysis can pick up this particular issue and redevelop it.[13]

One can cite, for example, the phenomenon whereby a problem which cannot be solved is forgotten or put on one side, and later a solution emerges effortlessly. In fact, this can happen overnight during sleep – one wakes up in the morning with a clear picture of something, which the night before was shrouded in obscurity. One can also cite human creativity as another example of the power of the unconscious: the artist may not have a clear idea of what the whole work is going to look like, or read like, but there seems to be 'something' in charge which is aware of the full picture. And of course, some people have that sense in relation to their life – the notion of 'destiny' captures this idea of a life-story or plan.

Such ideas are astonishing, for they imply that a 'higher power' exists in the mind which directs life according to a covert plan or plot. This is the 'alien' in our midst, and for some, maybe God in our midst. Therapy itself provides a compelling argument, for if one works with an individual over a number of years, one often gets the impression that gradually different areas of the personality – often those that have been neglected – are being brought forward for examination and renewal (or healing). But what is it that 'knows' which areas need attention, and what is it that organizes this in terms of time and space? Again, Jung talks of the 'inferior functions' which tend to demand attention in mid-life – but what is it that decides this?

Let us say that there is a tension in Freud between the 'chaotic' unconscious and the 'intelligent' unconscious, and this tension has been used by different analysis to take quite different stances towards the psyche as a whole.

The alien

Freud's term 'the id' is actually a translation of the German phrase 'das Es', which is literally translated as 'the it'. This perhaps gives a rather different flavour from 'id', suggesting as it does something within the human psyche which is almost non-human. And Freud describes it in such terms: it is 'dark and inaccessible', it is 'a chaos, a seething cauldron', it is primitive, irrational and amoral.[14]

These rather less technical descriptions give a more emotional flavour to Freud's description of the unconscious, and elsewhere he sees it as a positive danger to the ego.[15] The unconscious is something of an alien, hostile to civilization, uninterested in morality or issues of tact and sensitivity to others. Thus Freud opposes civilized society and the sexual instincts: the one demands the partial suppression of the other – 'the sexual life of civilized man is . . . severely impaired'.[16] Correspondingly, Freud has the notion that so-called 'primitive' human beings were in this respect at least, better off: 'primitive man was better off in knowing no restrictions of instinct.'[17] In fact, one should judge this view properly as a fantasy of Freud's – for example, one can point out that amongst many animals sexual life and aggression are both severely restricted; and that in many pre-industrial cultures (which are presumably more 'primitive' than industrial ones), sexual relations are hedged about with many restrictions.[18]

Freud sets up a sharp conflict between the instincts present in the unconscious on the one hand, and the ego and the superego on the other, these being seen as representative of society. The unconscious is dangerous precisely because of its amoral seeking of pleasure: this makes it very alluring but volatile and hard to handle. It is the task of the ego to do this work, and one of the great tasks of analytic psychotherapy is to permit the conscious awareness of the instinctual demands present in the unconscious whilst at the same time holding back on their acting out. For example, one may become aware that one is full of feelings of lust and rage towards others, but one is not compelled to act on such feelings, but neither is one compelled not to act on them! In other words, we have choice in these matters.

Freud makes a very explicit comment about this: 'analysis replaces repression by condemnation.'[19] This makes it absolutely clear that psychoanalysis does not aim for some libertine letting go of constraints, whether in relation to sexuality or aggression. 'Condemnation' means that one is now aware of a desire that was formerly repressed, but one chooses not to act on it. Of course, one can also choose to act on it, but that is within the scope of the person concerned and is not really a psychoanalytic issue.

Freud actually states that 'the man of prehistoric times survives unchanged in our unconscious'.[20] One might caricature Freud's view as follows: the unconscious is full of sexual appetite, destructive rage, envy, and so on.

This is a rather pessimistic view, for Freud ignores the evidence that the unconscious also contains feelings of love, compassion, connection with nature, spiritual openness and so on. For Freud, such feelings are 'aim-inhibited', that is, they are derivative of diverted sexual feelings. But what is striking about in-depth work with people in psychotherapy is that after working through very difficult barriers and blocks one often finds within people very powerful feelings of love and tenderness.

Freud's unconscious is something of a monster or an alien. It seems to growl within us like a primeval beast; or it tears down all pretence of feelings such as compassion, altruism and so on.

Perhaps I can put this opposition more starkly: Freud derives love from sexuality; however, many modern therapists would see sex as an attempt to find love. For example, the American analyst H. F. Searles, in his descriptions of therapy with very disturbed patients, argues that repressed love between parent and child is one of the key factors in precipitating such illnesses: 'I have found that it is essential for the patient to become aware of the presence of this love between mother and himself, in order to develop both a healthy self-esteem and a thorough-going resolution of his schizophrenic illness.'[21]

However, one should put Freud's theory of the unconscious in its historical and cultural context: no doubt, Freud was intent on puncturing the inflated claims of religion and morality and revealing the darker feelings that lurk in the human breast. He exposed what Jung was later to call 'the shadow', and no doubt this was a necessary correction to the overly moralistic kind of psychology which had flourished in the nineteenth century.

Repression

Repression is the key concept in Freud's thought, for through repression the unconscious is created. Furthermore, many other psychological processes flow from the base-line of repression. Thus, the resistances shown by patients in therapy are resistances to having repressed material brought to light. Resistance is therefore a special kind of meta-repression.

Repression also leads to a basic conflict in the psyche, or in fact, in the human being. Far from being a coherent unified entity, the person is shown to be involved in an internal civil war: the repressing agent versus the repressed desires.

However, one can also speak of the failure of repression – say in the case of a child involved in a seductive relationship with one parent. That child may well tend to repeat that kind of relationship in later life – tantalizing, frustrating, exciting but depriving. Here one can speak, as Freud does, of the 'premature satisfaction' of instinctual needs. Thus alongside the possibility of the repressing force being too powerful, thus cutting the person off from the energy and spontaneity of the id, there is also the danger of having too weak an ego, so that the individual is unable to resist the peremptory demands of the id. This is partly what happens with sexual abuse of children – the child learns that incestuous desires are not contained but acted out. Such children often become seductive themselves, and find it difficult not only to stop being seductive, but to appreciate that they are being so.

Too much ego or too little – these are the polarities which are found in people, and obviously there is a huge area in the middle, where an individual has a strong ego with regard to certain areas of life, but a weak one in other areas. It is interesting in this respect that acquaintances of mine sometimes express revulsion at the idea of being a therapist, and having to contain the intense and disturbing feelings and thoughts that people bring to therapy. This suggests that being a therapist has two major requirements: first, that one is open to the unconscious, particularly the more unwelcome or disagreeable aspects of it, which are normally shunned or denied; and second, one is able to contain these ideas without feeling deranged or over-excited by them. For example, in relation to sexuality, therapists have to be alive to sexual currents going on between therapist and patient and prepared to think about them and talk about them, but must also be able to resist their enactment.

An interesting example of the fragility of the ego concerns some obsessional people, who construct complicated series of actions and thoughts, which are gone through in a ritualistic way. It is clear with some people like this that the obsessive structure provides a skeleton identity which the patient hangs on to tenaciously. I recall one patient who could not bear to hear any discussion of the unconscious. He was terrified by the idea that if the unconscious is as powerful as is claimed, then he didn't exist. Spontaneity became equally terrifying, for if he carried out a spontaneous act, he couldn't identify an instigator of the act. In other words, he seemed to disappear, and then had to resurrect one of his complicated structures to re-establish his sense of self. Can we still speak of repressive forces at work here? In fact, this patient's whole childhood was a mystery to him, and he could make no connections at all between his present life and his past. Thus, he was laden with repressed material, which constantly 'leaked' out into his life and caused him great fear, for it seemed to emanate from some strange Other who was not himself.

At this point the issue of psychosis becomes important, for it has been supposed that this results from a failure of repression. In Freud's words, 'the maintenance of certain internal resistances is a sine qua non of normal life'.[22] If the unconscious emerges too much in an unmodulated form in waking life, we become disturbed and suffer from intense delusions: 'The precipitating cause of the outbreak of a psychosis is either that reality has become intolerably painful, or that the instincts have become extraordinarily intensified.'[23]

Thus the ego loses contact with reality under the impact of powerful unconscious forces, and/or the impact of a reality that is unbearable. In fact, the two processes frequently go hand in hand: that is, one way of escaping from an unbearable reality is to retreat into the inner world and there construct a more bearable one. The problem with this is that it is an intensely private world, cut off from normal social intercourse. I recall a patient of mine who claimed he had powerful relationships with the insects in his garden. He would describe to me how on the previous afternoon he had renewed acquaintance with a certain bee or fly, which had flown towards him in an acknowledgement of his importance.

One could detect in his poignant story a veiled description of his relationship with me – yet it is this which was unbearable or brought to light unbearable needs and feelings. Thus he retreated from this relationship into a more fantasized relationship with insects. Incidentally, I am not denying that one can have a very powerful relationship with nature – plants, animals, and so on. But for this man, these were the only relationships he could tolerate.

Ego and the unconscious

Repression was one of the factors which led Freud to realize that the distinction between 'being conscious' and 'being unconscious' was inadequate in a description of the relationship between the ego and 'the unconscious'. Put simply, Freud began to appreciate that parts of the ego, or some of its functions, are also unconscious. For example, even when a patient is told that he is dominated by a resistance, 'he is quite unaware of the fact, and even if he guesses from his unpleasurable feelings that a resistance is now at work in him, he does not know what it is or how to describe it'.[24]

This is a quite startling observation, because it must be assumed within the Freudian model that resistance flows from the ego, which is striving to prevent repressed material being brought to light. Freud concludes that 'we have come upon something in the ego itself which is also unconscious, which behaves exactly like the repressed'.[25]

The idea that part of the ego is itself unconscious at first seems to throw everything into disarray, but it is clear that ego and id cannot be distinguished on the grounds of 'being conscious' or 'being unconscious', but on other grounds – for example, the ego is the coherent part of the psyche, which has organizational powers. It is also connected with the body, in that it is able to carry out motor commands. By contrast, 'the unconscious' is incoherent and does not possess powers of organization. The unconscious is the primitive and irrational part of the psyche.

One must also remember that at all times Freud stresses that the ego is in fact part of the id which has emerged as a coherent organizing focal point: 'the ego is that part of the id which has been modified by the direct influence of the external world.'[26]

Death and the unconscious

Freud's concept of the death instinct is one of the most puzzling parts of his work. In his book *Beyond the Pleasure Principle*, he draws together a number of psychological data – the compulsion to repeat, the lowering of excitation in the nervous system, the need to protect the organism against excessive stimuli, an urge to restore an earlier state of affairs – which led Freud to propose that there is an instinct 'to return to the inanimate state'.[27] He is then able to connect this death instinct with the sadistic impulses in human beings, about which he had written at the beginning of the twentieth century – briefly, whereas the true death instinct concerns the destruction of oneself, sadism turns this outwards to others.[28]

I see one of the problems with this theory of death being to do with the use of the term 'instinct' – Freud even speaks of the 'aim of death' or the 'wish for death'.[29] No one can doubt that Freud is discussing something important in nature – the law of entropy seems relevant – the tendency of all things to fall into chaos or fragmentation.

But it is surely confusing to give the tendency towards death the same kind of categorization as the wish for love, sex and reproduction which is found in living things. In fact, the first tendency is the property of the whole of nature, including inanimate things, whereas Eros is the property only of living things. To say that both are 'instincts' seems to stretch the meaning of the term 'instinct' or 'drive' beyond recognition.

The position here is complicated by another crux for translators, for Freud's word *Triebe* has usually been translated as 'instincts', when its more natural English cognate would be 'drives'. The two English words do not seem synonymous, and it is possible that part of the problem with the 'death instinct' is to do with the use of 'instinct' here, which normally denotes a more biological concept than 'drive'. It seems less odd to me to say that there is a 'drive to death' in nature than an 'instinct' for death.

None the less, it strikes me that Freud has uncovered some important material concerning opposing tendencies in human beings. In particular, if we consider that unconsciousness is the normal condition of the whole of nature, then the struggle for consciousness appears in an heroic light. It is like a glimmer of light in an overpowering darkness, just as, perhaps, life itself appears amidst a great mass of inanimate matter.

Death can therefore be equated with inanimacy and with unconsciousness, and in Jungian terms, one can speak of the struggle of life amidst death, and consciousness amidst unconsciousness. However, Freud is loath to speak in such terms, as this conflicts with his asseveration that the death instinct is opposed by the libidinal instinct or Eros. But certainly, these remarks throw a fresh light on analysis or therapy itself: for in the therapeutic process, we endeavour to pierce the gloom of the unconscious and to bring light to it. There is much to oppose this endeavour, not least the patient's resistances and the tendency of many human beings to resist change and improvement to their lives.

Whilst, therefore, many analysts and therapists have been unhappy with the notion of a death instinct, there does seem to be value in the idea of a conflict between the movement towards life and an increase in consciousness, as against the movement against life and the effort to cling to unconsciousness. In fact, I have heard a number of patients express the wish for death, precisely when they are in the middle of a fierce psychic conflict. One might speak of a longing for death as a way of avoiding the pain of the conflict, and the necessity to separate from one's former neurotic personality and past. One can even speak of a longing for death as a way of avoiding life, change and new beginnings. It can also be construed as a wish to return to the embrace of the unconscious and escape from the exciting yet painful demands of adult life.

Not knowing

Put simply, the idea of the unconscious means that I do not know myself. One might adopt an optimistic spirit and argue that psychotherapy or analysis enables one to know oneself better. This seems to be true for some people, but I think one has to be very cautious about the claims that are made here. My own sense is that one can never 'know oneself', for there is always a huge amount that is unknown, no matter how much work one does on it. In fact, it might be more accurate to say that the unconscious is infinite and that we only scratch the surface of it.

People's reactions to that idea vary enormously: some are plunged into gloom, for it seems to suggest that we are condemned to wander in a fog of uncertainty. However, I feel this is too pessimistic: I believe one can get to know some of the main landmarks of one's own psyche, and this gives one a much better chance of navigating through life safely and without damaging other people.

Having said that, there is no doubt that the unconscious has an amazing ability to surprise us and shake us from our complacency. 'I thought I knew myself' is a common enough cry, when someone finds they are doing something or feeling something or saying something that is 'out of character'.

In fact, I am fond of the notion of 'not knowing'. I see it as a healthy corrective to the over-rational age we live in and the excessive emphasis placed on science and technology. It is rather refreshing to carry out an activity – I am thinking of psychotherapy – where *not* knowing becomes an achievement, rather than a failure, and where confusion and bewilderment can be allowed to stand as they are and are not 'solved'. Thus the idea that therapy 'solves problems' is quite wide of the mark – frequently, one has to hold a problem for long periods of time without a solution being obvious. Sometimes, one simply does not find a solution – the problem may dissolve, or one may learn to accept it, or it no longer seems to be a problem. I can cite as an example a married patient, who had gay affairs to satisfy the long-standing but denied homosexual side to his nature. He was in terrible torment over the conflict between loyalty to his wife and his sexual needs, but in the end he came to some kind of acceptance of the 'solution' he had found instinctively, since he felt he neither wanted to leave his wife nor deny his homosexuality. He also went through great conflict over whether to tell his wife, but decided not to. However, this work involved long periods of confusion and mental chaos before he came to some kind of peace.

This strikes me as a good example of the work with the unconscious in psychotherapy, in that one is attempting to form a relationship with it. This may sound either trite or sentimental, but it is revolutionary. I assume that most people have a very poor relationship with their unconscious, so that they could be said to have 'a stranger in their midst'. However, if one accepts Freud's proposals, there is no doubt that the unconscious sends a constant stream of messages to us – in the form of dreams, intuitions, irrational thoughts and images, strange life-events, and so on. For example, anyone who has ever fallen in love has been assailed by the unconscious! The patient cited above fell head over heels in love with a male prostitute – the unconscious certainly took a concrete form in his life and he had to come to terms with it.

One might generalize at this point and argue that our relationship with it is meagre and impoverished in Western industrial culture, and that the signs of this are all around us in the form of addictions of various kinds, lurid imagery in popular culture, religious cults, outbreaks of barbaric violence, and so on. In other words, the unconscious erupts because it is denied: what is more difficult to grasp is how collective symbols and rituals can be developed which help us to give expression to the unconscious in a safe manner. It seems to be true that one cannot cheat the unconscious – in the end, one has to settle accounts with it.

Another and more surprising way of expressing this is to say that when we are over-identified with the unconscious, our relationship with it is non-existent – we are not separate enough from it. For example, one often meets people who suffer powerful internal self-attacks. Their inner critic (super-ego) keeps up a continual stream of messages berating them for their failures. But what is quite startling to see is that many people simply accept the message – that they are hopeless, useless, and so on. It can take many years of intensive work before the individual is able to separate off from such unconscious material and appreciate that it is not necessarily the gospel truth. In other words, I can de-identify from my inner critic and resist its ferocious attacks.

Thus by separating from the unconscious, one is able to have a relationship with it. This may sound uncontroversial, but it is an extremely difficult project.

One of Freud's key perceptions was that one could not undertake this journey alone. In solitude, the individual's relationship to their unconscious becomes too messy and chaotic to decipher. We require a witness who can step in and help us – and sometimes give us support against the attacks mounted from an unconscious source, or on the other hand, permit an unconscious thought some space in which to exist, free from the heavy weight of repression.

I would argue, then, that those who deny the existence of the unconscious are completely identified with it, and therefore cannot distinguish it, but I am aware that this argument in itself might be shot down as a typically ingenious analytic rebuttal. In therapy itself, one sees its usefulness: the people who are most difficult to work with are those who are constantly identified with unconscious contents, which are then denied in a spirit of complacency and surprise. For example, I recall suggesting to certain people that they were angry with me – and eliciting furious denials! Or with some patients, one finds that the sessions are stormy, full of arguments, recriminations, and so on. Such patients tend to feel that this has nothing to do with them, but is a result of the therapy and its shortcomings. Of course, such problems are very common in people's intimate relationships.

It is to Freud that we owe a debt of thanks for mapping out for the first time the geography of the psyche in such a way that we could begin to grapple with the unconscious and could learn to negotiate with it. Then we are neither flooded by it in an uncontrollable manner nor are we forced to cast it into an outer darkness, from where its persecutions of us can become insufferable. The unconscious is an objective fact, just as much as gravity or the weather, and as human beings, we have to grapple with it, for it contains the source of our life's energy.

5
Forgetting, Repeating and Remembering

The themes of forgetting, repeating and remembering can be seen running through Freud's mature work as pronounced motifs: one could even argue that they are among the key principles of Freudian thought. Neurosis itself can be described as a form of repetition that both perpetuates an original traumatic situation or relationship and also tries to 'forget' it, in the sense of repressing it. Neurotic symptoms have a paradoxical quality therefore: on the one hand, they are like lumps of amber which contain some ancient creature perfectly preserved. For example, I had a male patient who had had a very seductive mother – she seemed to have been emotionally and sexually quite invasive, getting dressed in front of him, kissing him in an inappropriate way, talking about her orgasms, and so on. Throughout his adult life he had a series of relationships with women whom he perceived as seductive, and these relationships tended to be very stormy on both sides, with much recrimination, anger, feelings of revenge and so on. It seemed pretty clear that he was repeating some aspects of his relationship with his mother, partly in order finally to conquer the unavailable temptress, partly to be tantalizing to her (for revenge), and for other more obscure reasons – for example, at the deepest level he still felt like a little boy who wanted his mother to comfort him and not seduce him. In a sense, unconsciously he was still trying to solve the conundrum of this traumatic early relationship.

Freud used different kinds of imagery to describe this phenomenon, sometimes archaeological, at other times imagery derived from literature and publishing – 'new editions of old conflicts' is one of his celebrated descriptions of the transference relationship. He adds: 'the patient would like to behave the same way as he did in the past.'[1]

On the other hand, the neurosis also *obliterates* the original situation and its traumatic emotional quality: in the above example, it is because the man is cut off from his relationship with his mother and the hurt and anger it caused (and the love that is involved), that he is forced to resurrect it. To put it another way, the trauma exists in the unconscious, but the ego is not aware of it or refuses to be aware of it. The unconscious ripostes by evacuating the material into life – the man 'acts out' through a series of sexual relationships containing all the essential features of the original relationship, but which he is probably totally unaware of. No doubt much of our adult life recapitulates aspects of our infancy – this is not in itself a problem, but only becomes so when we repeat self-injurious patterns of thought, feeling and action.

One of the tasks of psychotherapy becomes clear at this point – to liberate the forgotten material, the repressed contents of the unconscious so that the individual can go through the various thoughts and feelings and work through the traumatic aspects of the relationship. If this is done thoroughly, there will be no need to act out, for the pressure has been removed from the unconscious. If you like, the unconscious constantly 'leaks' its repressed material: the solution is to open a channel to the unconscious so that the leak can become a steady flow between unconscious and ego. This is the process of 'remembering', only not remembering in a purely intellectual or detached way, but in an involved emotional manner. Freud makes the comment that the therapist must not respond to the patient's love, so that 'the patient... will then feel safe enough to allow all her preconditions for loving, all the phantasies springing from her sexual desires, all the detailed characteristics of her state of being in love, to come to light'.[2] The reason for the therapist's 'abstinence' are clear at this point: the alternative is to have a love affair with the patient, which would in fact, apart from the ethical considerations, stop the patient's fantasies and feelings 'coming to light'.

It can be seen that there are two types of 'remembering': first, the unconscious type, which involves repeating old situations without being aware that one is; second, the conscious type, when one is able to trace back such repetitions to their roots. Therapy takes the first type and attempts to transform it into the second.

Transference

'Remembering' and 'forgetting' are widespread phenomena in human existence, but in psychotherapy they achieve particular resonance in the transference, which Freud came to see as one of the central issues in the analysis and its resolution. That is, the patient brings to the relationship with the analyst old feelings, old ways of relating, yet this repetition is opaque since the feelings and ways of relating are unconscious. None the less the therapist has before him an invaluable array of material in the transference which preserves both the original traumatic relationship and its repression.

We can also adduce the theme of resistance: the propensity of the patient to fight against the insights of the analysis is another form of repetition. Resistance strives to keep the repression in place, so that the original traumatic thoughts and feelings are not brought to the surface.[3] Resistance is in fact very complex, as one also has to take into account the deep-rooted desire of many people to remain neurotic – if you like, their refusal to have a happier life. This conflicts with their unconscious guilt and need to be punished, and conflicts with other feelings, for example, the wish to punish other people by exhibiting one's misery and sickness. Thus there is an element of revenge in the wish to remain sick – 'Look what you've done to me' is a rough paraphrase of this attitude.

This brief summary indicates how complex the issues of remembering and forgetting are, and how deeply embedded in the Freudian project. For the aim of making the unconscious conscious means to lift the repressions so that one can 'remember' – 'remember' in the widest sense of 're-experience' – the traumatic relationships that produced one's neurotic attitudes to life. This equation can be expressed most simply as follows: those who do not remember the past are compelled to repeat it. Lacan describes this rather laconically: 'what is forgotten is recalled in acts.'[4]

Repetition

In fact, most of us most of the time are probably engaged in some form of repetition: we tend to follow the same career throughout our life; we pursue the same hobbies; we have friends of a certain kind; we are attracted to sexual partners of a certain kind. Human beings are remarkably conservative – but then, as Freud pointed out, life itself is conservative, unless it is forced to find a new way. Thus in the animal kingdom, there are species that are many millions of years old, even though it can be assumed that evolution is an ongoing process.

This led Freud to link the repetition compulsion with death itself, and what he called the 'death instinct', and many subsequent analysts have felt uneasy with this term. One can see why. It seems odd to call death an 'instinct', yet at the same time, it is clear what Freud was trying to express. It is not simply that everything is going to die, but that there is a tendency, or even a drive to death or inertia. For example, all of us have a primitive need to find a womb-like state of torpor, where we can escape the demands and rigours of the outside world. In large part sleep satisfies this demand, but the many addictive substances found in human culture also bear testimony to our craving for oblivion.

However, it may be preferable to separate the death instinct from the notion of repetition, since they seem to be quite different philosophical categories. None the less, Freud's research into repetition is quite profound and gives us many insights into the relationship between memory and identity. For example, anyone working professionally as a psychotherapist will become aware of the very powerful desire in many people to avoid change. Put another way, it is when the therapy is going well that many people start to back off and attempt flight. Those who are prone to suicidal feelings may be in danger of suicide precisely when they have recently felt some hope. Of course, if the therapist is prepared for this, it can be rectified, since therapist and patient are able to discuss it, probably even before it arises.

But the point I am making is that when I am confronted with change – even if it is change that I fundamentally desire – it strikes me as a threat to my identity. In fact, this is correct, since our normal sense of self can be assumed to be made up of many memories, many character traits and psychic structures that have acquired a sense of permanence. To put it crudely, depressed people dread not being depressed, for their depression is in large part who they are. In fact, I have heard people say to me: 'Don't take my depression away from me, it's all I have.' And this is not a joke; it must be taken seriously. Some people cannot go through change very quickly, otherwise the sense of disorientation and loss of identity are too great, and they may suffer a breakdown.

If we say, then, that repetition is one of the building blocks of human existence – and perhaps of life itself – we can also add the important point that most of the time it is unconscious. It goes on in the background, and only occasionally does it strike me that I have the same kinds of friends as I did 30 years ago, or that I am rereading books which I read as a student, and so on. Hence the unconsciousness of repetition is not a problem – except with self-damaging repetitions. Here we are faced with the task of exhuming them and making them more conscious, so that I regain some degree of choice over them.

I am reminded of one famous Zen story about suffering. A Zen trainee asks the head monk: 'Does Zen free us from suffering?', expecting the conventional reply, 'yes'. But the head monk replies otherwise: 'No, Zen gives us the freedom to suffer.'

I find this story quite profound and quite revealing of some of the liberating aspects of the Freudian project. For we act out partly to avoid the repressed pain inside us; therefore, the therapeutic task becomes one of releasing our pain so that we do not need to act out. The 'acting out' is the repetition which both 'remembers' the old pain by prolonging it, and 'forgets' it by destroying any insight we might have into it. For example, one sometimes meets in therapy people who have chaotic, melodramatic relationships, often with sado-masochistic elements. There is plenty of noise, arguments, reconciliations. The sex can be wonderful, but the despair very deep for both partners. Listening to descriptions of such relationships reminds me of opera – it has a certain magnificence, but who would want to live like that? Furthermore, why do people want to live like that? The answer is surely twofold: in part, they are both repeating patterns they learned as children; but also they want to avoid having any insight into their behaviour, and they want to avoid having any choice over it. One might say simply enough that they are avoiding intimacy, but then intimacy brings with it often the terrible danger of facing old wounds.

Repetition, then, lies at the heart of identity and in itself is not neurotic. Without it, there would be no sense of stable identity. But of course the psyche repeats everything, both the neurotic and non-neurotic aspects. We are interested in those forms of repetition – particularly in action – which maintain the repression of unbearable feelings. Our neuroses help us to avoid these feelings, whilst at the same time still causing us suffering through the self-damage or self-limitation that is found in all neurotic behaviour.

It can be seen how selective human beings are in their use of memory. There are those memories which help me to maintain my sense of myself – I know I am the same person who went to such and such a school, who got married at a certain age, and so on. Furthermore, I am the one having the memories. But at the same time, I repress those memories which would lead me to re-examine very deep wounds: these memories get acted out instead.

Freud's theoretical and practical work on repression and the lifting of repression produces a very subtle and dialectical approach to identity. The human being is like an iceberg, with nine-tenths of the personality below the water line, in the murky depths of the unconscious. People come to therapy with the hope of exposing some of those depths, but at the same time determined to resist such an uncovering. Our repressions are some of our dearest possessions!

Mourning

One of the strangest phenomena in psychotherapy is to see someone mourning their own neurotic past or former personality. That is, after someone has sufficiently penetrated their inner world to grasp concretely the neurotic core, and is thereby able to stop repeating certain self-destructive patterns, they often become very sad. It is likely that they are mourning their former self, who now has to be sacrificed if the person is to go forward to a new life.

But this phenomenon of mourning gives us insight into the dialectic of forgetting and remembering. One reason that we 'forget', and that we resist the movement forwards induced by psychotherapy, is that we are attached to both our old self and to those people who determined it. In other words, we are loyal to our parents, even though they may have instilled in us precisely those self-destructive tendencies that we have come to therapy to get rid of. Thus part of the resistance to therapy, and indeed to psychological growth, stems from this loyalty. It is difficult to cut the umbilical cord, even if this cutting promises us a new freedom. To go back to the example used at the beginning of this chapter, my patient with the seductive mother eventually broke through to very powerful feelings of grief and mourning for his mother. In some ways, his sexual relationships had acted to keep his tie with her intact. What he dreaded was to let go of his mother, even if that tie cost him so dearly; yet he also yearned to break free from her.

Thus our forgetting has the effect (and the aim) of tying us closely to our childhood and those important figures in it. Thus one often finds people at the beginning of therapy asserting stoutly that they had a 'wonderful childhood', that Mum and Dad were fine people, that there 'are no problems there'. This idyllic picture is often shattered later, but one has to overcome this powerful idealizing tendency, whose effect is to suffuse the past in a rather unreal glow, and also to keep the patient stuck in his neurotic patterns.

Unconsciously, the patient knows that the effect of 'remembering' will be to loosen these ties. If our aim is to become more autonomous, to become the person I am, rather than the person others may have determined for me, then this necessarily involves freeing myself of old injunctions, stipulations, and so on. Perhaps your father always told you you were useless; or told you that you were destined to be a politician, when secretly you always wanted to be an artist; or told you you were unattractive; or seduced you – all these actions and stipulations are imprisoning to people, and they seek to be free of them. But this means saying good-bye to that father and to the child of that father that one once was.

Remembering, therefore, often involves a degree of mourning for the past that one now remembers. For remembering leads to letting go, just as forgetting involved being identified with the thing that is forgotten. This is one of the most dazzling paradoxes at the centre of Freud's thought: by forgetting, we cling; by remembering, we become free.

Identification

One of the corollaries of the above paradox, is that, put baldly, we identify very strongly with the repressed. That is, I incorporate into myself and my actions those things that I am not aware of, that I have 'forgotten'.

There is, of course, an extraordinary paradox about this. It is the things I have forgotten or never knew that possess me, and as I become more aware of them I become less identified with them. How often does one meet people who are totally identified with one parent without knowing it? The identification is a means of attachment, and hence the patient will fight very strongly against any loosening of this tie and against any 'remembering' of it, for the remembering leads to letting go and mourning, and, quite likely, to feelings of abandonment, deep loneliness, and so on. Yet without this process, one cannot become an autonomous adult.

We can say, then, that 'remembering' is a kind of de-identification, and 'forgetting' is a kind of unconscious attachment. That is why remembering brings about mourning, and why forgetting is so resistant to enquiry. We do not want to remember what we have forgotten, because we do not want to give up those old ties, even if they are harmful to us.

These links between the repressed, acting out, identification and mourning demonstrate the complexity and subtlety of Freud's theory of the unconscious and the means necessary to liberate it. Here there is no simplistic opposition between the 'forgotten trauma' and the liberation consequent upon its recall, as is found in Hollywood films and some anti-Freudian critics. Rather, we find a titanic struggle in patients between those forces that want to exorcise and heal old wounds, and thereby attain some degree of freedom from them, and those forces that want to preserve the status quo. The human psyche contains both very conservative and very radical wings: the conservative wing wishes to keep things intact ('forgotten'), even if this involves the individual in a considerable degree of suffering and frustration; the radical wing wishes to be free of old restraints and inhibitions – wishes to 'remember' in other words – so that it can leave behind old modes of living and take up new ones.

The conservative aspect of the psyche can be related to Freud's concept of the 'death instinct', which he defines as 'the instinct to return to the inanimate state'.[5] I have no doubt that Freud unearthed something very important in human motivation: the desire for inertness.

One of the mistakes made by inexperienced therapists, whether consciously or unconsciously, is to take sides with the radical wing of the patient against the inertia which resists change. I vividly remember a mistake I made in this respect with a very talented artist, who was confronted with a new challenge in his career. He was paralysed by a fierce conflict between the desire to seize the new opportunity and develop his career, as against his intense fear of exposing himself to the public in a new way. In my inexperience, I began to cheer him on enthusiastically, whereupon he left therapy.

Of course, in hindsight it is clear what happened. As I applied more weight to one side of the conflict raging inside him, this actually produced a countervailing weight on the other side, which led him to stop the therapy. It is clear what I should have done – helped him to bring the conflict out more clearly, without putting a finger on one side or the other. The struggle between the new and the old must be allowed to go on, until it finds its own resolution. The novice therapist, obsessed with dreams of therapeutic success, tends to rush in and interfere with this process. That is not the responsibility of psychotherapy, however. This partly explains Freud's caution with regard to therapeutic ambition and 'cure'. On a number of occasions he indicated that he did not feel enthusiastic about this. Certainly, he must have learned from cases such as 'Dora' that his zeal and enthusiasm backfired, as so often is the case.

This phenomenon is shown brilliantly with those people who are deeply attached to their own negative view of life. Everything is hopeless, the therapy most of all. There is no point in any of it, and the patient only perseveres out of a kind of inertia. With patients like this, the worst thing that the therapist can do is be enthusiastic. Again, I recall instances when I attempted to dissuade such pessimistic people by pointing out that in fact we had made some progress. The next session would inevitably bring down a torrent of abuse and lamentation on my head. I had demonstrated even more clearly my ineptitude. Matters had become even more hopeless.

Such reactions bear testimony to premature interference by the therapist. One has to let such people find their own positive attitudes developing, often embryonically and with great fragility. The unconscious self-hatred of the patient is so intense that any suggestion of progress brings about a rapid revenge. The self-hatred also contains a hatred of others: hence, the denial that any progress had been made is intended to convey how hateful I have become. Of course, the more helpful I am, the more negative I seem to such patients.

These examples demonstrate very clearly how attached people are to their own psychological baggage, no matter how negative or self-injurious it might be. The baggage forms a key part of identity. There may well be a great fear here that 'I won't exist' if I give up my own neurotic patterns of thought and action, and this fear has to be given great respect. Certainly, there is a sense that the early analysts, including Freud, did not always show such respect, but rushed in impetuously, only to find that this had negative consequences.

Healing

I am really arguing that 'remembering' must be an organic process: it cannot flow from suggestion or more forceful pressure from the therapist. Of course, this brings up again the fascinating question as to how this organic development occurs in the psyche. One can say that there are two immense pressures: one is to keep things repressed; the other, to bring them into the daylight. There is therefore a mighty struggle between these two forces, and it is not clear which will come out on top. Some people work through a lot of painful material and attain a degree of freedom from their neuroses; others begin to back-track when they realize the implications of forward progress; some retreat into a fortress-like position, which repels all boarders. Thus any estimation as to the 'success' of psychotherapy has to grapple with this extraordinary fact – some people who come to therapy do not want to get 'better', and they will resist any such moves fiercely. In the end, that is their choice.

One can, therefore, take optimistic or pessimistic positions on the self-healing nature of the psyche. The optimistic position is that there is a powerful self-healing drive which is always pressing to remove blocks and neurotic frustrations; the pessimistic standpoint would deny this on the grounds that it turns the psyche into an image of God – something akin to Jung's view. Freud's position on this is complicated, as we have seen in the discussion of empiricism and anti-empiricism. Put crudely, at various times Freud puts forward both positions.

Nachträglichkeit

The role of memory within psychoanalysis is brought to a focal point in Freud's concept of *Nachträglichkeit*, which is usually translated as 'deferred action' or 'deferred effect', although the literal meaning is something like 'the quality of carrying on after the event'. With this concept, Freud claims that memory is itself a creative act, for in deferred action one retrospectively ascribes significance to an event or a situation which it did not possess at the time. Thus Freud distinguishes those 'forgotten' things which are known at some level, and those things which have never been known: 'something is "remembered" which could never have been "forgotten" because it was never at any time noticed – was never conscious'.[6]

The clearest example concerns traumatic incidents or situations occurring at a very early age, probably at a pre-verbal age. Psychologically, it is often assumed that the young infant is unable to process such incidents emotionally – or to put it simplistically, he is unable to know what he feels and he is unable to think about the incident. This is what the psychoanalyst Christopher Bollas refers to as the 'unthought known' – something which we know about but have never thought about. The aim of therapy is to help us to think about such unthought things, so that they are integrated into the whole personality.[7]

Nachträglichkeit is, therefore, a very sophisticated and even revolutionary concept, for it refutes the idea that memory is a kind of dead or inert recall of events and situations, much as one might look through an old photograph album. Memory is seen as creative and interactive, in the sense that the past assumes a different significance in the light of my present knowledge. We might even say that the past changes in the light of the present.

Freud uses the notion of deferred effect in relation to various phenomena, for example, the primal scene – children who see sexual intercourse between their parents – the castration complex, and the sexual abuse of children. Thus in relation to castration, he claims that the young boy who sees that his mother or sister does not possess a penis is at first unperturbed by this. But after he has learned about castration, through having threats of castration made to him, he is able to process his earlier observations and give them a more 'theoretical' status – that they are indeed evidence for actual castration – and now he is shocked and horrified by the visual testimony. The primal scene incidents are claimed to be meaningful only retrospectively in later childhood when the child has understood how human sex works.[8]

One does not have to have faith in either the primal scene hypothesis or the castration theory to see the value of the concept of 'deferred effect'. Indeed, a large part of therapy is taken up with the delayed comprehension of things which, at the time, were not comprehended. This also helps us to explain one of the motives for repetition: we are forced to repeat things we do not understand or we cannot think about, or we cannot feel, so that eventually the repeated situation can be acknowledged and understood, and not repeated again.

But how does deferred action come into being? In the first instance, one can speak of events occurring which the child's intellectual and emotional apparatus cannot process – they are too complex or too traumatic. Second – and this is a post-Freudian concept – there may be a failure by the child's caretakers to help it emotionally digest a painful experience, say the death of a sibling. In short, the adults have not performed the reflecting role so crucial to young children. In such a case, the event remains as an unprocessed 'lump' in the psyche and has to be processed later in life, sometimes much later. One might assume that for many people infantile experiences are never adequately worked over and remain as permanent 'tumours' in the psyche.

Let me give an example. A female patient of mine had a string of boyfriends who beat her up. Although she didn't like being beaten up, it was noticeable that she wasn't outraged by it. At some level she felt she deserved it. It also repeated the abuse – both physical and mental – which she had received from both parents.

The turning point in the therapy occurred when I felt so fed up with this sequence of abuse that I expressed my own sense of indignation and outrage. To my surprise, she began to be outraged herself, and after a very angry parting from her current violent partner, began to form different non-abusive relationships with men. I am not suggesting that my outrage 'caused' hers – rather, that her sense of indignation had been repressed when she was a child and was awoken by mine. Thus her outrage was 'deferred', and her understanding that her parents had abused her was likewise delayed by several decades. At the time, as a child it probably seemed inconceivable to her that her parents were treating her badly – she inferred, rather, that she was bad and deserved such treatment. It was only with great trepidation and guilt that as an adult she was able to turn the tables and retrospectively realize that her parents had ill-treated her.

We can see from this example that deferred action is not simply an intellectual process but also an emotional one. One does not just understand something for the first time, one may actually feel something for the first time. Thus the woman above felt outraged for the first time in her life and was able painfully to tear herself away from her addiction to abuse. She also concretely experienced how much she hated herself and also how much she loved herself and was exhausted by the self-hatred and ready to give it up. Another factor which helped her to do this was that our relationship was non-abusive, reliable and nourishing. In fact, she repeatedly commented that she found it very odd to be with a man who didn't abuse her, and it took her a number of years to get used to this and to realize that she liked it! At first, she felt quite scornful of me, and referred to me as a 'wimp' and so on – real men were brutal.

Normally, deferred action relates to such childhood traumatic events or situations. But it is likely that it goes on all the time in adult life. How often do we say 'I didn't realize it at the time', or 'I didn't grasp the significance of what he was saying until later'. A brief example: a woman notices casually that her husband, normally very punctilious in his appointments, misses several business meetings. It is only later, when she suspects him on other grounds of adultery, that she connects the missed meetings and infers that he was meeting his mistress. Examples like this are legion, but they are usually less dramatic and impressive than infantile ones, which can be seen as casting huge shadows over our adult lives. We have to keep going back to the situations (that is, repeat them) which were not processed. The adult examples also tend to seem less unconscious and less chaotic.

Let me recap. The concept of *Nachträglichkeit* forces us to abandon any simplistic notion of time and memory as linear, one-dimensional forces. Rather, we must grapple with a dynamic or creative concept of memory: when we 'remember', we are not simply recalling something as it were photographically, but we are reconstructing it, we are telling a new story about it. The past may be revised in the light of present knowledge; it may even be reshaped. Its emotional 'feel' may become quite different. Take a person who was genitally molested as a baby: memories of this are probably going to be very diffuse and unclear and difficult to verbalize. But it is likely that there will be some kind of repetition of them in the person's life, and by connecting these repeated events with the original trauma, we may be able to 'tell the story' of the original abuse. Again there are dangers here: that an over-eager therapist may rush to construct narratives which are not warranted by the evidence.

It might be thought that *Nachträglichkeit* is a relatively late development in Freud's thinking in relation to memory, but this is not so. We find him in the 1890s trying out various conceptions of memory, some of which are clearly precursors to the notion of 'deferred action'. For example, in a remarkable letter to Wilhelm Fliess, dated 6 December 1896, Freud makes the following analysis:

> I am working on the assumption that our psychic mechanism has come into being by a process of stratification: the material present in the form of memory traces being subjected from time to time to a *rearrangement* in accordance with fresh circumstances – to a *retranscription*. Thus what is essentially new about my thesis is that memory is present not once but several times over. (original emphasis)[9]

The term 'retranscription' is particularly interesting as it contains the metaphor of transcription or narration in relation to memory – the idea being that our memories are narratives which are 'retold' several times, according to later developments. We shall see in the next chapter that this idea has great importance in the overall concept of analysis as a form of narrative-construction which aims to fill in the gaps occurring in the 'mutilated' story which the patient first brings.[10]

Transference and counter-transference have an intimate relationship with *Nachträglichkeit*, for the way in which the patient treats the therapist gives us much information about the patient's early life and inner life. And to begin with this information will often be unknown to the patient and unknown to the therapist! Let me expand on this point: much of the information that I receive about a new patient cannot as yet be articulated by me. It is still deeply unconscious. Only gradually am I able to process it, think about it and eventually communicate to the patient what is it like being his 'object'. Of course, this often tells us also how the patient was himself treated as a child, since he tends to treat me in the same way, or tries to get me to treat him in the same way.

But this material is not understood by the patient, or to begin with, by the therapist. We might say that therapy consists of a long struggle to grasp the significance of such 'deferred' recreations, which in the first place are communicated from unconscious to unconscious. If you like, the relationship between therapist and patient is the central arena where *Nachträglichkeit* takes its effect. Thus in the example cited above of the woman beaten up by her boyfriend, it was the constant disparity between such abusive relationships and the non-abusive relationship existing between me and her which eventually forced matters to a head for both of us. In addition, her 'deferred' outrage caused me to block my own outrage for a long period, until I was able, after a fierce inner struggle, to liberate my indignation, which thereby permitted her to liberate her own. If you like, both of us were struggling with emotional anaesthesia.

Time, repetition and the unconscious

If we bring together Freud's notion of the timelessness of the unconscious with the notion of repetition, a very interesting connection occurs. From the point of view of the unconscious (if it can be said to have a point of view), repetition is not repetition, for the notion of repetition denotes a sequence of identical events in time. Thus if I keep slamming the door shut and then opening it, we have a series of discrete events which are perceived to be similar yet distinct. But in the unconscious, the repeated event or situation simply exists in an eternal present. If we think again about people who keep finding abusive partners, the abuse is being enacted in time and space, but the internal self-abuse exists in the atemporal world of the unconscious.

This can be related to ordinary notions of 'personality' and 'character', which are usually assumed to be fairly static, permanent sets of attributes. A certain amount of character structure consists of defensive formations, which were originally developed to protect the individual from dangerous or unpleasant impingements. Often such structures seem so solid that they are indestructible. But this is not true. One sees people go through extraordinary changes of personality – not, I hasten to add, because of psychotherapy, but because of the evolution of the individual.

We are presented, then, with the rather strange model of one part of the psyche (the unconscious) existing in a timeless state, containing certain objects and relations between objects which are as it were 'frozen', yet these interrelations are continually being projected into the concrete world of time and space, and here we have the perception of a 'repeated event' or a series of events. The person who has a series of abusive relationships is enacting the core abusive relationship which exists in the unconscious: the abusive partner takes the role of the inner abusive 'critic'. In fact, one often finds such relationships can easily flip round: some people actually alternate between relationships where they are the abuser and those where they are abused. But in terms of the present model it is easy to see how this can happen: the abuser and the 'abusee' both exist internally, locked in an eternal struggle, and both get played out in the external world. In terms of sado-masochism, the sadist can easily switch into playing the opposite, and in fact probably needs to keep switching in order to satisfy the melodramatic needs of the inner sadist and inner masochist.

The relationship between the timeless world of the unconscious and the world of time and space, where the ego has its domain, is yet another example of an idea in the Freudian *oeuvre* which remains undeveloped. In fact, Freud's references to 'timelessness' are scanty, and yet it is a crucial attribute of the unconscious. It is striking that in the 'Titan' metaphor Freud used to describe the impulses existing in the unconscious, he describes them as 'immortal':

> These wishes in our unconscious, ever on the alert, and so to say, immortal, remind one of the legendary Titans, weighed down since primaeval ages by the massive bulk of the mountains.[11]

One might go further and relate timelessness to death and the conservative instinct in human beings: can we not speculate that the psyche is witness to a huge struggle not just between death and Eros, or hate and love, but also between timelessness and time? That is, one of the chief duties of the ego is to pull us away from the seductive, frozen world of the unconscious dramas of childhood, so that we can stop repeating old patterns and begin to live in the present. The habits of repetition which are so deeply engrained in us are like those mythological monsters which must be slain if we are to find the hidden treasure. In this sense, timelessness must give precedence to time; death to life.

Psychoanalysis, therefore, points like an arrow, forward into life and away from the deadly coils of our own clinging to the past. To take the optimistic stance: there is a choice between life and death. Freud knew only too well that doing analysis or therapy offered no guarantee that the patient would choose life. Many do not. But at least such a patient might realize that death (or neurosis) was itself a choice and not an externally imposed doom. In addition, the Peter Pan part of all of us can be helped to come down to earth and begin to live a real, authentic existence, instead of floating forever in clouds of speculation and 'what ifs'.

6
Story-telling

It sounds rather banal to state that we approach Freud through his own writings and through what is written about him in the form of biographies, theoretical discussions, critiques, and so on. Of course, we may also stare with fascination at faded photographs of him or even some old film, but what 'Freud' means to most people is obtained via written texts. This is true of anyone with whom we grapple intellectually, studying their ideas, trying to evaluate their role in modern thought. It is however particularly true of Freud, since he was both a prolific and an eloquent writer – of letters, articles and books – and a massive amount has been written about him.

But there is more to 'knowing Freud' than this. We also have fantasies about him. For some, he is an heroic discoverer, in his own words, a conquistador. To others, he is an arch-villain and scoundrel, a corrupt purveyor of pseudo-science, a manipulator of unsuspecting patients. Such fantasies are not obtained from Freud's written texts, but from our own imaginations, indeed from our own unconscious. It is clear that in the twentieth century Freud occupied a prominent place in the fantasy life of many people, both intellectuals and non-intellectuals.

These issues do raise some interesting questions. Who is Freud? Which is the Freud you are familiar with, as perhaps opposed to the one I know? Into what context of ideas, feelings and fantasies do we place him? Why has Freud been so influential, when, for example, Jung, whose psychology is very rich and complex, has been much less so?

I think one answer to these questions is to do with Freud's ability as a writer and story-teller. Perhaps we should say not only that Freud is one of the most important thinkers of the twentieth century, but also one of the most important and influential writers. By contrast, Jung's writings are leaden and lugubrious.

Freud was a wonderful story-teller. His case histories are justly famous for their intrinsic interest, their construction, their wit, their suspense, and so on. But we can go further – story-telling is part of the psychoanalytic heritage, part of the 'therapeutic technique' which we tend to say that Freud 'invented'. And the 1980s and 1990s saw a widespread burgeoning of interest in the role of narrative within analysis and therapy.[1]

Psychotherapy consists, from one point of view, of story-telling between two people, and this story-telling undergoes some extraordinary shifts. As Freud says:

> I begin the treatment . . . by asking the patient the whole story of his life and illness, but even so the information I receive is never enough to let me see my way about the case. This first account may be compared to an unnavigable river whose stream is at one moment choked by masses of rock and at another divided and lost among shallows and sandbanks.[2]

Freud gives various reasons why the patient's story is incomplete – in part, to do with deliberate withholding, but also due to 'gaps in the memory'. But Freud concludes that at the end of treatment: 'we have before us an intelligible, consistent and unbroken case history.'[3]

Thus part of the psychoanalytic treatment consists in transforming the broken and incomplete initial story into a full and rounded one. How does this transformation happen? Clearly, the analyst helps in this process, and in Freud's early work it is clear that he was a zealous and hard-working 'editor'.

The 'Rat Man' case gives us many explicit indications as to how Freud saw this process of reconstruction. After the Rat Man has told Freud some of his story, Freud makes this comment: 'It was only when he told me the story for the third time that I could get him to realize its obscurities and could lay bare the errors of memory and the displacements in which he had become involved.' And Freud takes an active part in clearing up such obscurities and gaps: 'It was this last statement which provided me with a starting point from which I could begin straightening out the various distortions involved in his story.'[4]

But how does the analyst accomplish this 'straightening out', and what material does he use? Clearly, the analyst supplies the missing or distorted material on the basis of his interpretation of the patient's own associations. Thus, the Rat Man case reaches a critical juncture when Freud has been supplied with enough information:

> now the path was clear to the solution of his rat idea. The treatment had reached its turning point, and a quantity of material information which had hitherto been withheld became available, and so made possible a reconstruction of the whole concatenation of events.[5]

Thus the analyst does not simply rely on the production of greater and greater amounts of material from the patient, but also on his own analysis of it, which depends on the theoretical knowledge he possesses: 'With the assistance of our knowledge of infantile sexual theories and of symbolism . . . the whole thing could be translated and given a meaning.'[6] In other words, the mutilation of the life-story, which is due to repression, is healed by the analyst's ability to detect and recover the repressed material hidden in the story. Thus while overtly the life-story is incomplete, it also covertly supplies all the information needed to complete it. The analyst becomes skilled at elucidating the repressed parts of the story and eventually it is to be hoped that the patient too becomes skilled in doing this.

As Freud states, much of the repressed material is revealed symbolically, for example, in dreams, in the patient's actions, in memories and fantasies, and so on. A rather glaring example can be found in the Dora case when Dora brings a 'reticule' (a kind of handbag) to the session and keeps playing with it: Freud pounces on this as a symbol of masturbation. But Dora also supplies two key dreams, and much of the case history is taken up with an analysis of them by Freud, who subjects them to a highly sexual interpretation. In fact, symbolic material may be found anywhere, both during the session and outside it, in relation to the patient's dreams and fantasies but also their behaviour in the world, for example, relationships, sexual predilections, work, hobbies, and so on.

Clearly this method is open to abuse, if the therapist is over-zealous in his 'corrections' of the patient's story. At times, Freud does seem too energetic in his reconstructions: it is perhaps significant that Dora breaks off the treatment immediately after Freud's extensive interpretation of her second dream. Of course, this can be interpreted as a symbolic resistance to the interpretation, yet later therapeutic procedure would admit that the patient's sensitivity to interpretation must be respected.

A second danger can be seen in the previous quotation: 'with the assistance of our knowledge'. In other words, Freud is going to give a definite slant in his interpretations, and the patient has to like it or lump it. As we have seen, Dora was very resistant to Freud's zeal – after one of his interpretations, he comments: 'this explanation of mine was met by Dora with a most emphatic negative'.[7] This of course raises many issues to do with the therapist's activism, degree of intervention, interpretive zeal, and so on, and this formed part of an ongoing debate in psychotherapy during the twentieth century. It has also of course formed the basis for those attacks on therapy as a 'power-trip', in which an overweening therapist indoctrinates a submissive patient. The normal response to this is to argue that symbolic interpretations only work when they strike a chord in the patient; thus, one definitely does not impose them; that is clearly counter-productive.

Freud himself began to recommend that the analyst does not determine the 'themes' which come up, and argues that if the analyst analyses the resistances he sees in the patient's material, the patient is usually able to make the important connections himself.[8] This seems a far cry from the aggressive manner with which Freud conducted Dora's analysis.

Literature and psychoanalysis

Traditionally, the relationship between literature and psychoanalysis has been one of interpretation of the former by the latter. Psychoanalysis seemed to provide a set of tools and a set of ideas with which literature could be given a kind of 'depth' analysis. Latent meanings could be uncovered; the writer's particular unconscious configuration could be unearthed; perhaps the reader's own fantasies could be hypothesized. At times, of course, this hermeneutical use of psychoanalysis was rather crude and reductive. One of the problems with it is that the literary text might be approached in a rather naive way, for example, as if the characters in a play or novel were real people, thus ignoring the artifice of the work itself.

Another coarsening effect of psychoanalytic criticism lay in its misconstruing or ignoring of aesthetic effects: for example, *Hamlet* is not considered to be a great play simply because of its pronounced Oedipal theme; there is also the matter of its language, its organization, its portrayal of interiorization, and so on. 'Depth' criticism can easily miss the aesthetic effects on the linguistic 'surface'.

But if, traditionally, psychoanalysis has suggested that it might provide the key to a literary text, the understanding of psychoanalysis as a narrative-constructing enterprise reverses the relationship. The analytic construction or 'reconstruction' has an affinity to a literary text, and the analyst or therapist is in the position of a writer or editor, as indeed is the patient, so long as the analyst's zeal is not excessive and permits the patient his or her creative input to the process. It is possible, then, that psychoanalysis could be evaluated by literary critics in terms of its narrative abilities.

Can we suggest that psychotherapy is concerned with aesthetics, in the sense of being interested in the construction of 'smooth', coherent and intelligible texts? This does seem a rather remarkable approach to therapy, but it has certain points in its favour. For example, therapists often speak of the patient's 'satisfaction' with a particular interpretation. The satisfaction derives partly from a sense of truth or aptness – perhaps a gap in the 'story' has been partly filled by a suggestion from the therapist. But we can also suggest that the satisfaction is indeed aesthetic: the patient is dissatisfied with the present state of his life-story, which is broken and inconsistent, and yearns for a sense of harmony and internal consistency. This does not mean that we construct a 'happy' story or invent a false one, but we construct a story which fits together, which explains why one event followed another, which provides an internal logic to the story, whose logic has previously eluded the patient. People often wrack their brains over the enigma of their own lives: 'Why did I get involved with that man? Why did I take that job on? What on earth possessed me to do such a thing straight after something similar had ended in disaster?'

In other words, many people look for meaning in their lives, not some ultimate religious meaning, but an internal meaning, a meaning that connects the past with the present, that explains why certain patterns seem to repeat endlessly, and why certain feelings seem to haunt us. We can suggest, therefore, that these connections provide not only a sense of logic and meaning but also an aesthetic pleasure which is important. It can be paraphrased as follows: 'I see now. My life is not meaningless and illogical; it doesn't just consist of a heap of broken fragments; it is a creation with its own internal dynamics and laws.'

Perhaps here I am straying from a strictly Freudian world into a more Jungian one, yet it is arguable that Freud himself constantly brushed against such a world, even if he also expressed revulsion against it. Talk of life as a 'creation' brings up uncomfortable questions, such as who the creator is. Again, for Jung, this isn't a problem, since the Self is such a creator, but perhaps for Freud we have trespassed into the 'occult'. Yet it is implicit in Freud's theory of the unconscious that it is creative, dynamic and wilful.

We can put it more extremely: the story (or stories) told by the therapist and the patient *has (have) already been revealed* in the 'narrative' of the patient's life. But this life-story has been mutilated at the surface level, so that it does not 'make sense' to the patient; there are gaps in it, there are stuck points, where the narrative no longer flows on. Thus we can take Shakespeare's image of life being a 'tale told by an idiot, signifying nothing' and say that that is the initial appearance of life, especially the life of someone who is 'neurotic' or 'psychotic'. The task of therapy is to discover the deep underlying narrative of the person's life and *retell it* more explicitly. Psychotherapy can be seen in this light as a series of autobiographical sketches, which may in the end amalgamate to form a coherent account.

Such assumptions about therapy are bold, for they imply that there is an underlying narrative, that life has a sense to it, even a plan, that the external events of our lives correspond to an unconscious 'plot'. What is the plot? That is the question to be answered by the therapist/patient alliance.

Once again, these ideas seem to contradict Freud's explicit assertions that the unconscious is an uncoordinated aggregate, one might almost say, a rag-bag of impulses and desires. Yet the notion that the unconscious is coordinated and tells a story in the shape of the person's life is also present in Freud. Why else does Freud insist to his patients that there is a deep logic to the apparently chaotic events told to him? Why else does he tell Dora that her dreams of fire and 'jewel-cases' relate to her bed-wetting, her genitals and her love for her father and Herr K.?

In fact, one can argue that Freud went too far in such cases: he *imposed* a narrative on the patient, and in Dora's case, perhaps, this is one reason why she left the analysis. It is possible also that in the early years, before the theory of transference and counter-transference had been fully worked on, Freud made himself too much of a central character in the narrative by his insistence on certain interpretations, and by his unconscious identification with key characters in the patient's story. An example of this in the Dora case can be found at the point where Freud suggests that the kiss which Herr K. inflicts on Dora means more than a kiss – that in fact Dora was aware of Herr K. 's erect penis pressing against her. In terms of counter-transference, one might also suggest that it is Freud who is pressing his 'erect' interpretation against Dora, that Freud is unconsciously putting himself in the place of her father and Herr K., is unconsciously excited by Dora, and so on – in other words, a kind of mutual seduction is going on between Freud and Dora.

Such information would be routinely available today for the therapist who had been trained in the use of counter-transference, and who, for example, accepted being sexually aroused by Dora, realized that he had the wish to 'penetrate' her, whether literally or metaphorically, but was able to use this as vital information in the reconstruction of Dora's story. Without doubt, one would also have to consider the possibility of the therapist identifying with Dora and enjoying her tales of seduction by men.

Of course, the anti-Freudian has a nice argument in relation to these ideas – that life does not have a meaning, does not form a neat pattern, does not have an internal logic and inconsistency, and certainly does not have a creator, and that all of this forms the grandiose fantasy of inadequate people who compensate for their empty lives by working as therapists and inflicting their fantasies on their patients.

Sub-texts

Up to now, my formulation of the story-telling element in psychotherapy has been very simplistic. In particular, in suggesting that there is 'a life-story' which is to be reconstructed, I have ignored the very complex texture of stories which exists. Thus as well as the story of the patient's life, particularly the events of childhood, one must also describe the structure of the inner world, or relationships between 'internal objects'. Here one is very much concerned with the fantasies, dreams and other symbolic material presented by the patient, taken to be a reflection of the structure of the patient's psyche.

But these two stories intertwine: one cannot stipulate that the 'life-story' is objective and the inner story is subjective. Freud argues in quite a subtle fashion that our recollections are themselves shot through with fantasy, and also that 'dreaming is another kind of remembering'.[9] In the Rat Man case, Freud presents an explicit account of how fantasy and 'reality' are blended:

> people's 'childhood memories' are only consolidated at a later period, usually at the age of puberty; and that this involves a complicated process of remodelling, analogous in every way to the process by which a nation constructs legends about its early history.[10]

Another way of expressing this is that fantasies are as real as actual events, and it is not always necessary to distinguish them, and perhaps even that they cannot be separated.

There is a third sub-text: the story of the relationship between therapist and patient, and this story itself interconnects with the others. In fact, in reality one does not receive three stories at all, but a complex narrative which contains an interwoven texture, from which such subtexts can be hypothesized.

Dora's case shows Freud describing the first two stories, but omitting the third. First, he describes Dora as a 'perfect hysteric' who has blocked her sexual response to Herr K.'s advances. This is an 'internal' diagnosis – Dora's problems lie in her hysterical denial of 'normal' sexual vitality. The normal story of sexual development at puberty, leading to full intercourse, has (according to Freud) been interrupted by Dora herself, who has prevented the full dénouement taking place.

But Freud goes on to describe in great detail Dora's family situation and the relationships between her family and Herr and Frau K. In a sense, Freud is tacitly admitting that the 'internal' diagnosis – that Dora is repressing her own sexual responses – is quite inadequate, as she is in fact a pawn in a complex game of seduction and betrayal going on between her parents and the K. couple. Freud also admits that he has neglected to bring out the transference relationship between himself and Dora. It seems clear in retrospect that Dora's relationship with her father and with Herr K. is being repeated with Freud, and just as she repulsed the kiss from Herr K., she repulses Freud's 'advances' in the shape of his forceful interpretations. However, it strikes me as ludicrous to criticize Freud too much for these omissions: the Dora case occurred when psychoanalysis was at a fairly early stage of development.

A further point to be made about the complex interweaving of different stories is that different schools of therapy, and different individual therapists, favour one story over another. Thus the seduction hypothesis, formulated by Freud in the 1890s, is very much taken up with the reconstruction of historical events, perceived as traumatic to the patient. But then Freud made his 'turn inwards', and began to see neurosis as internally motivated. Later analysts became divided on this very issue: in crude terms, Melanie Klein continued the 'internal' shift and neglected the environment; object relations theorists such as D.W. Winnicott favoured the narrative of the patient's infancy and particularly the relations with the important caretakers (usually parents).

But patients also tend to favour different emphases: some are not very interested in their childhood; others are obsessed with it. The inner world feels very alien to some, but intuitively appealing to others; some patients are very resistant to any discussion of the present relationship between therapist and patient, but others find it fascinating and helpful. Thus as a psychotherapist, one finds oneself shifting one's narrative focus from one patient to another. And of course, one usually finds that several narratives are being told simultaneously, and frequently there is much confusion and many lacunae.

Reality and rhetoric

We have already seen that Freud disputes the objective reality of the patient's life-story. To put it another way, Freud expresses scepticism or agnosticism as to whether one is dealing with real events from the past or imagined events – the point being that in the unconscious this distinction is not important. However, one might certainly criticize this standpoint, since actual abuse received as a child does have devastating effects.

This issue has become very important in contemporary psychotherapy because of the 'recovered memory' movement. At times, this movement has seemed to take a rather naive view of memory, as if one can simply dig up memories of childhood abuse in an uncomplicated way. This is not the case: many people do not have sharp memories, but diffuse and blurred ones, often not of specific incidents, but of an atmosphere, a tension in the air, feelings that were veiled and unspoken. Thus one often meets patients who feel that one parent was quite seductive, but not in an acted out way.

None the less, it strikes me that there has to be a degree of 'realism' in the approach to the past. If a patient describes certain events in childhood, or certain emotional configurations, I have no reason to doubt this. The idea that one might reconstruct a life-story which afforded relief to the patient, *even if it wasn't true*, strikes me as bizarre, and again seems to demonstrate too much activism by the therapist. The therapist has no business reconstructing anything for which there isn't solid evidence. Hence if there are large gaps in the reconstruction of childhood, if there are hazy areas where nothing is clear, then that is what is, and it would be therapeutically quite dangerous and irresponsible to put something there or to make inferences which are not supported. The idea that any therapist, on the basis of a short acquaintance with a patient, might pronounce *ex cathedra* that the patient had been sexually abused as a child strikes me as extremely non-therapeutic and yet another form of tyranny.

In addition, it is important to state that many people have had confusing childhoods, and it would be not only absurd but counter-therapeutic to impose some kind of order on the confusion. Both patient and therapist have to live with the confusion and not try to make it too neat.

However, granted that a degree of realism must operate in psychotherapy, one must also grant that there is a certain relativity vis-à-vis reality. For example, if Dora were to go to a variety of contemporary therapists and present her two dreams, she would receive very different interpretations. Freud's out-and-out sexual interpretation might be repeated today by an orthodox Freudian, but other analytic therapists might see it in quite different terms, for example, as a set of metaphors to do with containment (the 'jewel-case', etc.). A Jungian therapist might extract a more mythological narrative, perhaps concerning something of great value that Dora possesses in her psyche. Some therapists would probably make no interpretation at all, but leave this to the patient.

Who is to say which 'story' is correct? Of course, the patient will probably lean more to some interpretations than others, yet even this is a relative phenomenon. I can recall patients' dreams which received different interpretations over a number of years, as the patient (and the therapist) were able to see more and more in the dream. Let me give a brief example: a male patient dreamt of a woman hanging in a wardrobe. Over a period of seven years he was able to make the following links to this dream. It represented his mother and her emotional self-destruction; it symbolized his own strangulated creativity; his own feminine side was shut away and half-dead; in fantasy, he cut the woman down and revived her. It is not possible to say that any one of these interpretations is 'correct' and the others 'incorrect'. The dream is rather like a precious stone with many facets: as one turns the stone different aspects catch the light.

This idea is covered by Freud's term 'over-determination', and its implications in relation to 'story-telling' are very important. In theory, a dream or another piece of symbolism has an infinite set of meanings, and our lives can be narrated in an infinite number of ways. Of course, it would be bizarre to set out to construct such an infinite set of stories, but the fact that it is theoretically possible is very important, and shows up the impoverishment introduced by positing a single objective 'truth' or 'reality'.

Let me give another example, which is rather shocking. A middle-aged man would often recount to me the horrendous story of being anally raped by a neighbour, when he was about four years old. This terrible deed elicited many responses from my patient, ranging from intense rage to fear and grief, and sometimes a kind of numbness. But he surprised me one day by telling me that he sometimes felt grateful to his assailant as he had made him what he was, for better or worse. One might call this 'forgiveness', yet it seemed to me to go beyond that, and to attain an extraordinary overview of life and its 'meaning'. In a sense, my patient was eventually able to find some meaning, some value, even in the most terrible event of his life. The story that he told about it changed subtly over time from one in which he was purely the victim to one in which he made something of it. One might say that his role changed from being the hapless victim of his life-story to being the story-teller, and indeed the author of his life.

Is it possible that the rape never happened and the patient had lied to me over seven years? It is theoretically possible, yet this would suggest a character structure (to do with compulsive lying) that this man did not possess. But again, those who are determined to find ammunition against therapy could argue that perhaps I had been duped by taking his story seriously.

Interpreting texts

I have already referred to the 'naive' use of psychoanalysis in literary criticism, involving the retrieval of 'latent' meanings in a text, which are hidden on its surface. The problems with such a view are quite striking and have been pointed out by many critics.[11] To argue that the value of any artistic work lies in its latent meaning is bizarre, for one is basically saying that a paraphrase of a novel is its meaning! Of course, this ignores the issue of aesthetics. Why is the artistic work valued as art? In other words, the texture of the 'surface' may be precisely the source of value, enjoyment, and so on. Postmodern criticism has delighted in the description of the 'superficial' aspects of works of art and has debunked the notion of 'depth-interpretation'.

Second, the theory of 'latent meanings' assumes a rather crude idea of meaning, as if there were one unambiguous meaning to a work, which every reader arrives at. This is patently false: one need only cite Shakespeare's tragedies, which have been given many different meanings over the centuries, some of which contradict each other. For example, for the psychoanalytic literary critic to argue that 'the central meaning' of *Hamlet* lies in Hamlet's Oedipal conflicts seems rather naive: for example, I find one of the most entrancing things about the play to be Hamlet's ability to examine his own process and communicate this self-examination to the audience.

Third, some literary critics have objected to the whole notion of interpretation as the central tool of criticism, for example in Susan Sontag's well-known critical work *Against Interpretation*.

Clearly, if psychoanalysis had contributed only such notions as 'latent meaning' to the criticism of literature and art, its value would be extremely limited. Psychological criticism as a whole is only one way of approaching art, along with many others. But my previous discussion of psychoanalysis as a form of story-telling shows us a more subtle approach to works of art. For the 'story-telling' which goes on in psychotherapy is a joint effort, which takes place within the ambit of an intense relationship. This gives us an interesting idea about art criticism: what is the actual reading of the text like? How does the relationship between text and reader take place? How does the structure of the text affect the reader? How much is the reader able or inclined to be creative about the text, to create his or her own text, if you like? These ideas can be related to the development of 'reception theory' in literary criticism – a concern with the role of the reader in the literary process.[12]

In other words, just as the uncovering of lost memories turns out to be a more creative process than first appears, so the interpretation of texts can be seen likewise, not just as the passive reception of something that is ready made, but as a kind of joint production between the text and the reader. Here the role of free associations and fantasies seems interesting, for again, just as the interpretation of a dream (or a memory) flows from all the associations that are connected with it, so the critic or the ordinary reader no doubt avails himself of similar material. This might strike some critics as leaning towards arbitrariness and moving away from the text, but it is surely not a new process, but one that has always gone on. All schools of criticism in this sense can be said to prescribe a certain group of fantasies about texts as preferable to other fantasies! For example, the interest in 'characters' shown by a critic such as A. C. Bradley has been frowned on in contemporary criticism, which prefers to focus on the 'language' of the text, or perhaps its socio-political context, and so on.[13]

In this context, I recall John Berger's experiment of showing paintings to school children, who came out with both naive and also very perceptive comments. But Berger was using shock tactics to demonstrate the kind of fresh responses found in those who are not used to sophisticated art criticism. However, even that can be defined as a particular set of associations and fantasies.

Language

Freud makes the point that the unconscious becomes conscious partly through the use of words.[14] The word is a sensual medium, which passes between two people and causes a change to both. For example, it is striking in relation to feelings of love how powerful 'words of love' become, not just in 'expressing' the feeling but in giving it life. Love comes into being through the word of love! This becomes a definite issue in certain relationships, where words of love are not spoken. One partner may complain: 'Of course, you know I love you, even if I can't say it.' However, the other partner has the very legitimate response to this that love consists in part in the speaking of love. In other words, love is not just a 'feeling'; it is also a kind of performative art. Thus, if I love you, I speak words of love, I carry out deeds of love. It is not adequate for me to argue that I 'feel' love for you. Is that love?

Again, in relation to artistic works, this issue of sensuality or 'performative' effects is very important. The text is a sensual object which has effects on the reader's body as well as mind. This is obviously why poetry uses such devices as rhyme, rhythm, and so on. These are sensual arrangements of sounds, which can have intense effects on the reader.

Such approaches to texts are well known and have been found in various schools, such as New Criticism. The point I am making is that psychoanalysis offers us a quite subtle approach to texts, since its main work is concerned with texts, particularly the text of the unconscious and the spoken texts going on in the therapy room. Psychotherapy can itself be described as a performative art or ritual: its aim is itself. If one sticks at therapy for a long period, one comes to realize that its goal is always realized, even if a particular session feels like a 'failure'. One might say that here is another example of Freud's prescience: his invention of analysis points forward to the postmodern emphasis on the representation of things and on performances.

Of course, one cannot push the 'aesthetic' aspect of therapy too far. After all, we are dealing with people's intense feelings and difficulties; we are not engaged in a kind of elegant exercise in conversational wit. But the whole point about 'story-telling' is that those intense feelings and difficulties have to be dealt with by being talked about; and the relationship between the therapist and patient has to be conducted in part through language. I would not say it goes on solely through language: that would ignore the non-verbal aspects of communication between human beings – the use of the body in particular. Doing therapy or counselling by telephone can be done but it certainly lacks something – above all, the physical presence of both parties. But analysis and psychotherapy are undoubtedly linguistic and communicative events, and much of the power and curative properties associated with them stem from the completion of unfulfilled communications. That which could never be said can now be said; that which could never be asked can now be asked; the unspeakable is spoken; that which has existed inside me for all of my life in a latent fashion can be actualized and witnessed by another. If we accept that therapy deals with unbearable truths and unbearable feelings and thoughts, then through our communication we find that we can bear the unbearable together, when we could not bear it alone.

7
Instincts and Environment

One of the fundamental tensions in Freud's work is between the instinctual drive – conceived of as an inner force or source of energy, emanating ultimately from the body and impinging on mental events – and the individual's relation with the environment. Generally, it is held that drive theory dominates Freud's main work and that later post-Freudian psychoanalysis takes up and develops the field of relational theory, for example in 'object relations'.[1] However, it is certainly true that Freud himself was interested in relations between people – the Oedipus complex consists of precisely that. One might argue that ultimately Freud synthesized drive theory with a relational theory, in that in the Oedipal situation, the inbuilt drives or instincts are mediated, thwarted, expressed, given shape, in the particular relations existing in the child's family.

However, that is an idealized picture of Freud's ideas: realistically, one finds a more fragmented presentation as Freud wrestled with complex sets of ideas, attempting to integrate them into a coherent model. There is also a sense of development: very early Freud, with the advancement of the seduction theory, could be said to focus on relationships; then he moves much more to a theory of drives propelling individuals towards certain actions and objects; but then he contextualizes this within family dynamics. This is not a particularly coherent or smooth line of development – how could it be? – but there is a sense of enrichment and increasing complexity as Freud has to grapple with material which does not conform with existing theories.

The opposition between drives and objects, or more accurately drives and relationships, is clearly important in psychoanalysis, as it is in Western thought. It corresponds to two ways of looking at reality: the first takes the individual as a given, with its instincts and its needs directing that individual into relation with others. Thus, to take the classical picture of the mother–baby dyad, one can argue, in this model, that the baby is hungry and therefore looks for a source of nourishment and finds the breast. Freud quite frequently seems to takes this point of view, but also stipulates that the infant is seeking pleasure:

> we learn that infants perform actions which have no purpose other than obtaining pleasure. It is our belief that they first experience this pleasure in connection with taking nourishment but that they soon learn to separate it from that accompanying condition.[2]

But in his later theoretical work, Freud takes a rather different point of view: that out of our relations with others, aspects of identity emerge. For example, the super-ego emerges as an internalized form of prohibition acquired from parental prohibition: 'the super-ego retains the character of the father.'[3]

The most interesting context for the working out of these ideas in practice is of course analysis itself. Here, purely drive-oriented interpretations tend to fall flat, for appealing to someone's biological make-up somehow seems to ignore them as a living human being. But, apart from the type of interpretation that is given – and Freud seems to give both drive-type interpretations and relational ones – the existence of analysis itself is a kind of homage to the importance of relationship. For the analysis is a relationship, and clearly this relationship has effects on the patient and on the analyst which are deeply important to the progress of the analysis.

Therapy is therefore dyadic not monadic, and this we owe to Freud. Therapy is a dialogue not a monologue by patient or therapist. In therapy we affect each other, and these affects and effects are supremely important to the course of the therapy and its success. Of course, Freud did not fully work out the implications of this in terms of transference and counter-transference, but he certainly established a context in which this could be done. Arguments as to whether Freud at times behaved unethically within the frame of analysis seem to me to be irrelevant, for the frame itself would survive any such infringements. We know in fact that infringements are inevitable, just as they are inevitable within medicine and law and other professional areas. A more serious argument would be that the analytical frame itself is inherently power-driven, unequal and exploits the patient.

The Other

At this point it is relevant to point to the early evolution of Freud's ideas, which took place within the ambit of his relationship with Wilhelm Fliess, with whom he communicated by letter for 15 years, and periodically met for intense discussions of psychology, biology and other areas of common interest. Today Fliess is seen generally as a rather bizarre figure, who put forward ideas about numerology and the importance of the nose, which are widely discredited. However, to consider only the intellectual relationship between Freud and Fliess misses the importance of Fliess in Freud's development. We can say that Fliess filled the role of the Other, who listened, responded, empathized, criticized, and so on. Thus Freud's 'self-analysis' took place very much in the gaze of someone else. In fact, one has to speak of the mutual love between the two men, and without doubt this love – and the giving and receiving of it – was crucial in Freud's development at this period.[4]

One might say simply that Freud needed someone to bounce off, but it goes further than that. Freud could only develop in relation with others, and his important relationships often involved antagonism as much as friendship. There is an archetypal relationship in Freud's life: an intense friendship which eventually cools and turns to hostility. This is found with Fliess, Jung, Ferenczi, Rank, Adler and other more minor figures. Whatever its personal origins, it seems to be involve a dialectical process. First, two people are attracted to each other and find what they have in common, and then they discover that they must separate in order to develop fully. This is certainly true of the Freud/Jung relationship.

One can, of course, speak of the love and hate involved in these relationships, or of the father/son aspects, but I think even more pertinent is the factor of intimacy and separation. Two people come together in a spirit of intellectual excitement and personal affection, but then have to move apart in a spirit of antagonism and mutual suspicion. One might well argue that that is a basic process in human development: for example, one can see it in the separation which adolescents have to make from their parents, which often involves the formers' scorn towards the latter. Without doubt this is a healthy scorn, enabling the adolescent to break his infantile dependence on his parents.

Of course, similar processes are found in therapy, where both intense positive and negative feelings can be experienced by both parties. However, rather than leading to friendship or estrangement, the feelings are hopefully contained within the frame of therapy, so that they can be worked through and understood.

Clearly, Freud's discovery of the importance of the Other in self-development was not theoretical! It was a concrete fact in his own life, and no doubt throughout his life he hungered for that contact and found it with many people, such as his beloved Lou Andreas-Salomé.[5] One might even argue that his invention of psychoanalysis stemmed from that need for contact with people. There is little doubt that Freud was not the cool neutral figure which he eventually believed the analyst should attempt to be. Rather, one gets the impression from the case-studies and from patients' reports that Freud was a passionate man who at times permitted his passions expression in the analysis – for example in his analysis with the writer Hilda Doolittle ('H.D.').[6]

Drives/objects

Let me return to the notion of the drives: Freud assumes that they make inner demands on the organism, which has to reduce the tension they cause. Thus Freud talks of 'an incessant and unavoidable afflux of stimulation', which the nervous system has to get rid of. In fact, the nervous system is defined as an 'apparatus which has the function of getting rid of the stimuli which reach it'.[7]

This is a very 'inner-directed' scheme: noticeably, the organism is not in contact with the environment. This seems at odds with evolutionary theory, in which the organism evolves so as to make a 'fit' with its physical context. Thus instincts themselves presumably evolve accordingly – or perhaps it is better to speak of 'instinctive behaviour' which is elicited by certain cues in the environment. But Freud makes a sharp division between inner and outer worlds, and sees them evolving separately. In this light, it is interesting to note that he quite often makes reference to Larmarckian notions of inheritance, whereby the organism can make an adaptation which is then handed down, a kind of self-willed evolution. This tends to contradict Darwinian evolutionary theory, which maintains that random changes in the organism are 'selected for' by the environment. The pressure for change comes from without, not from within. It is not surprising that Freud was a Larmarckian, believing in the possibility of the inheritance of acquired characteristics. In Freud's words: 'constitutional dispositions are also undoubtedly after-effects of experiences by ancestors in the past.'[8]

Within the Freudian model of drives the relation of objects to instincts is quite strange. Objects are approached because they offer the promise of reducing the inner tension caused by the pressure of instinctual demands, or needs. For example, Freud's theory of anxiety in part attributes it to the realization by the child that its needs may not be met if its mother is absent:

> the situation, then, which it regards as a 'danger' and against which it wants to be safeguarded is that of non-satisfaction, of a *growing tension due to need*, against which it is helpless. (original emphasis)[9]

In this model, the 'object' is subordinate to the inner need for 'detensioning', which is a goal of the pleasure principle. I say this is a strange idea, since objects become subordinate to instincts; that is, I approach them in order to satisfy my needs. What is missing in this account is that the child is attached to its mother and fears the breaking of that attachment.

Again, from an evolutionary point of view, one might argue against Freud that instinctive behaviour evolves so as to cope with the various objects in the environment. For example, if we accept that babies 'instinctively' smile at a very young age, one might assume that this behaviour evolved through natural selection favouring smiling, because smiling produces better contact with adult care-givers, and this contact improves the likelihood of the infant's survival. It would seem very odd to argue that the 'instinct' for smiling evolved in isolation from other people, since it is a response to them.

Or to take an even more glaring example: do babies take to the breast because it satisfies their need to suck? Or shouldn't we rather say that the sucking reflex evolved in response to babies frequent contact with breasts? Again, it would be very odd to say that sucking exists in isolation as an inner-directed demand, which seeks satisfaction from the nearest available suckable object! This is a very Hegelian approach to reality, and tends to subordinate the material world to forces acting upon it which are quite independent and indeed have prior existence.

The most notable omission from Freud's model is any account of the interaction between organism and environment, and between the organism and others. For Freud, the organism seems to be isolated, and its instincts or needs seem to have no biological function apart from reproduction.[10]

For Freud *behaviour occurs as a result of an organism seeking to discharge built-up tension arising from inner needs*. The problem with this as a model of energy and behaviour is that it ignores the interaction with the environment. Consider the example of a bird carrying out 'broken wing' manoeuvres when it sees a predator near its nest, so that the predator will be drawn away from its young. If the predator leaves, the manoeuvres stop. It seems perverse to describe this sequence of actions as caused by first, an excess of energy, and second, the subsidence of that energy. This ignores the behaviourial pattern shown by the bird in the face of a predator, which, one can assume, is genetically programmed and has arisen through evolution: to put it crudely, birds that began to carry out the manoeuvre had a better chance of their genes surviving.[11]

Human examples are similar: consider a baby crying when its mother leaves the room and then falling silent when she returns. Again, to argue that the crying is caused by a build-up of energy and the silence by a diminution is perverse, since it ignores the relationship between baby and mother.[12] Of course these arguments, and others, have led to the formulation of object relations theory, which diminishes the importance of drives or instincts in favour of social relations.

Freud's theory of energy derived from models prevalent in the nineteenth century, but they remained unchanged in psychoanalysis. This theory of energy tends to isolate the organism from the environment, so that behaviour arises as a result of inner processes, not as a result of interaction between organism and environment. It tends to isolate the organism from others – for example, Freud argues that children become attached to their mother because she feeds them. Attachment is therefore a secondary result of nutritional needs.

We can speak of a tension in Freud between the consideration of the individual in isolation, beset by various instinctive demands which must be dealt with in some way, and the view of the individual in relation to others. This tension parallels the division between theory and practice in psychoanalysis, for whereas Freud's metapsychology tends to be based on the individual, analytic practice is concerned with the relationship between two people in the room. Such notions as transference show the importance of this relationship, for the patient 'transfers' past conflicts onto the new relationship.

The Hungarian analyst Michael Balint makes this point very forcibly:

> Our theory has been mainly based on the study of pathological forms which use internalization extensively and which have only weakly cathected object-relations; our technique was invented and has been mainly developed when working with pathological forms such as hysteria, sexual disorders, character neurosis, all of which have strongly cathected object-relations. This, however, is only natural, as our true field of study is the *psycho-analytical situation*, a situation

> where relations to an object – admittedly a very peculiar object – are of overwhelming importance.[13]

Clearly, the divergence between theory and practice stems in part from Freud's earlier career as neurologist, and his predilection for 'scientific' methodology and formulation. However, analytic practice could not develop within a biological framework, but had to proceed within the framework of the relationship between analyst and patient. Whereas in his metapsychological theorizing Freud could doubt whether instinctive drives originally have an object, this view might seem strange in the therapeutic context, since the situation has been set up so that the object is there! On the other hand, one comes across patients who are not very aware that anyone else exists, so that drive theory might prove useful here, in the sense that such people could be said to be existing at a very primitive stage of objectless narcissism, wherein one's own needs are paramount and the existence of others doubtful or merely a necessary accessory to the needs. Sometimes it is said that such people exist in a state of 'pre-ruth': they have not developed concern for others.

The history of psychoanalysis has therefore seen a struggle between 'drive theory' and 'object relations', and it can be stated in general terms that the latter has tended to oust the former, although not entirely. But certainly many of the major postwar analysts, such as Melanie Klein, D. W. Winnicott and W. R. D. Fairbairn, emphasized the child's relationship with others, particularly its mother. None the less, it is arguable that the tension in Freud's thought between individualism and relatedness, as with other tensions found in him, gave his ideas tremendous energy, for Freud struggled to amalgamate ideas which seemed contradictory.

This tension can be related to Freud's description of the 'pleasure principle' and the 'reality principle', which are in conflict: the ego learns to postpone immediate gratification if the objective situation demands this. What is striking about this formulation is that Freud places this conflict at the heart of psychic life: 'the ego . . . has dethroned the pleasure principle which dominates the course of events in the id without any restriction and has replaced it by the reality principle, which promises more certainty and greater success.'[14]

One cannot simply equate the reality principle with the presence of others – it embraces the whole of one's environment and its demands – but it is clear that the tension between the individual's drives and the impingement of the outside world not only runs as a thread through the history of psychoanalysis, but according to Freud dominates the development of human beings.

Neurosis

Freud's theoretical writings give little importance to the environment in the creation of neurosis. He seems more interested in the internal conflicts between the 'instinctual impulse' and the repressive forces in the psyche:

> the ego defends itself against the instinctual impulse by the mechanisms of repression. The repressed material struggles against this fate. It creates for itself, along paths over which the ego has no power, a substitutive representation (which forces itself upon the ego by way of a compromise) – the symptom.[15]

There is something unsatisfying about this picture, for one wants to know why the conflict is set in motion in the first place. Freud goes on to argue that the ego, in its repressive capacity, is actually taking the part of the super-ego, which in turn is formed from 'influences in the external world'. But we are still left pondering the question as to why some people are more neurotic than others and whether certain family environments are more likely to create neuroses. Freud is clearly not theoretically interested in the influence of family – this can be seen in one of his clinical vignettes, concerning the development of a perversion:

> The subject was a man who is today quite indifferent to the genitals and other attractions of women, but who can be plunged into irresistible sexual excitement only by a foot of a particular form wearing a shoe. He can recall an event from his sixth year which was decisive for the fixation of his libido. He was sitting on a stool beside the governess who was to give him lessons in English. The governess, who was an elderly, dried-up, plain-looking spinster, with pale-blue eyes and a snub nose, had something wrong with her foot that day, and on that account kept it, wearing a velvet slipper, stretched out on a cushion. Her leg itself was most decently concealed. A thin, scraggy foot, like the one he had then seen belonging to his governess, thereupon became (after a timid attempt at normal sexual activity at puberty) his only sexual object, and the man was irresistibly attracted if a foot of this kind was associated with other features besides which recalled the type of the English governess.[16]

This description explains little in fact, for there is no indication as to why at the age of six this man was compelled to make such a narrowly focused attachment. Why, for example, was he not interested in his mother's feet? Why could he not form a more rounded emotional and erotic attachment to the governess? Is it possible that his relationship with her was the most intimate in his life and that the sexual fixation is a perpetual record of this? In other words, in today's therapeutic environment, one would suggest that this story conceals as much as it reveals, and that much earlier damage had been done to the individual's ability to form relationships. The governess incident, in other words, is itself a symptom not a cause.

Freud frequently argues that neurosis arises as a result of three factors: a constitutional disposition, some kind of environmental trauma, and the degree of repression induced by upbringing and education. But in practice he seems to give more weight to the first and third factors than to the second. This bias can be seen to an alarming degree in the comments of his followers: for example, in her seminar notes, Lou Andreas-Salomé makes the following comment:

> On traumas of childhood. Not important in themselves. An unsheltered child exposed to all manner of traumas might often remain healthier if his later way of life is untroubled than a protected one, who in later life is confronted by greater cultural renunciations.[17]

This comment is echoed in Freud's story of the working-class girl and the middle-class girl, who experiment with each other sexually as young children and then learn to masturbate. Freud maps out two different paths for these girls: the working-class girl will be 'free from neurosis', while the middle-class girl will renounce sex out of feelings of disgust. Why is this? Freud asserts that the latter

> came under the influence of education and accepted its demands. From the suggestions offered to it, her ego constructed ideals of feminine purity and abstinence which are incompatible with sexual activity; her intellectual activity reduced her interest in the feminine part which she was destined to play.[18]

In fact, it seems likely that working-class children are just as likely to suffer negative influences as middle-class children, but perhaps a more important point here is that Freud sets the traumatic repression quite late in life ('the influence of education'), whereas modern therapists might say that inhibitions of sexuality and other areas of self-expression can begin from birth and are very closely tied up with one's relations with both parents. Specifically, the way one's body is treated as an infant will partly influence the way one treats the body later in life.

The same kind of emphasis can be seen in Freud's observation on breast-feeding, which, he asserts, is for the infant mainly a source of pleasure:

> infants perform actions which have no purpose other than obtaining pleasure . . . Sucking at the mother's breast is the starting point of the whole of sexual life, the unmatched prototype of every later sexual satisfaction.[19]

Post-Freudian discussion of breast-feeding would no doubt emphasize the fact that the infant is also intensely involved in relating to his mother and that the way this relationship is handled will no doubt be influential in later life. Freud, however, argues that 'the infantile object-choice [is] only a feeble one'.[20] Of course, such a conclusion flows inexorably from Freud's drive-theory – that we are only interested in others because they offer us the chance to relieve our tension, caused by a build-up of frustration.

Perhaps it is futile and anachronistic to criticize Freud for being too concerned with drive theory and not enough with object relations, but I think it is important to bring out his philosophical tendencies. He does tend to see the individual in isolation, as a collection of drives which force us to make contact with others, in order to dispel the displeasure of frustration. There is a rather autistic flavour to this view of human beings, and no doubt in part it is a relic of nineteenth-century positivism. But in the wider context, it is one half of a duality of views which has characterized Western attitudes to human beings.

Introduction of the object to the Freudian model

One cannot say that Freud's model of the individual ever becomes a true 'object relations' model, since Freud continues to argue for the primacy of the drive, and the derivative nature of the object. Writing in 1915, he states:

> The object of an instinct is the thing in regard to which or through which the instinct is able to achieve its aim. It is what is most variable

> about an instinct and *is not originally connected with it*, but becomes assigned to it only in consequence of being peculiarly fitted to make satisfaction possible . . . It may be changed any number of times in the course of the vicissitudes which the instinct undergoes during its existence. (added emphasis)[21]

But Freud's theory of the drives does not remain objectless: one can trace the gradual intrusion of the object into Freud's theoretical schema. To begin with, it is negligible – in *The Interpretation of Dreams* (1900) it is absent; in *Three Essays on the Theory of Sexuality* (1905) it has a minor role. But a series of papers – on narcissism (1914), on mourning and identification (1917), on the Oedipus complex (1924), on femininity (1931) – begin to give greater prominence to the object, as Freud's initial concept of the drive without an object changes to a more object-related one. The paper on mourning argues that faced with the loss of a 'love-object', the object is incorporated within the psyche in the form of an identification:

> an object which was lost has been set up again inside the ego – that is, an object-cathexis has been replaced by an identification.[22]

To take the most obvious example: my love for my parents ('cathexis' meaning 'investment' or 'interest') changes to an identification as I get older and become more separate from them. I actually become rather similar to them: so the identification is a form of connection with them, preventing too absolute a separation or loss of them. I remember them by becoming like them.

Later, the notion of the superego will also assume that certain objects can be internalized into the psychic structure of the individual. The superego plays a vital part in the Oedipus complex, for it is its relic, when the complex has been destroyed – the parental prohibitions on incestuous sex are internalized as a critical voice:

> the child's parents, and especially its father, were perceived as an obstacle to the realization of his Oedipal wishes; so his infantile ego fortified itself for the carrying out of the repression by erecting this same obstacle within itself.[23]

Perhaps most dramatically, in his papers on femininity – the 1931 paper 'Female Sexuality' and the 1933 paper 'Femininity' – Freud has to confront the change in object-choice made by girls from their mother to their father. Freud's consistent focus on male development had tended to obscure the importance of object-choice, since little boys could be assumed to retain the same love-object – their mother – from birth to adolescence, and beyond. Freud struggles to explain how girls switch from mother to father, and advances a series of rather unconvincing phallocentric arguments – for example, that girls are disgruntled at not being given a penis by their mothers and so turn to the father. Whatever counter-argument one puts forward here – and the rather obvious argument might be that girls are innately attracted to the male – the role of the object has again forced itself into the foreground.

Most striking of all in Freud's later period is his description of the ego's propensity to internalize those objects which it is involved with (which it has 'cathected'):

> when a person has to give up a sexual object, there quite often ensues an alteration of his ego which can only be described as a setting up of the object inside the ego . . . the process, especially in the early phases of development, is a very frequent one, and it makes it possible to suppose that the character of the ego is a precipitate of abandoned object-cathexes and that it contains the history of those object-choices.[24]

Freud adds that this process of identification can also occur before the object is given up. This is quite a radical adaptation in psychoanalytic theory and flows in part from Freud's previous work on mourning and melancholia. Its main application is in relation to the Oedipus complex, since it can be assumed that both boys and girls make identifications with mother and father. But Freud is happy to apply the theory outside the Oedipal relations, and comments for example that certain women betray past love affairs by 'vestiges of their object-cathexes in the traits of their character'.[25]

These passages, written in 1923, when Freud was 67, represent a significant move away from a purely drive-oriented psychology, for the ego itself is now said to be partly made up of the residues of former relationships. Perhaps one cannot exaggerate the importance of this shift, for while Freud himself never abandoned the base-line of the instinctual drive, these theoretical formulations concerning identification give the green light to the later development of object relations. Implicitly, drive-oriented psychology was moving into the background in favour of a more relational approach.

A duality in Western philosophy

In their influential book *Object Relations in Psychoanalytic Theory*, Greenberg and Mitchell draw a distinction between two approaches to human existence found in Western thought:

> Man is an essentially individual animal; man is an essentially social animal. The history of Western social and political philosophy has revolved around the tension between these two views of the nature of human experience. One school of thought, finding its fullest expression in British eighteenth-century philosophy (which formed the basis for the political institutions of the United States), takes as its premise that human satisfactions and goals are fundamentally personal and individual. Human beings pursue their own separate aims, argue Hobbes and Locke, and these atomistic, discordant pursuits are likely to interfere with each other... A second school of philosophy, with roots going back to Aristotle, developing through the work of Rousseau, Hegel and other continental philosophers, culminating in Marx's vision of human history, takes as its premise that human satisfaction and goals are realizable only within a community. Man is intrinsically social; he cannot be said to exist meaningfully apart from others.[26]

The authors add that 'in the pessimism of his later years, Freud becomes most fully Hobbesian'.[27]

I find this historical and philosophical overview very useful, as it helps to explain the shift from Freud's ideas, which very much assume the first philosophical stance – that the human being is isolated – to the contemporary object relations schools of analysis and therapy, which reject Freud's 'Hobbesian' views in favour of a more 'relational' view. We might simply say that the pendulum has swung away from Freud's individualism, so redolent of nineteenth-century laissez-faire ideas, towards a more radical and social view, in which the individual is seen intrinsically as a social unit, almost unimaginable outside relationships. Yet Greenberg and Mitchell make a further illuminating point as to how we select between these views:

> The evaluation of psychoanalytic theories is a matter of personal choice. The theory stands or falls on how compelling it appears to be, on its underlying vision of human life. Does the theory speak to you? Does it seem to account for your deepest longings, fears?[28]

This is a valuable point, for the choice between an individualist psychology such as Freud's, and a more 'socialized' psychology such as object relations, is very much a subjective one. It is also correct to say that both points of view are valuable. Rather than trying to pick winners and losers, it is preferable to keep both philosophies in mind as useful tools in the description and explanation of human existence.

My personal view is that object relations psychology has gone too far in its emphasis on family environment. I have a certain sympathy with Freud's more 'internal' approach to neurosis, or at least I tend to believe that there is an interaction between environment and innate disposition in certain people. For example, I have often noticed that patients who come from large families seem to be the most introverted of all the siblings and often the most sensitive. This seems to make them more open to the negative things going in the family, whereas other brothers and sisters are more immune. To use Freud's language, one might say they have a greater 'disposition' to neurosis.

One can say the same of schizophrenia – that while there may be stressful factors in the family environment, there may well be an innate disposition to the illness. This argument amounts to saying that confronted with a similarly stressful childhood, some people will react with fortitude and will get on with life, while others will get depressed and neurotic, and some may feel rather crazy.

This argument also has implications for the growth of personality. Again, I believe that while family environment is obviously important in the construction of character, there are also important innate structures. For example, there is some evidence from studies of foetal life, that individual foetuses are already behaving differently in the womb.[29] It is surely not in dispute that certain abilities – music, mathematics, languages, art – can be innate and form important influences on the individual's personality.

At times, these arguments can have weighty and alarming consequences. For example, many analytic organizations refuse to train gay men and lesbians as psychotherapists, on the grounds that they are too damaged to work with patients, particularly heterosexual patients. However, this argument rests on the premise that homosexuality is caused by some kind of family dysfunction or a failure to traverse the Oedipus complex, and so on. If, on the contrary, homosexuality is genetically acquired, then this argument falls to the ground, but many analytic organizations have clung to the idea that homosexuality is a perversion.[30]

In the end, Freud's struggle to reconcile drive theory with a more object-oriented approach cannot be dismissed as a hangover from nineteenth-century thought or as an outmoded conflict which psychotherapy has satisfactorily dealt with today. I think that every day in one's work as a psychotherapist one has to deal with this paradox: that each one of us stands alone, with our own needs, likes and dislikes, our own drive for life and self-expression; and at the same time, we exist in an environment that partly shapes us, and particularly we stand with others, who have the same needs and ambitions, and whom we need. Of course, this tension exists outside psychotherapy, and surely all human beings have to grapple with it. In crude terms, one finds that some people appear too selfish, but also that others are not selfish enough. The struggle to integrate these two sides of life is a considerable one. In Freud's work we find an extraordinary theoretical record of it.

8
Dialectics in the Psyche

One of Freud's most startling and brilliant observations about the therapeutic process concerns the 'negative therapeutic reaction'. This involves the patient who resists or sabotages the progress of the therapy, who in fact becomes negative when things are going well. However, this principle is widened by Freud to include those who cannot tolerate good things in their life or who are 'wrecked by success', to use his memorable phrase.[1] He also refers to the 'need to suffer', a paralysing and agonizing problem for some people, who have a kind of quasi-addiction to suffering and find happiness or even a moderate degree of contentment unbearable.

In the therapeutic milieu this problem is widespread and presents many problems. The therapist learns with such patients not to make positive comments or express confidence or hope about how the therapy is progressing – retribution is often swift and severe.

It is likely that all these phenomena have guilt in common, but Freud's theory of guilt is sophisticated and complex, and would be developed extensively by later analysts such as Melanie Klein. It is not simply a matter of having a 'bad conscience' – Freud is able to relate guilt to aggression or hatred, internalized forms of prohibition, excessive loyalty and loss. Above all, Freud's theory of guilt, crime and punishment is dynamic. It concerns internal relations in the psyche. The ego is persecuted by the ego ideal – the superego – which can adopt an attitude of extreme harshness, so that the ego becomes abject and victimized. However, Freud also observes that this harshness seems to draw into itself all the aggression or sadism in the individual. In short, when we are guilty we hate ourselves and punish ourselves instead of punishing others. One part of us punishes another part, particularly if it seems to be in possession of something good or enjoyable, or there has been a successful outcome in some endeavour. The ego actually comes to dread anything good happening because of the inevitable retribution. The best solution can then seem to stick to a life of austerity and stoicism – in that way, at least punishment is avoided.

Mourning

In relation to mourning, Freud states that the mourner loses interest in normal life and concentrates attention on the lost person, who has to be let go of in a gradual fashion if the individual is to turn back to life. If mourning is carried out successfully, the mourner is able to let go of the dead person, and is able to turn outwards to new interests and new relationships.[2]

Melancholia – or depression – seems to carry this a stage further, since it is the ego itself which is seen as lost in a more permanent manner. There has been a kind of narcissistic identification or fusion between the object and the ego, so that faced with the loss of the former, it seems as if the ego itself is emptied out, impoverished or destroyed: 'an object loss is transformed into an ego loss.'[3] People suffering from intense depression feel annihilated, worthless or even non-existent, such is the extent of the erosion of their sense of self. It is an awesome experience to meet such people regularly, as they seem to exist in an almost non-human state, or in a state of non-being. Their despair is also infectious – one starts to wonder how one can ever reach them or find out what is going on inside them. Whereas conventional mourning relates to the death of another, melancholia seems to involve a mourning for the death of oneself.

But Freud points out that the destructiveness involved here may also be targeted at a love-object in a kind of covert aggressive attack, veiled by suffering:

> we perceive that the self-reproaches are reproaches against a loved object which have been shifted away from it onto the patient's own ego.
>
> The woman who loudly pities her husband for being tied to such an incapable wife as herself is really accusing the husband of being incapable.[4]

In many cases of intense depression, one can eventually detect undercurrents of rage and revenge, frequently against the person's parents. The term 'grudge' is useful here, but the grudge involved can be so massive as to take over the entire existence of the patient: everything is devoted to it. It is likely that the depression is a kind of revenge: 'I had such bad parents that the only satisfaction I can find now is to demonstrate how bad they were by ruining my own life.' I have met very creative people who felt determined not to permit themselves any success in case that gave pleasure to their parents or suggested somehow that their parents had not been entirely useless. At the same time, there is often a deeply buried wish to be reconnected with the parents, whose love seems to be lost forever. Thus a vicious circle can be set up: the contact that is yearned for is sabotaged by the individual's destructiveness and hatred. At its most extreme, this can lead to suicide.

Freud has highlighted a group of psychological phenomena which employ the technique of incorporation and identification. At first glance, this seems straightforward enough: when a loved one dies, we go through a prolonged and painful period of letting go of them, whilst at the same time retaining inside ourselves some enduring images of the dead person; but in pathological mourning or in severe depression, the loss is felt as a loss of oneself or an emptying out of oneself. In fact, this phenomenon can be seen in romantic love, and especially in cases where one partner jilts the other: the jilted person may go through a period of intense depression, when it feels as if one has lost one's own identity and one's reason for living, such has been the close identification with the partner. This process is not felt to be pathological, unless it goes on for an inordinate length of time.

As we have seen, Freud also notices that certain forms of melancholia are in fact aggressive or persecutory – they are designed to punish someone else. Here aggression is being meted out to others, but in a concealed way. One might say that the masochism has a sadistic core, or the suffering has a core of hatred. The same can be seen with certain people who fall ill – their illness has a persecutory flavour, and also solicits large amounts of attention from others. The example with which I began this chapter is apposite here – the patient who resists positive progress is not just sabotaging the therapy out of guilt, or fear of punishment by the inner critic, but also as a punishment towards the therapist. In fact, some people are so incensed by being helped, or so envious of the help they receive, that they will expand enormous effort to sabotage it. 'Since I started therapy, I feel worse' is a not uncommon accusation, often couched in the most bitter of tones.

In fact, these examples show a subtle relationship between guilt and envy: such a person feels guilty about receiving help, but also envies (and hates) the person who is able to give it. We might say that there is an internal envy at work: the superego envies the ego for the benefits it receives. In other words, some examples of guilt arise out of hostile feelings of envy being directed from one part of my psyche to another, which then feels depressed and expects punishment or even feels that it deserves punishment, and *in extremis* demands punishment.

Many of these ideas concerning envy were to be considerably amplified in the postwar era by Melanie Klein, who argued that the infant may experience envy towards the mother's breast, since it is able to give so much, but also seems able to keep so much back for itself. But this envy can lead to guilt or anxiety over the possibility of having damaged the breast with its envy.[5] Such work may seem more dramatic or exotic than Freud's, particularly as Freud did not theorize about the very early relations between mother and infant, but it is arguable that Klein's theory of envy is commensurate with Freud's earlier work on guilt, aggression and the death instinct.

The use of depression as a method of punishment also shows us the complexity of intra-psychic relations: the aggression or hatred which is felt towards the other person is hidden by being incorporated into the critical part of the psyche – the superego. Thus I punish myself in order to punish you:

> the self-tormenting in melancholia, which is without doubt enjoyable, signifies ... a satisfaction of trends of sadism and hate.[6]

Freud uses this analysis to show how people use illness itself to torment others; and how suicide often involves a return of 'murderous impulses against others' against the self.[7] One might suspect also that romantic love conceals a degree of aggression or hatred towards the loved person. How irritating it is that someone should excite such need and dependency in oneself!

The same kind of analysis can be used in relation to guilt itself: that the aggression that the child feels against its parents (which often cannot be directly expressed) is reversed and incorporated into the critical agency – the superego – from where it can persecute the ego of the individual concerned. To put this in simple English, instead of being angry with you, I turn my anger against myself and feel depressed and guilty. Freud comments:

> the original severity of the super-ego does not – or does not so much – represent the severity which one has experienced from it [the object],

> or which one attributes to it; it represents rather one's aggressiveness towards it.[8]

Thus, as well as involving incorporation and identification, many of these phenomena involve a reversal: I punish myself instead of you; or I kill myself instead of you; I love you instead of myself; I lose myself as well as you. Freud's crowning claim is that the superego itself is the inheritor of the Oedipus complex, which, once destroyed in the face of parental prohibition, is incorporated into the psyche in the form of the destroyer – or in simple terms, the superego takes a harsh parental role towards the ego. The parent–child relationship is replicated inside the psyche. Again, we can note the intense identification which occurs here: even if my father is harsh or cruel towards me, I will incorporate those aspects of him inside myself and treat myself as he treated me. If I am hated, I will hate myself.

Thus a basic principle is at work here: that separation or loss leads to an identification with what is lost. In relation to mourning Freud says that 'the existence of the lost object is psychically prolonged'.[9] In the course of normal mourning this prolongation is finite, since in the end the mourner lets go of the deceased person and turns their interest to other people. But in other areas, the psychic prolongation is permanent: our guilt is a solidification, if in reversed form, of our aggression; the super-ego is the heir to the Oedipus complex; depression perpetuates something that has been felt to be lost. In a sense, when I am depressed, *I lose myself.*

There is clearly a delicate balance in the relations between ego and objects, and in situations such as intense depression, the ego becomes lost in the object, or in Freud's words, 'the ego is overwhelmed by the object'.[10] This would normally be considered to be a masochistic position, yet, many people encounter it when they fall in love. The person one is in love with assumes a grandeur and beauty that strike other people as inflated or bizarre and may well strike oneself as odd in later years. There is a temporary kind of loss of ego, confronted with the inflated object who seems to possess all virtues. We might argue that the ardent lover empties himself out and puts the good aspects of himself into the loved one, who is then adored by the abject suitor.

The other common situation where the ego is depleted in this manner is suicide, when the ego is able to treat itself as a hated object, and, one might imagine, destroys itself in place of someone else, or as a means of exacting revenge on someone else. Suicide shows the paradoxical structure of reversal most acutely: that I negate myself or hate myself, or indeed destroy myself, *in place of the hated object.*

Projection

Clearly, we are talking about the psychological phenomenon of projection, but projection of a complex and sophisticated kind. Freud's analysis of phenomena such as guilt and hatred demonstrates how dialectical his approach to the psyche is: all the time, human beings are sending parts of their own psyche out into others or bringing aspects of others into themselves. For example, according to Freud the Oedipal infant is internalizing the prohibitions received from the parents (particularly the father), and these will form a permanent fixture in the psyche; at the same time, the infant is turning his aggression towards the parents into a form of aggression towards itself. At the same time – and this is rather post-Freudian – the love and care that the infant receives will be internalized and form a crucial aspect of identity – that I am able to love myself. Conversely, any deprivation and harshness received also becomes a dynamic part of the personality – I become harsh towards myself and others. No doubt, parental harshness also activates feelings of injustice and aggression in the child, which may then also produce intense guilt.

Confronted with such complex interplays of feelings, projections and introjections, one might well wonder how individuals ever sort out what belongs to them and what to others, and in an in-depth psychotherapy such an investigation is crucial. Many people are confused about who they are, since they are so full of psychic contents projected from others, and also see the world very much in terms of their own inner values. There is a constant interplay between self and other, so that each contains qualities and processes which originate in the other.

These psychic processes also have profound philosophical implications for the nature of human identity: it is clear that the I or the self is inherently relational. In particular, the human infant has an enormous plasticity towards its environment and particularly towards other people.[11] As soon as it is born – and perhaps even before it is born – it both begins to internalize the communications received from others and begins to see the outside world in terms of its inner world. We might argue that intense paranoia illustrates this phenomenon perfectly: for the paranoid person – who projects her own hostility and mistrust onto others – tends to find that she is treated badly, thus confirming the correctness of the paranoid view. Indeed, at the unconscious level one can argue that paranoia seeks out ill-treatment and avoids love, for it is love that is dreaded above all and must be shunned. Paranoid people are righteously unhappy. What is very difficult is to get them to admit that they have set up the whole system of distrust, hostility, punishment, and so on.

But in a sense we are all paranoid; we all have an unconscious view of the nature of the universe and we project that view outwards. Indeed, one can argue that we construct our lives so that this basic attitude is confirmed, whether it be a benign or malign one. Of course, psychotherapy provides us with a space in which such unconscious attitudes can be recovered, but this is very difficult work, not only because the attitudes are unconscious, but also because it is often a very painful process. After all, withdrawing projections means taking responsibility for one's own life, which is usually a humbling, even shattering, experience. It might mean admitting that one has a choice over such projections, which can be an extremely frightening point to arrive at. Instead of blaming others for my life – which for many people is a fairly comfortable position – I can take responsibility for it and assert that I create it. To see the world as a friendly or unfriendly place is actually a choice which everyone has, but this idea can shatter one's set of assumptions about reality and one's existing personality structure. It is not therefore lightly or easily arrived at.

Such statements may appear to go beyond what Freud would have felt comfortable with, yet at the same time again one can suggest that they flow from his work on projection and introjection. For example, his description of criminals as very guilty people who must constantly seek out dangerous activities in order to be caught and punished suggests a practical solution: to help criminals become conscious of, not their wrong-doing, but their guilt, their sense of worthlessness, their underlying depression and no doubt their rage against others. If this is done, the need to be punished should diminish, and hence the need to act out criminally. In other words, the dialectical view of the psyche put forward by Freud offers many concrete solutions to apparently intractable psychological and social problems, such as delinquency, crime and other types of anti-social acting out. Of course, one cannot force the criminal to work on his or her guilt! As with alcoholics and other addicts, the individual has to have hit rock bottom and then seek help in a genuine fashion. But help is available. Those who scoff at therapy should perhaps read some of the material written by those who work with such individuals. It is subtle, sophisticated work, but it is also down to earth and offers hope to those who are in despair.[12] Above all, it offers a measure of self-worth, for it states that such projections originate in ourselves and that we are not hapless victims of fate. This strikes me as a very dignified view of human beings.

Transference

Therapy can help in the unscrambling of these complexities in part because the transference relationship actually brings the patient's projections into the room, or indeed onto or into the therapist. For example, the paranoid person will tend to be distrustful of the therapist, will suspect the therapist of plotting against him and so on, the seductive person will attempt to mesmerize the therapist, the guilty person will see the therapist as a critical figure, and so on. Whether or not the patient can eventually come to see that these perceptions and strategies stem from their own unconscious is another matter, for without doubt we all hang on tenaciously to our view of the world, and resist any suggestion that we are the author of it. It just seems that that is the way the world is, and there's nothing we can do about it. Freud makes the comment that:

> the patient regards the products of the awakening of his unconscious impulses as contemporaneous and real; he seeks to put his passions into action without taking any account of the real situation... The struggle between the doctor and the patient, between intellect and instinctual life, between understanding and seeking to act, is played out almost exclusively in the phenomenon of transference.[13]

In the struggle against acting out or against blind projection, therapists do have a certain amount of ammunition on their side. For one thing, many patients will have exhausted themselves already in their life by going through a series of repetitive situations. For example, the patient who sees the therapist as critical may agree that most figures in their life seem to be critical; or the patient who feels hurt because the therapist is not sexually excited may agree that such disappointments have been common in their life. The compulsion to repeat has not been initiated by psychotherapy, but has been going on throughout everyone's life. Therapy simply attempts to focus on it consciously, and many people who come to therapy feel desperate because of the repetitive disasters in their life and are therefore relatively open to the idea that these disasters have a close connection with their unconscious material – more bluntly, that we create the disasters in our lives as well as the triumphs. Those who are particularly guilty create the disasters to atone for the triumphs!

The great subtlety of Freud's thought is illustrated in his claim that the transference is also a resistance to the analytic process:

> Instead of remembering, he [the patient] repeats attitudes and emotional impulses from his early life which can be used as a resistance against the doctor and the treatment by means of what is known as 'transference'.[14]

In other words, the transference onto the analyst is designed to hide material which is more difficult and painful to deal with, and which the patient does not want to make conscious. But Freud also points out that if the transference is a form of resistance, then it provides a very rich vein of material for the analyst. In other words, the transference-resistance shown by the patient is without doubt a permanent part of their personality and will probably occur in all significant relationships. So far from resistance being a deterrence to the analyst, it becomes one of the focal points for investigation:

> we are aware that these resistances are bound to come to light; in fact, we are dissatisfied if we cannot provoke them clearly enough and are unable to demonstrate them to the patient. Indeed we come finally to understand that the overcoming of these resistances is the essential function of analysis and is the only part of our work which gives us an assurance that we have achieved something with the patient.[15]

In post-Freudian language, one can say that ultimately such resistances attempt to prevent intimacy between therapist and patient, for it is intimacy which nearly all patients crave and also dread. The transference projections arise then as barriers to intimacy, and it is the job of the therapist to help the patient see this.

Much work has been done since the 1920s on these phenomena, but we should still pause and consider what a considerable contribution Freud has made to our understanding of the subtlety and complexity of human defences against love and authenticity. For here, in the examination of the transference-resistance, Freud shows how patterns repeated from childhood are used to stop the individual succeeding in his push forward to life and love. In other words, one part of the psyche is firmly against this project and wishes to remain bogged down in the morbid fantasies derived from childhood, even while another part wishes to let go and begin to live in the present. Of course, the analyst or therapist cannot simply be aligned with the forces of life against the forces of morbidity for this in itself can provoke a massive backlash from the latter. Rather, the therapist is in a position to demonstrate to the patient how such a conflict rages inside the psyche – in simple terms, between the need for love as against the resistance to love. There is no guaranteed solution to this conflict. One cannot promise anybody that life will triumph over death, or that 'therapy will cure', for again that is the individual's choice and without doubt some people prefer death to life, or, more mundanely, prefer depression to love.

But it seems clear that Freud has unlocked the door to very dark places in the personality – our propensity to project unwelcome feelings and thoughts onto others, or onto the universe itself, thus absolving ourselves of responsibility for our lives. For example, I quite often hear patients complain that there are no eligible potential partners around: 'there are no decent men'; 'all the decent women are married'. Such complaints provide clever hiding places for one's fear of intimacy and fear of what intimacy might bring up in oneself such as feelings of vulnerability, rage, disappointment, and so on. It's not simply that we blame others for our own shortcomings – that insight can be found in the New Testament after all – but that we set out very ingeniously to construct a world order which guarantees our failure at something, particularly in relationships, work and creativity – and then blame the world order as a kind of objective 'fate' over which we have no power, and towards which we feel a kind of martyred rage. Freud was a master at unravelling such intricate forms of camouflage and laying bare our resistances, not just to therapy, but to life itself.

In the end, Freud is saying that our neuroses are our defences against authenticity and love, and for that reason amongst our dearest possessions. Or even that character itself is a protective defence. So it is that in the deepest forms of psychotherapy parts of the patient's character are dismantled and laid bare, if the patient so wishes. Obviously, this kind of work cannot be done against someone's will – that would be absurd and actually counter-productive for the defences simply get stronger. We see this happening in Freud's case-study concerning 'Dora'. Freud hammers at Dora with his interpretations, demonstrates his zeal and cleverness – and she leaves! In a sense, her sexual abuse at the hands of her parents and their friends is repeated in Freud's quasi-rape. However, I do not infer from this that Freud was an irredeemable tyrant and power-monger – that would be an undialectical judgement. No doubt like all analysts and therapists Freud had to make his way partly by his own mistakes, not least with that omnipotence which is the pitfall for many tyro-therapists. At the same time, the Dora case exemplifies another phenomenon – counter-transference, the analyst's own responses to the patient – which Freud mentions briefly in his writings, but which would later assume a greater and greater significance in the handling of depth psychology.[16]

Transference illustrates beautifully the themes of this chapter – that the inner and outer worlds of human beings interpenetrate and are liable to mutual reversals. The transference shows the inner world being projected onto the outer. Thus, the over-guilty patient tends to see the therapist as a critical tyrant – this represents the projection of an inner figure who tyrannizes the patient. But we can also argue that this inner figure is itself made up of congealed forces, partly from the outer world – the parental prohibitions, for example – and partly from the inner – the child's aggressive feelings against such figures. It is also likely that the patient feels critical of the therapist, but is able to conceal this by reversing the equation. Perhaps also the patient craves the therapist's love and therefore dreads punishment or wishes for punishment. I cannot publish an exhaustive list of such incorporations and reversals, since there is no recipe book for psychic configurations. Suffice it to say that such complex interplays between inner and outer characterize human beings in general, and are not the property of 'neurotic' people. Our inner world is made up of intrusions from outside; our outer world is made up of emanations from within. The therapeutic task is to lift the veil which masks such fusions between self and other and to begin the painful business of separating oneself out as an autonomous being.

9
Contradictions in Sexuality

In his book *The History of Sexuality* Michel Foucault presents an arresting thesis: not just that sexuality has become an obsession in modern Western culture, it has become a means of acquiring knowledge and power, a way of seeing reality, a way of communicating about reality, one might even say a way of being a self. Foucault refers to a 'great sexual sermon' which has 'swept through our societies', and in which sex is hailed as 'the revelation of truth, the overturning of global laws, the proclamation of a new day to come and the promise of a certain felicity'.[1]

But Foucault is not referring to Freud or psychoanalysis – he argues that this 'discursive explosion' has been going on since the eighteenth century. In fact, Freud is mentioned only briefly in Foucault's *History* – Foucault makes the point that those who saw Freud as the originator of this movement were unaware of the long build-up which had occurred before the Freudian project was constructed: 'what they had attributed solely to the genius of Freud had already gone through a long stage of preparation.'[2]

Foucault's ideas seem relevant to psychoanalysis in at least two ways: first, that Freud saw sex in some ways as 'the revelation of truth'. Certainly, he put forward a notion of sexual etiology: the idea that the neuroses have a sexual origin. In Freud's words, 'people fall ill in one way or another of frustration, when reality prevents them from satisfying their sexual wishes.'[3] But Freud goes further, since he claims that the sexual drives are dominated by the pleasure principle, which states that 'our total mental activity is directed towards achieving pleasure'.[4] In his *Outline of Psychoanalysis*, Freud gives a succinct summary of the operation of this principle:

> the core of our being ... is formed by the obscure id ... Within this id the organic instincts operate, which are themselves compounded

> of two primal forces (Eros and destructiveness) in varying proportions ... The one and only urge of these instincts is towards satisfaction.[5]

Later in the same passage, Freud states categorically that 'the id obeys the inexorable pleasure principle'. In his gloomy work, *Civilization and its Discontents*, he states that 'what decides the purpose of life is simply the programme of the pleasure principle'.[6]

Of course, matters become much more complex in the Freudian schema, since for example the process of sublimation can be used to divert the sexual drives into non-sexual areas such as art, intellectuality, and so on. None the less, Freud offers us a rather stark picture of human existence, dominated by the urge to satisfy our instincts, but opposed by the demands of civilization, which curb our pleasures so that we are able to channel energy into social life. Freud comments rather bleakly that 'one feels inclined to say that the intention that man should be "happy" is not included in the plan of "Creation"'.[7]

One might want to offer numerous objections to this description of human life – that it is too pessimistic, or too dualistic, perhaps – but more pertinently that it eroticizes existence too much. Perhaps the key issue here is to do with sublimation, for with this concept Freud is able to claim that the sexual drives lie behind many non-sexual activities. This is one of the chief objections which Jung raised to Freudian psychology, and Jung preferred to speak in terms of a generalized libido or life-energy, not sexual, which could be said to be the driving force behind both sexual and non-sexual activities. But for Freud, there is a sense in which the sexual is the key to the identity of everyone, their neuroses, their way of conducting life, their chances of happiness. In this sense, in Foucault's words, 'we demand that sex speak the truth ... and we demand that it tell us our truth'.[8]

The other aspect of Foucault's theory of sexuality which seems relevant in any consideration of Freud is Foucault's insistence that sexuality itself is constituted by the 'discourse on sex'. In other words, sexuality is not a pre-existent sociological or political phenomenon in human existence but is produced by the 'putting into discourse of sex'.[9] Elsewhere Foucault speaks of the 'production of sexuality':

> sexuality must not be thought of as a kind of natural given which power tries to hold in check, or as an obscure domain which knowledge tries gradually to uncover. It is the name that can be given to a historical construct.[10]

Freud's own work is marked by a veritable 'discursive explosion' – perhaps no one else has written so much about sex – I have already commented on Freud's restlessness and his constant revisions to his theories. Furthermore, the invention of psychoanalysis produced a space where people could turn their own 'sex into discourse' – in the last chapter, I remarked that analysis and therapy are above all linguistic events where stories are told and retold. And Freud is insistent – today we may suggest, too insistent – that the patient's stories and the analyst's stories focus on the sexual history of the patient.

Foucault's description of the confessional in the church springs to mind here: 'the confession was, and still remains, the general standard governing the production of the true discourse on sex.'[11] Foucault goes on to argue that the confessional was gradually secularized and spread into education, psychiatry, the justice system, literature, medicine, and so on. Arguably then, Freud's invention of psychoanalysis as a means of helping patients through the 'talking cure' has as its antecedents these ancient procedures for putting sex into discourse.

Substantive issues

Should we say, then, of Freud that he was simply, amidst this discursive explosion about sex, the master story-teller, one of the great writers about sex, and the facilitator of our interminable confessions and conversations about it? Or did Freud change our conception of sex and sexuality, as well as our ability to talk about it and confess to it? In other words, are there substantive issues in Freud's theory of sexuality?

In fact, Freud took a radical approach to human sexuality. To say that he deconstructed it is an understatement: he shattered it. First, he separated it from reproduction, and argued that the sexual instincts are driven by the need for pleasure. This in itself marks a considerable liberation from those quasi-biological, semi-theological arguments – still found, for example, in the Catholic Church – which have always connected sex with the production of children, and thereby indicated that the pleasures of sex are fortunate by-products to its real meaning and purpose. Freud turns this upside down, and no doubt delights in upsetting core Christian ethical principles.

Second, he described human infants as sexual beings, who pursue pleasure not genitally, but all over their body. Thus, the genital aim in adult sexuality is a much delayed development, and many people retain many pre-genital desires. The notion of infantile sexuality has always caused consternation, but one can see that it ties in logically with the first principle: for if children can be said to have sexual sensations and pleasures, they are obviously enjoying sex of some kind long before they are reproductively active. Freud is also able to demonstrate quite elegantly that the so-called perversions in adult sexuality consist of the perseveration of ancient infantile predilections. In this sense, everyone is perverse to a degree and the distinction between normality and perversion becomes a spectrum rather than a polarized opposition. According to Freud, sexual foreplay – with its non-genital play and caressing – embodies perverse infantile pleasures.[12]

Third, Freud opposes civilization to sex in a quite dramatic fashion, arguing as he does that culture must carry out a massive repression of the sexual drives, which cannot be allowed immediate satisfaction, if cultural and social life is to have any stability. We can argue that Freud has introduced two key fantasies here: first, he imagines that sex would become destructive and anti-social if left to flourish unchecked; and second, that many neuroses are caused by the repressiveness of culture – 'they would have been more healthy if it could have been possible for them to be less good,' he says of those afflicted by neurosis.[13]

The first fantasy is quite prominent in Freud's writings, and involves the idea that early human beings enjoyed unrestricted sex and were therefore non-neurotic. I have already pointed out in chapter 4 that this connects with his conception of the unconscious as a rather dangerous part of the psyche, containing as it does such unbridled instincts; and also that Freud's fantasies about 'primitive' human beings may be incorrect. One point that Freud seems to miss here is that most mammals have a very restricted sexual receptivity amongst females; and that therefore one might conjecture that the evolution of unrestricted sexual receptivity amongst early female humans may well have gone hand in hand with those cultural and social phenomena which Freud sees as restrictive on sexuality. In short, it is possible that there never has been a time amongst animals or early humans when sex was unrestricted.[14] If this were true, then either neurosis has always existed amongst humans (since they have always had sexual restrictions placed upon them) or Freud is wrong in assuming that neurosis stems from sexual frustration.

Fourth, he claims that sexuality is closely tied to the unconscious, since many repressed desires are retained there, in a 'forgotten' state, but still exerting a pressure on the individual. Again, there is an interlocking connection with infantile sexuality, for our ancient sexual wishes were repressed in infancy and still exist in the timeless world of the unconscious. Thus for Freud the unconscious is infantile in its essence and preserves many sexual desires which are at odds with the adult world.

This also means that sexuality is closely connected with fantasy. Since many of the things that we want are forbidden, we have to enjoy them in a hallucinatory manner – we dream about them, fantasize about them unconsciously, convert them into symbols or symbolic actions, and so on.

Fifth, Freud is able to connect such 'frozen' sexual wishes and fixations with the development of character itself so that one can speak of the anal character, the phallic character, the oral character, and so on. In this way, a whole characterology becomes possible, based on the various types of underlying sexual interest shown by individuals.

Sixth, in the Oedipus complex he postulates a family drama in which sexual desires and prohibitions are played out in painful, even tragic, ways. It is in this theatre that we first learn that many desires cannot be fulfilled, are considered anti-social or arouse anger in our parents or invite punishment. The little boy feels threatened with castration if he dares to prolong his sexual interest in his mother; the little girl learns that she is already castrated, and can only long for the penis that will never be hers. Thus the Oedipus complex brings sexuality and gender together: masculinity and femininity are partly shaped through its restrictions and identifications.

A radical model?

Perhaps the first thing to be said about this model of sexuality is that it is intellectually satisfying – it is an elegant model. This might make us pause and wonder if Freud prizes elegance above empirical reality: there is a sense in which it is too neat. In fact, the neatness begins to fray at the edges, for example, in the description of female sexuality and femininity which cannot be confined within the mould of the phallic Oedipal model, as we shall see in the next chapter. I have already mentioned the way in which the concept of sublimation gives Freud an escape clause: he can maintain the omnipresence of the sexual drives by suggesting that they can be diverted into non-sexual channels. The notion of 'the sexual' begins to widen dramatically in Freud's later writings.

Secondly, as a model of human sexuality it is so radical that contemporary students of sexuality – for example, in feminism and the gay movement – still find it an invaluable source of ideas. It is radical because it strips away much of the Christianized moral attitude which has arguably inhibited the study of sexuality in Western culture: instead of investigating what is, studies of sexuality have often been obsessed with what should and should not be. Of course, Freud was not exempt from such biases, but he was scornful of over-ethical approaches to sexuality.

It is also a radical model in detaching human sexuality from reproduction, and hence from biology. This seems rather ironic, since Freud was often at pains to point to the anatomical or biological foundations to human sexual desire, but in his construction of a truly psychological psychology he turned towards the study of desire, pleasure and inhibition and away from the reproductive bias of biological studies of sex.

Psychoanalysis offers a radical approach to sexuality in yet another way: its postulate of the repressed unconscious which must be released from bondage if the individual is to be freed from a debilitating constriction throws down the gauntlet to the forces of conservatism. Of course, psychoanalysis has often served these forces, and has for example, at times pilloried homosexuality.[15] But there remains a radical core to Freud's theory which can be reclaimed. The link between infantile sexuality, perversion and the pleasure principle, and the opposition hypothesized between sexual fulfilment and a repressive civilization – these features produce a model of sexuality quite at odds with the ethical models that have existed in the Christian West for centuries, and that still exist. And Freud's own attitude often shows this radicalism: for example, he is sympathetic to homosexuals and is much less homophobic than some of his later followers; he expresses concern for the plight of women who remain sexually unsatisfied despite being married – unlike men, they have no recourse to adultery or prostitutes. Of course, Freud also exhibits quite conservative attitudes towards both homosexuals and women – he is clearly ambivalent towards sexual dissidence or 'free love'.

Freud's *Three Essays on Sexuality* shows in its structure the revolutionary aim of the writer, for Freud begins, not with a consideration of adult sexuality, but with a section on 'Sexual Aberrations', followed by a section on 'Infantile Sexuality', these two sections occupying 80 pages in the modern editions. Only then do we find the third section devoted to 'The Transformations of Puberty' which details the development of genital sexuality. In other words, the structure of the *Three Essays* is a deliberate mirroring of sexual development: genital sex arrives late and last. There is a long period of preparation for it, when intercourse and reproduction are not in the picture at all, and when the pleasure principle drives the human infant to seek bodily pleasure, unless and until it is forbidden to do so by adults.

Freud's thoughts on the role of sexual repression, as found in education, religion and moralizing about sex, are not in doubt. In his essay

'The Sexual Enlightenment of Children' he makes the comment, in relation to children's sexual curiosity, that

> if it is the purpose of educators to stifle the child's power of independent thought as early as possible, in favour of the 'goodness' which they think so much of, they cannot set about this better than by deceiving him in sexual matters and intimidating him in matters of religion.[16]

His article '"Civilized" Sexual Morality and Modern Nervous Illness' should be read as one of his most mordant comments on the damage brought about by morality, which, according to Freud, produces mass neurosis among those who are unable to find sexual fulfilment. Marriage itself is not seen as a solution by Freud: he comments in relation to women who feel sexually unsatisfied in marriage that 'the cure for nervous illness arising from marriage would be marital unfaithfulness'. But this is forbidden to most women, who have no other recourse but to become ill, that is, neurotic: 'nothing protects her virtue as securely as an illness.'[17]

In such comments we see a rather bleak, even bitter, Freud, unable to see any solution to the conflict between the individual's need for sexual happiness and the demands of a society intent on suppression and inhibition. In a sense, he is saying that sexual happiness is almost impossible, except for those libertines who flout conventional morality and take their pleasures where they may.

It is interesting to look back at these comments 90 years after they were written. After the permissive explosion of the 1960s and the subsequent relaxation of puritan morality towards sex, what would Freud say now? Undoubtedly people today are able to enjoy sex before marriage much more freely than then; sex is taken for granted by some young people as one of life's pleasures; contraception has eradicated the fear of pregnancy which haunted Freud's generation. But has this produced a greater happiness in people? It strikes me as arguable that sexual neurosis is still widely prevalent today, in the sense that many men and women are afraid of sex, are afraid of being open in sex, are afraid of being intimate, and so on. In addition, it is not obviously true that those who enjoy unlimited sex without fear of pregnancy are happier people than Freud's generation!

It seems likely that Freud underestimated the non-sexual aspects of sex. By this I mean that what brings people to therapy today is a failure of intimacy, rather than a failure in sexual availability or sexual technique. And perhaps he also underestimated the non-sexual aspects of neurosis: arguably civilization produces neurotic people in large numbers quite apart from the degree of sexual repression that is involved. For example, we might speak of a 'loss of meaning' to be found in modern industrial society – but this takes us into quasi-spiritual areas of human life with which Freud felt distinctly uncomfortable.

None the less, it is difficult to deny Freud's place in history as a sexual radical, often distorted and denied by his own followers, who have sometimes brought back into the study of sexuality those ethical concerns which Freud so much despised.

Bodily desire

Freud describes the human infant as full of desires – desires for bodily pleasures above all. In a sense, this infant almost seems to aim for orgasm, or at any rate the fulfilment of its intense physical needs. But this means that human beings are seen as desiring animals, even if their desires are circumscribed by a civilization which cannot allow the raw satisfaction of their instincts. They are therefore both desiring and proscribed animals, constantly struggling between the twin poles of sex and repression. This can be seen as either a tragic or a bleak view of both sexuality and human existence – I have already cited Freud's remark that happiness is not really allowed for in the scheme of things. Repression is inevitable, satisfaction is fleeting. This connects with the aims of psychoanalysis, which do not include the satisfaction of our libidinal desires directly, but being able to acknowledge them consciously, so that they no longer lurk like wild animals in the unconscious. We cannot have what we want, Freud says, but at least we can become aware of wanting it and understand that and the reasons we cannot have it. This is therapeutic pessimism indeed!

Although there is no doubt that Freud's sexual theories have been considerably diluted in the last 50 years, his stress on the instinctual side of human beings still seems valuable. Many people who come to therapy seem to have developed their thinking ability, but have neglected their bodies and their need for sex and love – indeed, frequently they have experienced powerful prohibitions on sex and love in childhood. One also meets people who are puzzled by the idea that they are allowed to have wants, needs and desires, especially of an instinctual kind. In this sense, although Freud's out-and-out sexual etiology seems quite inadequate today, his stress on the instincts and on sex remains an important strand in the therapeutic armoury.

Let me give an example. Jim has been talking with me for several years about the lack of meaning in his life, although he has work he enjoys, he is quite creative musically and he has a good relationship with his girlfriend. But something nags at him, a sense of something lacking. A series of dreams seem to be the harbinger of something new: he dreams continually of animals such as tigers, lions, reptiles, snakes. To me, these images seem to indicate the instinctual side of Jim, which in the past has been suppressed in favour of the mental. Jim is very good at thinking things through!

Then he complains to me that love-making with his girlfriend is rather 'polite'. When I ask for clarification, he becomes embarrassed, but tells me that their sexual life consists almost entirely of perfunctory acts of penetration.

I also begin, in my own fantasy life around Jim, to get a sense of his penis rising up in the air! This image is at first rather uncomfortable, but Jim himself begins to talk about his penis, and his shyness, fear, diffidence about it. It seems rather vulgar, and his undoubted desire to penetrate his girlfriend makes him feel uneasy. I suggest to him that he is partly uneasy about the rawness and crudeness of the desire and the physical organs involved. There is a growing sense of a man who has been sexually constricted all his life.

I will curtail this story, only to add that things did improve for Jim and his girlfriend, and that they came to enjoy a much more open and frank sexual relationship, where they did not need to hide their bodies as much as formerly, and where they could enjoy each other's body in a more uninhibited fashion.

There is a further interesting spin-off to this story: Jim's creativity also changed during this time and he began to develop a new interest in spirituality. My interpretation here is not Freudian – I do not see the creative and spiritual impulses as stemming from the sexual, but rather that Jim had been able to liberate his 'life-energy' across the board.

But my main point here is that Jim's sense of lack stemmed partly from an incomplete relationship with his own body and an inability to enjoy his body and its desires in the company of another. He had feelings of shame and fear around this, but he was able to partly work through these.

I think this story is not uncommon. In our culture, there is such a premium placed on thinking, decision-making, abstract conceptualizing, and so on that the raw aggressive energy of the body can be lost sight of or squashed. In this sense, Freud's emphasis on the instincts and the bodily origins of the instincts is invaluable.

If you like, the Freudian paradigm points us to the primitive aspects of life as being life-enhancing, one might say life-giving. This teaching had enormous value for the twentieth century which placed such value on the mind and on technology and science. These things leave us feeling hollow if we do not attend to the more animal aspects of ourselves, in particular our bodies.

Oedipal traumas

The Oedipus complex is familiar to many people outside the world of psychotherapy: certainly the idea of a romance between boys and their mothers, and girls and their fathers is widely understood. But perhaps we have become inured to the more extraordinary aspects of Freud's Oedipal theory – in particular, that it posits that at the heart of human sexual identity and development lie traumatic disturbances. Loss, prohibition, threats of violence, rivalry – these are the language of Oedipal triangles. Consider that the little boy is apparently threatened with the loss of his penis and warned off the woman he loves – his mother. The little girl learns that she is already castrated and also finds that her would-be mate belongs to someone else. Sexual desire and love itself are surrounded by very dark feelings – deprivation, loss, jealousy, abandonment.

We might say that the little boy learns a very hard lesson: what I have, I may lose, and what I want, I cannot have. For the girl, matters seem even worse: I have already lost something of great value and must forever mourn my castrated state, and what I want, I cannot have. Without doubt, if we accept that these are the foundations of human sexuality, then it is a fractured sexuality. Human beings are forever haunted by the unattainable and the spectre of loss. And Lacan was to extend this sense of loss even further, by arguing that we do not even possess a stable sense of self, but must constantly and feverishly seek identifications with other things in order to maintain an identity. The ego itself, for Lacan, is a phantom.[18]

Lacan's views on sexuality and its potential for satisfaction are notoriously sceptical – for example, he comments that 'the act of love is the polymorphous perversion of the male', and even more nihilistically, 'love rarely comes true, as each of us knows, and it only lasts for a time. For what is love except banging one's head against a wall, since there is no sexual relation?'[19]

The key question in relation to these themes is whether they are transhistorically viable, or whether they are applicable to particular cultures or sub-cultures. Some radical critics have argued that Freud mistook the sexual mores of the European middle class for a universal structure, and in particular failed to see that in a patriarchal society, the prohibitions of the father appear like tablets of stone. For example, the idea that the man's wife 'belongs' to him can be characterized as a patriarchal and perhaps capitalist idea and not a universal one. The notion that father and son contest ownership of the mother seems to be derived from capitalist laws of property.[20]

Furthermore, the traumatizing aspect of the Oedipus complex is accepted by Freud as part of the human condition – indeed, Freud argues that this complex is the source of neurosis itself. But is it? Again, sexual and political radicals can argue that the complex is itself a product of psychological damage, in the family, and in society – not that a disrupted Oedipal trajectory causes neuroses, but that the Oedipus complex is itself neurotic, or is the result of psychic damage. For example, one can argue that the nuclear family is the hotbed of Oedipal conflict. But is the nuclear family universal and unchanging?

This critique has particular relevance to the theory of female sexuality, which in Freud's model appears as a kind of second prize awarded to those who were not given first prize: the penis. If the little boy is faced with the threat to his genitals, the little girl learns that for her the catastrophe has already happened. In the next chapter I shall argue that Freud universalizes and biologizes this aspect of female psychology, and fails to historicize it or place it in its socio-political context.

The same objection can be raised by gay radicals, who can object to the analysis of homosexuality as a kind of failed Oedipal trajectory – instead of (correctly) identifying with his father and loving his mother, the gay boy has done the reverse and this is perverse. But clearly the whole structure of the Oedipus complex guarantees that many people fail: homosexuals, those who prefer not to be married or have children, those who live alone, those who have unconventional sex lives, and so on.

It seems ironic that Freud complains about the shackles placed on human sexuality by human culture, and then seems to invent a theoretical shackle or straitjacket. Of course, Freud would retort that he did not 'invent' the Oedipus complex, but merely discovered it. One cannot dispute that, but one can dispute Freud's claim that it is somehow wired into human relationships.

However, the pre-Oedipal development of post-Freudian psychoanalysis has cast another shadow over the Oedipus complex, which can no longer be seen as the key to the neuroses, since many of them seem to have roots in the first months and years of infancy. In fact, it has become a truism in psychotherapy that people who are severely damaged cannot accept Oedipal interpretations since their damage goes further back, and first one has to help them to repair their damaged sense of self before one can even contemplate venturing into areas such as rivalry, sexual attraction, and so on.

Some evidence of these phenomena can be found in Freud's case study of 'Little Hans', which shows Freud determined to prove that Hans's problems are derived from the Oedipus complex. Yet Freud's description of the family show parents who seem quite unhappy, who beat their children, threaten to leave them, threaten Hans with castration and generally treat him harshly. One cannot really criticize Freud for not seeing this, since presumably many children were treated similarly and showed neurotic symptoms in childhood or later. In fact, I have no doubt that many children are still treated in this way. Is Hans's suffering derived from the Oedipus complex or from harsh and unreliable parents? To put it another way, is the Oedipus complex itself derived from harsh and unreliable parenting?

I have certainly known families where the love-affair between one child and a parent was not treated harshly, but with love and understanding. Of course, one cannot deny that some degree of disappointment must be involved for the child when it realizes that it cannot actually sexually possess the loved parent, but let us not forget that there is also a relief in this, for the child probably senses unconsciously that it is not time for it to enter into a genital relationship with anyone. In other words, the 'prohibition' which Freud makes so much of may also be welcome to the child and not as traumatic as he claims. What cannot be disputed is that many children have been raised in a very harsh manner, and still are – but is this an inevitable part of child-rearing, or is it again a particular feature of our culture?

Eros

One of Freud's interesting characteristics is that after a major disagreement with another analyst, for example Rank or Jung, and after he has explicitly stated his objections to their ideas, he often begins to incorporate part of the rejected ideas into his work. Thus after the split with Jung, partly over the question of Jung's non-sexual libido, or 'life-energy', we find Freud beginning to discuss the 'desexualized' libido. Similarly, the notion of birth anxiety can be found in Freud's work after the split with Rank.[21]

Undoubtedly, the concept of the sexual drive becomes more metaphysical later in Freud's life. He speaks of Eros as a force 'binding things together', contrasted with the death instinct, which tends to disintegrate them. The original thesis of the sexual instincts, which are eventually directed towards an object, begins to be amplified in various ways. For example, with the concept of narcissism Freud asserts that 'the ego now found its position among sexual objects' – in other words, libido is not directed outwards towards another object but towards the ego itself.[22]

But then Freud begins to speak of a 'desexualized Eros', from which flows a source of energy which is available to the organism. Freud even relates this to the process of thought:

> If this displaceable energy is desexualized libido, it may also be described as sublimated energy; for it would still retain the main purpose of Eros – that of uniting and binding – in so far as it helps towards establishing the unity, or tendency to unity, which is particularly characteristic of the ego. If thought-processes in the wider sense are to be included among these displacements, then the activity of thinking is also supplied from the sublimation of erotic motive forces.[23]

Clearly, Freud's use of the term 'Eros' is quite different from his early use of the term 'sexual instincts' for now these instincts can be displaced, defused, desexualized, sublimated. In the end, we seem to end up with a kind of life-energy, opposed to the destructive instinct (or death instinct). Freud has stretched the concept of 'the sexual' a very long way, so much so that one can legitimately wonder if there is any normal sense of the word left. It is difficult to avoid the suspicion that Freud, consciously or not, is ceding ground to those of his critics, including Jung, who had objected to the monistic sexual etiological framework of early psychoanalysis. Of course, one problem with the 'Eros' concept is that it has become so generalized as to seem almost meaningless.

Gender and sexuality

Freud's theoretical work on the differentiation between boys and girls has been severely criticized by gender students for its phallocentric bias, and yet the basic schema of psychoanalysis has been used in many contemporary theories of gender and sexuality. Freud's work on gender has been enormously influential, particularly as it has been emended by the French analyst Jacques Lacan, who in fact retained the 'phallic' tendency in Freud's approach.

What seems of great importance in Freud's work on gender flows from the notion of the unconscious: Freud's ideas go against any kind of social realism or empiricism, which might claim that children simply imitate their parents, or are 'trained' in various gender positions: boys are trained to be masculine, girls to be feminine, and so on. But as Jacqueline Rose points out:

> psychoanalysis becomes one of the few places in our culture where it is recognized as more than a fact of individual pathology that most women do not painlessly slip into their roles as women, if indeed they do at all.[24]

The same can be said for men: the masculine ethos is not uniformly or painlessly adopted by men. Far from it – many men find masculinity an agonizing straitjacket.[25] But the key thrust of psychoanalytic thought is that there cannot be an effortless 'training' or 'learning' of gender positions, for the unconscious is not educable in this way. If you like, the unconscious resists any pedagogical instruction or indoctrination. If you demand of me that I should be 'feminine' or 'masculine', I may outwardly obey, but there is little doubt that in the unconscious will be found positions that are quite different and probably antithetical. The same can be said of the heterosexual/homosexual divide: we know little enough about how these positions are arrived at, but it seems pretty clear that one cannot 'cure' people of their homosexuality. As Rose says, 'the unconscious constantly reveals the failure of identity.'[26] Another way of putting this is that Freud's model of the psyche posits contradiction at its heart: contradiction between ego and id; but also contradiction in the id itself and in the ego. If my conscious mind likes to say 'black', then it is likely that the unconscious is murmuring (or maybe screaming) 'white'. Furthermore, another part of my unconscious may well be screaming 'red'!

A classic example of this is homophobia: the man who screams loudest about the sickness of homosexuality can be suspected of some secret sexual quirk of his own: witness the strange story of J. Edgar Hoover. Another clear example can be found in the anti-pornography movement: it never ceases to amaze me how blatantly many of its followers spend huge amounts of energy looking for pornography, writing and speaking about it, and even showing it to others! This is a more sophisticated version of the tabloid newspapers which under the headline, 'Shock, horror, scandal' give us our daily dose of titillation. No doubt we are shocked and horrified – at our own sexual excitement over the scandal being described.

Lacan has considerably dramatized the contradictions in psychoanalysis, but one cannot disagree with his stipulation that the ego is not simply incoherent, but necessarily incoherent.[27] This suggests to me that those students of gender and sexuality who reject any kind of psychoanalytic input – I am not saying that they have to become root-and-branch Freudians – are bound in the end to fall victim to some form of empiricism. But empiricism can never explain the vagaries and mysteries of gender/sex: not only can it not explain why many women (and men) fail to fit smoothly into their stipulated gender positions, it cannot explain why even those who do can become so desperately unhappy. Psychoanalysis offers us the premise of a psyche divided against itself: therefore if, as a man, I adopt various extreme 'masculine' or 'macho' traits, I may well end up being persecuted by those parts of myself which want to go in another direction. This may make me persecute others – for example, by beating up gay men, being scornful towards women, and so on – anything to get rid of the dreaded Other inside myself.

This is the dialectical vision of Freud, and when we have criticized and rejected some of the substantive aspects of his model of sexuality we are left with the invaluable notion of psychic opposition or negation. This states that *I am what I am not* – hence the little boy adores his mother and wants to marry her – but we can also suggest that he would love to get pregnant by his father. The little girl adores her father – but would also love to impregnate her mother. The heterosexual male has a passionate desire for his lover – but secretly (unconsciously) yearns to possess her breasts and her womb in his own body, as she yearns to possess his penis. Of course, this list is endless, and for those who are unsympathetic to Freudianism will no doubt seem wilful and perverse. But it is the perversion present in us all that Freud points us to. In this context, I am not using the term 'perversion' in a moral sense, but simply to denote that which is antithetical to my conscious desires and my public personality.

10 Femininity, Feminism and Psychoanalysis

Female sexuality has been seen as problematic in patriarchal culture for thousands of years. In some cultures, women have to shroud their bodies in public places; in others, clitoridectomy is carried out to prevent their sexual pleasure; in Western culture the twin themes of Madonna and whore intertwine to form a bizarre schizophrenic picture. The Virgin Mary represents one extreme: a sexless mother who can give birth with an intact hymen; at the other extreme, one thinks of the many women persecuted in the witch-hunts and other barbaric suppressions. Attitudes to menstruation are also revealing: the menstrual woman is often seen as a deadly figure, who will kill flowers, spoil the hunt, put spells on animals. Western pornography gives us another slant: one senses in it a strange mixture of infantile fascination with the female body combined with hatred and horror.[1]

Desire and revulsion, fascination and dread – these attitudes still seem quite common amongst men today, for example in many obscene jokes which treat women's body as deadly mantraps or as objects to masturbate into.

The reasons why female sexuality, and femininity in general, arouse such polarized feelings are beyond the scope of this book. However, it strikes me that men have often seen the feminine as a great threat to the masculine. If we accept that masculinity is not something one is born with, but something that must be arduously achieved, then regression to a primitive identification with mother, and mother's body, is seen as a threat to that task. In other words, the feminine is very dangerous, since it might seduce one from the onerous duty of being masculine. One thinks of Ulysses resisting the song of the Sirens. Of course, speaking in the language of depth psychology, such dangers partly arise because men secretly wish to return to a feminine identification such as they once enjoyed with their mothers. If they did not, why would such a regression be so feared?[2]

One can also argue more simply that in patriarchy, woman is conceived as the Other, and therefore simultaneously arouses need, desire and hatred. For example, many of the cultures surrounding the Mediterranean seem to contain this mixture of extreme machismo and very ambivalent attitudes to women – for the greatest danger for a man is to be in any way like a woman. Hence homophobia is intense in these cultures.[3]

Mention of machismo provides us with an insight into the commonest strategy employed by men in the face of the dangers posed by women, their sexuality and feminine identity – to deny it and to cover it up. For example, the machismo found in Mediterranean and other cultures specializes in a virtual extirpation of any feminine traits in men and an obliteration of feminine aspects of culture. One often finds a severe segregation between the sexes – in many countries in southern Europe, women are the church-goers; men the café-goers. No doubt this segregation is useful to women as well, but it provides for men a vital removal of feminine influence, which is perhaps more dominant at home.

When we turn to the treatment of femininity and female sexuality in psychoanalysis, it would be odd if it did not bear the hallmarks of patriarchal culture. And without doubt Freud's theories concerning girls and women, and the development of feminine identity and female sexuality, are shot through with phallocentric and masculinist ideas.

In the first place, Freud takes the penis as the primary sexual organ, and in relation to pre-pubescent children, as the only sexual organ. He claims that both boys and girls have a phallic sexual identity, and that since girls are not yet aware of the vagina, but only of the clitoris (conceived of as a diminutive penis), they are conscious that their 'penis' is inferior to the boy's, who in turn is aghast to realize that penises can be removed, since apparently the girl has lost hers.[4]

One thing that is striking here is that the breast is largely absent: yet pornography again shows us how important an icon this is in the male conception of women. If little boys and girls are said to be fascinated by superior and inferior penises, one would also expect them to be fascinated by breasts, since many of them have an intimate contact with them from birth. But Freud is relatively silent about this and men's possible envy of women's breasts. Instead he speaks of the 'universal premiss of the penis'.[5] Hence, in the Freudian model of sexuality the clitoris assumes great significance, not as an independent female organ of sexual pleasure, but as an 'inferior' penis, about which women harbour feelings of shame and humiliation. Thus, the development of a feminine identity and of a feminine sexuality in girls is completely overshadowed by the looming presence of the penis, and a universal phallic sexuality. In Freud's notorious words, 'the little girl is a little man'.[6]

At puberty, according to the Freudian schema, girls begin to become aware of the vagina, but here again, Freud adopts a phallocentric attitude: the function of the vagina is to 'receive' the penis and obtain pleasure from the penis. Now Freud claims that the mature woman must give up clitoral pleasure and accept the pleasures of intercourse, and eventually pregnancy and childbirth. Freud goes so far as to claim that 'sexual anaesthesia' in women is caused by holding on to the pleasures of the clitoris:

> The process of a girl's becoming a woman depends very much on the clitoris passing on this sensitivity to the vaginal orifice in good time and completely. In cases of what is know as sexual anaesthesia in women the clitoris has obstinately retained its sensitivity.[7]

There are other aspects of the theory of the feminine which strike one as biased towards a masculinist ideology: for example, women are seen as passive and masochist; femininity is seen as a kind of compensatory development, achieved almost in chagrin at the failure to become a man. The little girl's attachment to her father occurs in a state of pique at the failure of her mother to give her a penis.

It strikes me that Freud's logic in his deployment of such arguments is deeply flawed – the claim that the clitoris is an inferior penis seems to beg many questions, but Freud states it as a basic assumption. Remarkably, Freud cites children's views on sexuality, amongst which are the view that everyone possesses a penis. Freud almost seems to suggest that this is evidence for its veracity.[8]

Freud also seems to shift from anatomical to psychological arguments with a disturbing sleight of hand: he cites the physiological evidence that the clitoris is 'homologous' to the penis and moves from that to argue that the clitoris is a 'masculine' organ.[9] This is like arguing that because men have nipples like women they are therefore somehow feminized.

In relation to boys' castration anxiety, one might also wonder if the shock felt by boys at the sight of women without a penis stems from an unconscious wish to be like them. In other words, castration anxiety in men can be plausibly connected with their own unconscious wishes. But since this is an example of feminine identification in boys, Freud largely passes over it.[10]

One could go on with more criticisms of Freud's theory of female sexuality, but in a sense they are beside the point – the point being that many of Freud's claims are ascribed to biological or instinctual processes, whereas today one might want to adduce political factors – in other words, the argument that women have been traditionally passive, ashamed of their own sexuality, envious of men, and so on, because those are the effects of the oppression exerted by a patriarchal society. Freud is fiercely opposed to this and sees actual castration – the lack of a penis – as the universal origin for all types of female development:

> the discovery that she is castrated is a turning point in a girl's growth. Three lines of possible development start from it: one leads to sexual inhibitions or neurosis, the second to change of character in the sense of a masculinity complex, the third, finally, to normal femininity.[11]

But femininity itself is seen to be closely associated with passivity – in a sense, to become a woman, the young girl has to renounce her claim to aggression and activity.[12] Freud's account of female development is therefore a tightly locked inner circle of anatomical and psychological milestones, which seems to have little relationship with socio-political structures. Indeed, Freud comments about this that:

> Children have, to begin with, no idea of the significance of the distinction between the sexes; on the contrary, they start with the assumption that the same genital organ (the male one) is possessed by both sexes; they do not begin their sexual researches with the problem of the distinction between the sexes, *while the social underestimation of women is completely foreign to them.* (added emphasis)[13]

This, written in 1914, is highly significant, since if children are assumed to be socio-politically innocent, especially as regards the 'social underestimation of women', then it is logically correct that the foundations of sexual and gender identity – assumed in the Freudian model to go back to infancy – are built without political influence. Indeed, one has to argue within this scheme that the political oppression of women flows from their anatomical and psychological inferiority, not the other way round. Since women are 'naturally' passive, full of shame and humiliation about their castrated state, and since men are aggressive, sexually potent and above all inheritors of the phallic order, it is not surprising that men have dominated women. Furthermore, according this model, this domination is unchangeable.

In a sense, Freud is loath to distinguish the possession of a penis from membership of the phallic order: the first being an anatomical attribute, the second a socio-political one. Or one can express this by reversing Freud's logic: Freud says that having a penis gives men a certain superiority in life; but one can reply, it is because men have had a traditional dominance over women socio-politically, that having a penis is therefore construed as being superior.

In 1925, Freud wrote a short article with the significant title 'Some Psychical Consequences of the Anatomical Distinction between the Sexes', in which he makes the following comment:

> After a woman has become aware of the wound to her narcissism, she develops, like a scar, a sense of inferiority. When she has passed beyond her first attempt at explaining her lack of a penis as being a punishment personal to herself and has recognized that that sexual character is a universal one, she begins to share the contempt felt by men for a sex which is the lesser in so important a respect.[14]

Freud could not really set out his position more clearly: women's castration is universal and leads to a sense of inferiority and self-hatred – in fact, Freud is really stating that women are inferior! In his 1931 paper, 'Female Sexuality', Freud, unusually, cites some of the objections raised by other analysts to his views on femininity, and comments tersely, in relation to Karen Horney's arguments: 'This does not tally with my impressions.'[15]

One can see why Freud was unwilling to allow his critics, such as Horney and Ernest Jones, any ground in the controversy over female development, for if Freud allowed for either a notion of 'primary femininity' or a notion of political influence on female identity (and, of course, male identity), then the edifice of phallocentrism would begin to topple.

And topple it did: if femininity is a thorn in the side of Freudian thought, one can argue that eventually it produces a huge counter-revolution in psychoanalysis, in that the phallocentric or father-centred nature of Freud's original formulations is overturned in favour of a mother-centred psychology, expressed most cogently in 'object relations' theory. To put it another way, Oedipal psychology is downgraded in favour of pre-Oedipal psychology, where the relations between mother and infant assume great importance. In this psychology, the breast does loom large for both sexes, and the object relations therapist may well speak of the symbolic breast being offered to the patient, who accepts it gratefully, or spits it out, or bites it cruelly, and so on.

Yet Freud was not unaware of these developments – one can say he anticipates them in his late papers on femininity, where he can be seen struggling with the theoretical problems posed by the development of the young girl and her love and desire for her father. He seems to sense the coming importance of maternal care, which had been overshadowed in his classic theoretical statements of the phallic nature of human sexuality.

But the question of femininity also leads to bigger questions: if Freud's analysis of female development can be accused of being transhistorical, overly anatomical and insufficiently attentive to socio-political issues, then the same charge can be levelled against psychoanalysis as a whole – that, in crude terms, it instinctualizes or biologizes the political and the cultural. Sexuality in the postmodern era has come to be seen by radical thinkers and writers as a set of political constructions – for example, the rise of the nuclear family, the exile of homosexuality and other forms of sexual 'deviance', the degradation of female sexuality, the link between procreation and property – these features of Western sexual life are not seen as universal, biologically-based phenomena, but historically determined and transient. Surely this analysis is confirmed by the fact that there have been changes in gender and sexuality in the postwar era: homosexuality has been to a limited extent destigmatized; women's sexuality is less hidden and proscribed than it was; women have become more assertive in public life. According to Freud's model, such changes are impossible, for they go against the biological and psychological edicts of the castration complex and the Oedipal complex.

Yet one can also argue that Freud began this revolution in the study of sexuality, for it was he who separated sexuality from reproduction and connected it with the pleasure principle. And it is Freud who argues that civilization is deeply hostile to sexual pleasure. Once again we see a paradox in the Freudian body of thought: Freud is both political and anti-political. In one area of his work he fiercely denounces the cultural suppression of sexual pleasure; yet in another area, he denounces any attempt to link women's 'passivity' with socio-political structures. It is Freud who castigates the sexual deprivation of women in marriage; yet the same Freud stipulates that masochism is 'truly feminine'.[16]

Moreover, it is more than a little absurd to condemn Freud for not having produced a fully worked out or consistent socio-political theory of sexuality. One might as well criticize Newton for not having anticipated Einsteinian relativity theory. There is a kind of anachronism at work here. Freud produced a patchwork of quasi-political (or 'cultural'), anatomical and psychological motifs in his model of sexuality, and no doubt one can perceive awkward juxtapositions and downright contradictions in the model as a whole. But without doubt it is the first model of *psycho-sexuality*.

The spectral mother

One of the fascinating aspects of Freud's attitude to women and femininity is the 'missing mother'. In other words, Freud's Oedipal theory sidelines the mother and converts her into a passive object. Thus in the classical formulation of the Oedipus complex, the little boy loves and desires his mother, but is thwarted by his great rival, his father, and eventually renounces his incestuous desires under the threat of castration. What is striking here is that the mother's own desire is obscured – she is the 'object of desire' for both son and father. Yet it is surely an important part of a child's life that it is – or is not – adored by its mother, physically held and comforted by her, seen as her surrogate, punished by her, toilet-trained by her, engaged in dialogue by her, and so on. The little boy is therefore not simply a would-be seducer of his mother, but the object of her quasi-seduction. Freud is not unaware of this fact, and reports that many actual seductions occur at the hands of women servants, nannies and so on, but this interesting phenomenon does not find a place within the metapsychological framework of psychoanalysis.

Could we argue that Freud is theoretically aligning himself with the notion of the passionless woman, prevalent in the nineteenth century? Freud seems ambivalent about this: on the one hand, he suggests that men are more aggressively committed to the sexual act, and some women may be 'constitutionally' frigid.[17] Yet Freud also accepted that women have strong sexual desires – he describes Dora as 'completely hysterical' because she does not respond favourably to the sexual advances of an older man.

One can suggest several other reasons for the 'missing mother'. First, Freud's own 'mother complex', which compelled him to deny the power and aggression of the seductive mother as an active sexual being, to whom both sons and fathers respond. Second, one could argue that Freud's is a patriarchal theory, which attempts to obliterate women as active agents – as subjects – and render them passive objects, subject to both male desire and the scientific enquiry of psychoanalysts. Third, one can also suggest that Freud describes the actual obliteration of women under patriarchy.

There is also the rather mundane fact that Freud tended not to see the psychoanalyst as a motherly figure, and probably found that role uncomfortable himself – he reports that women analysts found it easier to elicit the mother- transference.[18]

Little Hans

The question of feminine identification not only pertains to the development of little girls, but boys also. Thus in the Little Hans case there is a large amount of material concerning the little boy's maternal identification, and this material sits awkwardly within Freud's paternal theory. For example, Hans is obviously in love with his mother and is quite seductive towards her:

> This morning Hans was given his usual daily bath by his mother and afterwards dried and powdered. As his mother was powdering round his penis and taking care not to touch it, Hans said 'Why don't you put your finger there?'
> *Mother* 'Because that'd be piggish.'
> *Hans* 'What's that? Piggish? Why?'
> *Mother* 'Because it's not proper.'
> *Hans* (laughing) 'But it's great fun.'[19]

Hans is obviously in tune with the pleasure principle! But Hans's love for his mother also takes the form of an identification with her: for example, he has many fantasies about having children and looking after them:

> 'This morning I was in the W.C. with all my children. First I did lumf and widdled and they looked on. Then I put them on the seat and they widdled and did lumf, and I wiped their behinds with paper. D'you know why? Because I'd so much like to have children; then I'd do everything for them.'[20]

These fantasies persist in the teeth of his father's constant reminders that children, especially boys, can't have children:

> [*Father*] 'You had Grete in bed with you yesterday, but you know quite well that boys can't have children.'
> [*Hans*] 'Well, yes. But I believe they can, all the same.'[21]

At one point Freud makes an extraordinary comment about Hans's maternal fantasies:

> There is no necessity on this account to assume in Hans the presence of a feminine strain of desire for having children. It was with his mother that Hans had had his most blissful experience as a child, and he was now repeating them, and himself playing the active part, which was necessarily that of his mother.[22]

This note seems totally contradictory. Freud first denies that there is a feminine identification in Hans, but then argues that he is repeating infantile experiences but taking the part of his mother! Clearly, Freud is trying to get over the awkward fact of Hans's femininity, for this does not fit in very well with Freud's main masculinist thrust: that Hans is dominated by fear of his father, and will therefore eventually identify with him and renounce his mother. But here in Freud's own case-study one finds strong evidence for an intense attachment to the mother – material which many years later could be used by both object relations theorists and political feminists as ammunition for their respective arguments.[23]

Hans's horse phobia is also of great interest, since both Freud and Hans's father see it as an image of Hans's fear of his father. Yet there is some evidence that Hans equates horses and other large animals with the female. For example, furniture vans and other heavily laden vehicles seem to represent pregnant women, and Freud concedes this.[24]

There is a strong sense in this case of Freud and Hans's father bending the material towards a paternal theory, so that Hans's story fits into the classical Oedipal structure: he loves his mother, but fears his father's prohibition. But there is a large amount of evidence in the case-study that Hans also has a powerful identification with his mother and wishes to have children like her, is afraid of being abandoned by her, and so on. There is a strong sense of Freud obfuscating inconvenient evidence which does match his phallocentric theory.

At first glance, this seems puzzling, for Freud has provided a perfectly adequate theoretical explanation for such phenomena: the negative Oedipus complex, whereby a child identifies with the parent of the opposite sex and fantasizes a relation with the same-sex parent. Freud also argues that these contra-sexual identifications are remarkably resistant to enquiry in analysis.[25] But it is likely that the 'Little Hans' case has a hidden sub-text: to defend Freud's ideas about the Oedipus complex and the notion of the infantile origin of neuroses:

the general idea Freud wanted to enforce with this case study was that 'Little Hans'' childhood neurosis corroborated the conjectures which Freud's adult neurotic patients had encouraged him to explore.[26]

Freud expresses this himself more eloquently at the end of the case study:

> When . . . an adult neurotic patient comes to us for psychoanalytic treatment . . . we find regularly that his neurosis has as its point of departure an infantile anxiety such as the one we have been discussing, and is in fact a continuation of it; so that, as it were, a continuous and undisturbed thread of psychical activity, taking its start from the conflicts of his childhood, has been spun through his life.[27]

Feminine space

It would be incorrect simply to posit a Freud who is anti-feminine and anti-female. Rather, one should speak about his ambivalences towards the feminine. In fact, Freud's creation of psychoanalysis strikes me as a kind of 'feminine' creation, for this space is contemplative rather than active, it nurtures reflection, feeling and intuition rather than extrovert aggression or action. It strikes me that many men find therapy particularly uncomfortable for this reason, for it leads them into a world with which they are not familiar. Furthermore, the therapeutic space fosters attentiveness to the patient's own 'inner space', which again strikes me as a more feminine than masculine faculty.

Of course, when terms such as 'feminine' and 'masculine' are used in this way, one must be aware that they are relative rather than absolute terms – they have been given certain values in patriarchal society, such that the 'feminine' side of the polarity is often denigrated in favour of the 'masculine' side. But this in itself shows the revolutionary quality of Freud's contributions. He got closer to the heart of living people than academic psychologists were able to.

There is something ironic about the contradiction in Freud between the scientist, determined to bring the psyche into the scientific arena, and the creative artist, who invented psychoanalytic as a living encounter between two people, who are both radically changed by it.

Feminism

I have already indicated that Freud's masculinism produced a volte-face within psychoanalysis: object relations psychology eventually raised the banner of the spectral mother and began to grant her much more weight in the formation of children's psyches. Arguably, the repressed feminine, which Freud analysed very much in terms of a failed or negated masculinity, was beginning to emerge from the shadows and claim its own psychological space, its own identity, separate from the phallic order. Furthermore, it became apparent that the psychological analysis of masculinity had to grapple with the fear of the feminine in men: one might almost say that the tables were turned, for now it could be said that male identity in part functions as a defence against the feminine, both internally and externally.[28]

These developments are paralleled by the rise of political feminism, which originally, in its postwar renaissance, scorned Freud as the arch-patriarch, but eventually came to see psychoanalysis as one of the most important tools at its disposal in the analysis of patriarchal society and the relations between men and women in that society. In fact, it seemed that no other body of ideas could adequately describe and explain the puzzling features of patriarchy – Marxism had generally ignored it, as had academic sociology and politics. But psychoanalysis had patriarchal relations at its core: as we have seen, Freud's analysis of the distinction between the sexes often took a pronounced anatomical bent, and Freud is unmoved by any political analysis of women's subjugation, but feminism was able to excise the anatomical aspects and preserve the psychological analysis of patriarchy. In Juliet Mitchell's words, in her influential book *Psychoanalysis and Feminism*, Freud's work 'was not a recommendation of patriarchy but a description of it'.[29]

Mitchell argues that a lot of early (1960s) feminist discussion of Freud was crude and inaccurate, but more to the point, it couldn't see the wood for the trees: the fact that Freud was imbued with patriarchal thinking is not surprising, and does not mean that his insights into the patriarchal social/sexual system are invalidated. One might argue the opposite, that he had a remarkable grasp of the relationship between gender, sexuality and the family within patriarchy. Furthermore, it became apparent that within psychoanalysis a number of women had challenged some of the Freud's more sexist assumptions about men and women – Karen Horney, for example, objected to the notion of penis envy, not so much in itself, but because it ignored the fierce envy that men showed towards women, which she noticed in her male patients.[30] In other words, it was possible within the psychoanalytic system to argue against Freud's excessive bias towards phallic psychology.

Psychoanalysis is also well known as a profession where women had become influential, and had not seemed to suffer because of their sex –

Melanie Klein is one of the most original post-Freudian theoreticians within psychoanalysis. Hence it became clear that psychoanalysis is not a monolithic orthodoxy, where the words of the Master could not be challenged. In fact in the 1920s and 1930s it was precisely the issue of femininity which aroused much controversy within psychoanalysis, with analysts such as Ernest Jones and Horney challenging Freud's ideas about women.

The key difference between those feminists who rejected Freud and those who began to accept that psychoanalysis was an invaluable tool in the analysis of sexual difference and patriarchal dominance lies in the attitude to the unconscious. Anti-Freudian feminists have tended to adopt a kind of 'social realism' or a type of existential libertarianism. For example, in her work *The Second Sex*, Simone de Beauvoir argues that psychoanalysis ignores the choices that confront women:

> I shall pose the problem of feminine destiny quite otherwise: I shall place women in a world of values and give her behaviour a dimension of liberty. I believe that she has the power to choose between the assertion of her transcendence and her alienation as object; she is not the plaything of contradictory drives; she devises solutions of diverse values in the ethical scale.[31]

This assertion has to suppress the notion of the unconscious, which throws into question all ideas about 'freedom', 'authenticity' and 'choice'. It does not necessarily lead us to argue that freedom and choice are impossible, but that they are not simply a matter of conscious rational decisions. Hence de Beauvoir has to assert that woman 'is not the plaything of contradictory drives' – for of course, if she is, then it becomes much more difficult to conceive of the project of choice and authenticity. In particular, the idea that women can choose not to be 'alienated objects' strikes me as question-begging, for how can one do this if one is unaware that one is an alienated object? Indeed, being alienated surely implies that one is unconscious of one's alienation?

This is the project which psychoanalysis has set itself: to change alienation to 'transcendence', in the sense of returning choice to the apparently choiceless. De Beauvoir seems to see this as an act of will, but psychoanalytically speaking, the will finds itself continually subverted and attacked by forces in the unconscious, which cannot be removed by a further act of will. If you like, the unconscious is an objective fact, which one has to grapple with. It cannot be dismissed by fiat.

However, de Beauvoir is putting forward a fairly sophisticated argument based on her existential philosophy; some anti-Freudian feminists have advanced a cruder empiricist or realist approach, arguing that psychoanalysis ignores the environment where 'real' change can occur, and from where our beliefs and attitudes derive:

> Psycho-analysis, whatever individual therapists may say, does tend to encourage conformity which may amount to something likes brain-washing. If you are unhappy, the tendency is not to look at your situation and change that, you look within yourself and try to adapt yourself to the situation.[32]

This position simply wipes out any idea that human existence is shot through with unconscious fantasy: for example, that the child's gender and sexual identity are not simply imitations or reflections of those around it, but also comprise a complex tissue of fantasies about what being masculine or feminine involves. This approach has the merit of explaining why many people find it difficult to achieve a stable gender position, or find their own gender to be fragile or unsatisfactory. The idea that one can 'look at your situation and change that' sounds very positive and bracing, but in practice many people find it impossible, precisely because of the internal barriers against change or against 'looking' which exist. Those barriers are often unconscious, which is not to say they are not hugely influential. But it is impossible to change something in one's psyche which is unconscious, unless one is prepared to do the laborious work of in-depth analysis. In fact, it is impossible to 'look at your situation' initially, for looking at the unconscious is a skill that has to be learned gradually.

The crux of the matter in this debate is that Freud theorized about gender and sexuality: he was not content simply to observe and record. For example, where hysteria had been treated as a set of bizarre behaviours, Freud began to enquire as to the underlying meanings of these behaviours. As he says in the Introductory Lectures: 'It was discovered one day that the pathological symptoms of certain neurotic patients have a sense.'[33] But the empiricist cannot tolerate the idea of an 'underlying' sense or level of reality which is distinct from the surface and which has to be inferred.

A further problem within 'second-wave' feminist theory is that the position of men is either idealized or at least is seen as uncomplicated compared with that of women. In particular, the idea that masculinity might itself be a precarious and dangerous accomplishment is ignored.[34]

Again, this kind of view rests on a sort of surface analysis of events – the notion of the unconscious is desperately missing here, for only with that tool can we begin to examine the contradictions within gender and sexuality. For example, as we have seen, one of the insights of psychoanalysis had been that as well as achieving an identification with the father, boys also have an identification with the mother. Post-Freudian research seems to show that this pre-Oedipal tie is involved in very complex ways with the assumption of a masculine identity, which partly protects the male against the maternal identification.

Of course, Freud's analysis lacked something which feminism contributed in abundance: a political examination of gender and sexuality. Freud's apolitical theory cannot really explain why women are seen as inferior in human societies – Freud is forced into some rather desperate appeals to biology and anatomy. Thus women are seen as inferior because they have an inferior penis. The circularity of this argument is patent, but did not seem to embarrass Freud, who fiercely opposed any attempt to bring political arguments into the equation, although elsewhere he was a critic of those cultural repressive forces which denied people sexual happiness.

Hence the bringing together of feminist ideas with psychoanalytic thought produces a very powerful body of ideas, for feminism can give psychoanalysis an underpinning of political ideas. One can turn Freud's discussion of penis envy round: the reason that women are reckoned to have an inferior penis is because everything about them is considered to be inferior in a patriarchal society. But psychoanalysis can also point out that this in itself is too monolithic and undialectical an assertion: if women are believed to be inferior, we might conjecture that underneath that belief lurks its opposite: men also fear women and see them as very powerful.

It strikes me then that the split which has existed in Western thought between political and psychological analysis has been partly healed in the coming together of feminism and psychoanalysis. Freud rejected politics as having anything interesting to say about sexuality; originally, political feminism rejected the postulate of the unconscious, with its corollaries that gender and sexuality are riven with fantasy, contradiction and conflict. But when these two apparently opposite systems of ideas are brought together, the result is very powerful.

We might hypothesize that the unconscious can be considered to be not just a repository of forbidden instinctual impulses or desires, but also the container of socio-political information which has been repressed. For example, such an approach throws an interesting light on racism and sexism: one of the problems with anti-discrimination laws and campaigns is that they find it difficult to deal with 'unconscious racism' and 'unconscious sexism'. One cannot deal with such phenomena simply by launching oneself at them or delivering an accusatory harangue to those deemed guilty, who may be genuinely unaware of their prejudices.

Relations between the sexes throw up an immense amount of interesting material, when one adopts such an approach. I often notice how hatred for the opposite sex lurks beneath the surface in many people. People feel guilty, ashamed, embarrassed, about this hatred, but as with other unconscious thoughts and feelings, it leaks out in all kinds of subtle ways. How much healthier it seems to exhume them and allow them some air – to make one's hatreds conscious can be a very liberating experience and also tends to leave room for positive feelings.

Clearly, such phenomena as racism and sexism cannot be considered purely psychologically or purely politically: they are politico-psychological complexes. But arguably, many of Freud's ideas about sexuality and gender, such as castration anxiety, the Oedipus complex, penis envy, identification with the aggressor, and so on, can be considered to be politico-psychological structures and processes.

11
Dreams, Jokes and Films

According to Freud, dreaming tells us something of great importance about human beings – not simply that we have irrational images and thoughts as we sleep, but that something unconscious presses upon our consciousness, and under conditions where our resistance to that pressure is reduced, this 'something' erupts.

Freud saw dreams as prime evidence for his theory of the psyche, and his book *The Interpretation of Dreams* stands like a massive frontispiece to his whole work. It is his *opus major.* Freud never wrote such a weighty volume about neurosis or psychoanalytic technique, which are given shorter and more technical treatment. But dreaming – along with other aspects of ordinary life such as jokes and slips of the tongue – shows us that the Freudian notions of the unconscious and repression, and the distorted expression of the unconscious, do not simply apply to neurotic states of mind but pertain to a great many mental events. Indeed Freud states that 'psychoanalysis is founded upon the analysis of dreams'.[1]

Freud's description of dreams becomes quite complex and technical, but at the heart of it there is the key notion of conflict in the psyche:

> There must be a force here which is seeking to express something and another which is striving to prevent its expression . . . the conflict has ended in a compromise, so that the communicating agency has, it is true, been able to say what it wanted but not in the way it wanted – only in a softened down, distorted and unrecognizable form.[2]

Here we find in a most explicit form one of Freud's major ideas about the psyche and about human beings: that we are intrinsically fragmented into warring factions. One part of us – the unconscious – wishes to communicate its wishes, in fact, wants its wishes carried out. But another part wants to repress these wishes, and certainly stop them being carried out. But in sleep, a kind of reconciliation occurs: the forbidden wish is expressed, but in disguised form. A kind of partial satisfaction is granted to both sides: the unconscious wish achieves some kind of expression – a hallucinated fulfilment; yet the censor also is satisfied since the wish is heavily disguised and distorted.

Of course, this is a highly dynamic picture of the human being, who is said to be made up of antagonistic forces, which cannot be homogenized. This is a very difficult idea to grasp, not intellectually, but emotionally, for I am sure that we all wish it were not so. We wish that we were homogeneous, integrated, unified. Freud is saying that we are not, and cannot be. What we can do is bring the conflicts inside us out into the open, and learn to live with them.

The fundamental antagonism in the dream, according to Freud, is between the child and the adult, for the unconscious wish is infantile, but cannot be granted expression in the adult world. One can also refer here to a clash between our desires and civilization, for society cannot permit us to enact our most primitive wishes, for example to kill others, or to have unrestricted sex. But the prohibitions of society are internalized in the shape of the repressing force within us, the superego or the censor.

If the dream is a compromise, it is also a kind of temporary psychosis, an hallucination which takes us over, as the contents of the unconscious are allowed a kind of release, although not a complete one. Dreaming can therefore be linked with neurosis and psychosis, and indeed with analysis and psychotherapy. We can say that in neurotic and psychotic states the relationship between the repression and expression of the unconscious is not successfully managed; by contrast, we hope that in therapy our forbidden wishes and feelings are permitted expression, not in action, but in words and emotional release. In other words, we come to have a satisfactory relationship with the unconscious.

Analysis and therapy are therefore a kind of dreaming with another, a release of forbidden material before a witness who will neither condemn nor seduce. In this sense dreams offer us the hope that the irreconcilable elements in the psyche can be brought to a state of truce in our waking life as well as in sleep.

The child of night

As I have mentioned, Freud's technical description of dreams becomes rather recondite. However, it can be summarized as follows: at the root of the dream, there is an unconscious wish or impulse, which Freud terms a 'child of night' – consciously, we repudiate it.[3] However, while we are sleeping, this impulse is able to hitch a ride on the coat-tails of an inoffensive thought or image derived from the day's events: in other words, the unconscious wish disguises itself:

> a train of thoughts has been aroused by the working of the mind in the daytime, and retained some of its activity, escaping from the general inhibition of interests which introduces sleep and constitutes the psychical preparation for sleep. During the night this train of thoughts succeeds in finding connections with one of the unconscious tendencies present ever since childhood in the mind of the dreamer, but ordinarily repressed and excluded from his conscious life. By the borrowed force of this unconscious help, the thoughts, the residue of the day's work, now become active again, and emerge into consciousness in the shape of the dream.[4]

To put it the other way, the unconscious wish takes on the mantle of the 'daytime thought' as a kind of camouflage, so permitting its veiled expression in the dream. In *The Interpretation of Dreams* Freud uses the image of the entrepreneur and the capitalist:

> A daytime thought may very well play the part of an entrepreneur for a dream; but the entrepreneur, who as people say, has the idea and the initiative to carry it out, can do nothing without capital; he needs a capitalist who can afford the outlay, and the capitalist who provides the psychical outlay for the dream is invariably and indisputably, whatever may be the thoughts of the previous day, a wish from the unconscious.[5]

Let me give an example: I dreamed that I was having tea with a friend, and found to my disgust that the tea-pot brought to the table had twelve tea-bags in it. I fished six of them out, but still felt disconsolate as I was still faced with very strong tea. In fact, that week I had had tea in a café, and had found two tea-bags in the teapot, and had taken them out instantly, as I like my tea quite weak. Here is the 'day-time thought' which the dream borrows, and which is relatively inoffensive. But of course this idea has been changed dramatically – now there are twelve tea-bags in the pot given to me by a friend. Eventually I was able to relate this image to the feeling that I had been spending too much time with my friend, that I felt tired with his company and really wanted a break from him. This is the forbidden wish – to get rid of him – which in the dream is disguised by means of the tea-bags.

Here at once one encounters one of the weighty objections to this mode of dream interpretation: that it seems arbitrary. Freud's theory of psychic determinism asserts that the associations that come to mind concerning a certain dream must of necessity be relevant to it, but of course the only judgement about this is inevitably a subjective one. For example, I might have many associations to the above dream – for example, I think that I like Earl Grey tea, that I don't like tea-bags anyway, that I like cafés, that London has seen a huge growth in the number of cafés in recent years, that tea is one of the old colonial products brought to Britain from countries such as India, that I have a number of tea-pots, and really prefer metal ones to china ones – obviously, this chain of associations is potentially endless. It is therefore my own choice as to which associations are particularly relevant, and those critics who see psychotherapy as a whole as a rag-bag of messy unverifiable claims can mount their attack with some confidence.

Yet the dreamer has a subjective key to the dream, and there can be no objective key – to equate 'subjectivity' of interpretation with arbitrariness strikes me as lazy thinking. Indeed, the links that we make between dream-images and other thoughts or images often seem very powerful and, as it were, inevitable. It's rather like the tip-of-tongue phenomenon: when I temporarily forget a word for something, I usually know without doubt which words are incorrect. Similarly, I know which associations are irrelevant to my dreams.

Wish-fulfilment

Many people criticize the wish-fulfilment aspect of dreams, yet it is central to Freud's ideas, for it flows from his idea that the unconscious is full of desires or wishes. Many criticisms centre on nightmares, frightening dreams or other kinds of negative images in dreams. How can they represent wishes? Here the dynamism of Freud's theory of the psyche comes into its own, for it is quite clear that frequently one part of us wishes damage to another part.

For example, whilst working with creative people, I have often noticed that when they are in the middle of a creative success, or just after it, they are subject to negative feelings about their work, and are liable to have frightening or horrific dreams. The 'wish' here stems from the destructive element in the psyche, which envies the success being enjoyed by the creative side and wishes to sabotage it. Clearly the notion of 'wish-fulfilment' does not coincide with our happiness! The devil in us is able to dream as well as the angel.

None the less, in contemporary dream analysis, it would often be assumed that there are many unconscious feelings which can be expressed in dreams, such as fear, love, horror, and that the concept of wish-fulfilment is too narrow. Freud might still have a good riposte here: that a dream full of fears has satisfied the wish that the fear be brought into the open! Even those dreams which repeat some traumatic event – for example, a car accident, or events in war-time – could be said to represent the wish to go over this material in order to defuse its horror.

Interpretation

Dreams are not transparent. They often resist interpretation. This presents many problems to do with dream analysis, and for thousands of years there have been complicated systems of interpretation in different cultures, often to do with premonitions of the future. As we have seen, Freud uses the method of free association – and the dreamer's own links to the dream in question are the key material:

> we ask the dreamer...to divert his attention from the dream as a whole on to the separate portions of its content and to report to us in succession everything that occurs to him in relation to each of these portions.[6]

In the example above, I made the link between having too many teabags and having spent too much time with a friend – of course, this link is entirely subjective and not predictable by anyone else.

This is a key step in psychological theory and technique, for instead of an external authority dictating to us the meaning of our dreams and other material in our life, we find that we ourselves are the experts. We cannot publish lists or books of dream symbolism, for this rides roughshod over the subjectivity of the dreamer's unconscious wishes. No doubt at times Freud himself rode roughshod over his patients, yet this does not figure in his codification of analytic technique!

The non-transparency of dreams also presents certain fascinating theoretical problems concerning their germination. How have they become so opaque? Here Freud develops at length the notion of mechanisms such as condensation, displacement and distortion, and he is able to demonstrate the split-level origin of dreams: one level, where the 'dream-thoughts' originate, and then another level, where they have been obfuscated or disguised. Freud even speaks of the 'evil' nature of dream wishes – 'actively evil and extravagantly sexual wishes, which have made the censorship and distortion of dreams necessary'.[7]

Of course, this seems particularly true of sexual or aggressive wishes, but one finds a wide range of experiences which people cannot permit themselves to experience consciously and which have to be dreamed about. For example, I am sure some people are unable or unwilling to face up to their emotional needs for contact with others: and this can appear in dreams in the shape of ravening animals, primitive beasts, and so on. Or others cannot accept feelings of love, and they may appear heavily disguised in dreams. In other words, I think Freud is wrong to speak of 'evil wishes', unless one grants that for some people the wish for love is an evil wish. We might argue that anything can appear in a dream in disguised form which for that person runs counter to their dominant personality: thus for the angry person, sentiments of harmony and peace may be impermissible; for the sexual athlete, tenderness and care, and so on.

The dreamer

Freud has a certain problem with complex dreams, for the question of their origin poses a profound question about the nature of the psyche. How is the complex dream formed? Who is the dreamer?

Here again we have the suggestion that the psyche is both creative and organizational, for some dreams form very impressive narrative structures, whose elucidation provides us with a kind of aesthetic pleasure. Freud makes the comment that such dreams are evidence of a sophisticated ability:

> we have found evidence in the dream-thoughts of a highly complex intellectual function, operating with almost the whole resources of the mental apparatus.[8]

In other words, the dream is not just produced by the unconscious, but by an interaction between the unconscious and other organizational parts of the mind. Freud can therefore reject the Jungian idea of the Self, which is the organizing centre of the whole psyche and which can direct dreams to the attention of the ego. Instead, Freud is able to argue that unconscious and ego join together to produce the dream. This still leaves us with the question of the ultimate 'narrator' of the dream – where is it located? Certainly dreams are neither chaotic nor random.

Poetry or prose?

Perhaps the most cogent criticism of Freud's dream theory would stem from a totally different concept of the unconscious, more akin to Jung's. Whereas Freud's unconscious is full of repressed infantile wishes, which are striving to break out in some form, Jung's unconscious also contains material which has never been conscious because it represents the latent or unfulfilled potential of the individual. In addition, Jung's notion of the archetype – a kind of instinctual pattern – suggests that our dreams may be expressions of archetypal forces.[9]

One of the interesting aspects of this opposition concerns the distortion or opacity found in dreams. Freud basically argues that dreams are disguised wishes, disguised because the repressing force strives to prevent their naked expression. But from the other point of view, the distortion may also be a result of the embryonic nature of the content, which cannot be expressed directly because it is not as yet known directly in the psyche. And in relation to dreams which relate to archetypes, the dream has to be 'distorted' in a sense, since it is impossible to have a direct representation of an archetype.

To put this more simplistically, it is possible to argue that some dream-thoughts can only be expressed symbolically or through images. For example, how can we dream of God? We have to dream of some image of God. Or how can we dream about fate or destiny? Again, we can perceive this only through metaphors. Or if you wish to dream about your life's journey, and its twists and turns, and its wrong turnings, and its possible outcome – this would have to be done via some kind of image, just as I have had to write about it metaphorically as a journey.

This argument tends towards an interesting thesis: that the reason dreams are 'distorted' is that the dreaming function is basically a metaphoric function, not just for reasons of disguise or censorship, but because that is how that part of the psyche works. In other words, the dreaming part of us functions more like poetry than prose. We cannot ask a poet 'Why have you disguised your material in all these images and metaphors and obscurities?' The question is absurd, because that is what poetry is like. Poetry is not disguised prose, and perhaps dreaming is not disguised thinking. We know that the meaning of a poem is not equivalent to a paraphrase of it, and it is therefore worth considering that the meaning of a dream is not simply our interpretation of it. The dream then is like a work of art, which has its own existence *sui generis*, and which cannot be fully interpreted intellectually. As I gaze at a favourite painting in a gallery, or listen to some music, I cannot summarize my response to it with a few phrases or some interpretative gloss. The image is the image, with its own being. The dream is the dream. And indeed, one finds sometimes in therapy that it is best not to interpret a dream, that it should just be left to exist as itself, with all its mysterious qualities and facets.

This argument does not invalidate Freud's theory of dreams, which is surely applicable to large numbers of dreams, but suggests that there are also dreams dreamed by an original imaginal force in the psyche. Here Freud shows his rationalism, when he speaks of 'dream-thoughts', because this ignores the possibility that the unconscious contains or produces primitive images which cannot be reduced to anything else, least of all a thought or idea. This seems to connect with the psychological analysis of art: isn't it likely that an artist such as Picasso is able to access directly primitive images in the unconscious? In other words, he is not translating unconscious thoughts into images but taking the images directly from the source.

The theoretical implications of these arguments are clearly considerable, for Freud's notion of dreams rests on the idea of the censor, from which the dream escapes, as it were, in a disguised form. However, the above argument suggests that there are dreams which are not trying to escape the censor but which simply exist in their own form, or that there are 'dream-images' which cannot be expressed any other way. It is interesting to consider whether babies and animals dream, for one might consider that they dream in the absence of a repressing force.

Jokes

Jokes, according to Freud, reveal similar mechanisms to dreams. That is, a forbidden thought or wish is concealed in the joke, but of course is also revealed – for example, many jokes contain hostile feelings 'softened down' so that they become more palatable. In a sense, we get to have our cake and eat it; we are able to express the hostility yet we are somehow absolved from full responsibility for it. There is a well-known saying in comedy circles: no victim, no joke. This is also expressed in the old saying: if you fall and break your leg, it's hilarious; if I stub my toe, it's a tragedy.

For example, soon after the death of Princess Diana, a spate of quite sadistic jokes appeared concerned with the details of her death. However, although the content of such jokes appears to be simply aggressive, they may also cloak other feelings, such as grief, horror, fear, and so on.

Perhaps jokes about death make us able to deal with the incomprehensibility of it a little bit more easily.

But Freud takes a narrow approach to so-called 'tendentious' jokes:

> there are only two purposes that it [a joke] may serve, and these two can be subsumed under a single heading. It is either a hostile jokes (serving the purpose of aggressiveness, satire, or defence) or an obscene joke (serving the purpose of exposure).[10]

However, a large part of Freud's book *Jokes and their Relation to the Unconscious* is taken up with the ways in which jokes allow us to relax our inhibitions on pleasure. For example, he argues that we take a childish pleasure in word-play and verbal nonsense, which tends to be inhibited in adulthood, but jokes permit the release of this inhibition. For example, a lot of the pleasure derived from watching comedians such as Morecambe and Wise, and the contemporary crop of stand-up comedians, stems from their verbal ingenuity and use of absurd word-play. They are literally playing in front of us.

Freud also points to the formal similarities between dreams and jokes:

> We found that the characteristics and effects of jokes are linked with certain forms of expression or technical methods, among which the most striking are condensation, displacement and indirect representation. Processes, however, which lead to the same results ... have become known to us as peculiarities of the dream-work.[11]

This leads Freud to the very interesting thesis that jokes, like dreams, take us into the unconscious, or to use his term, 'plunges' us into the unconscious, with the aim of producing pleasure:

> Thought is put back for a moment to the stage of childhood so as once more to gain possession of the childish source of pleasure.[12]

Thus Freud is able to point to the infantile nature of the pleasures attained through jokes, just as he was able to point to the infantile nature of the wishes expressed in dreams. One has to admire the global systematicity of Freud's theories, yet at the same time, there is perhaps a sense in which Freud is 'over-determined' to find global solutions. In other words, he has a passion for theorizing, but there is a danger here that this passion will overlook empirical facts which contradict the overall theory. I have already pointed out one awkward fact, that some jokes – for example, jokes about AIDS or Alzheimer's disease – seem to represent our wish to distance ourselves from terrifying or horrifying aspects of life. Freud might reply to this objection that such jokes permit the release of our sadistic feelings towards sick people, which normally must be cloaked. Let me give an example of a fairly cruel joke, which has been in circulation for several years in England:

> A man is lying in a hospital bed, and is very ill. He has had many tests done to ascertain what's wrong, and now the consultant comes to tell him. The consultant says: 'I'm very sorry, Mr Brown, but you have two very serious conditions. First, you have AIDS, but also, I'm afraid you have Alzheimer's.'
>
> The patient stares at him, then sighs in relief: 'At least I don't have AIDS.'

I have tried this joke out on a number of people. Most people laugh at it, but some also express a kind of disapproval, yet it strikes me that the two are connected: part of the comic effect of the joke is to do with making fun of people we're not supposed to. However, the joke also has an idiotic side: the man says 'I don't have AIDS' immediately after being told he has. But in addition there is our search and eventual grasp of the cause of this misunderstanding: the reason he's forgotten he has AIDS is because he has Alzheimer's, which notoriously causes memory loss. In this case, the memory loss is very rapid – by the end of the consultant's sentence the patient has forgotten the beginning of it.

One can therefore speak of different facets to this joke: part of the comic effect seems to stem from working out a puzzle – why does he deny what he has just been told? Presumably there is the pleasure at working out the puzzle for ourselves. Then there is the sadistic pleasure in making fun of people with AIDS and Alzheimer's. This has an extra edge, since we know this is very wrong, therefore perhaps unconsciously we enjoy it even more. In other words, it's a joke in bad taste. But we can also suggest that jokes such as this provide a relief from the horror of such illnesses – that is, we laugh in the face of suffering and death. There may also be unconscious feelings of triumph that we are healthy while others are not.

This strikes me as a very complex set of comedic attributes, some of which seem to fit Freud's notion of jokes expressing the unconscious – particularly our sadistic or triumphant feelings towards sick people – others which seem to pertain to playfulness (the puzzle aspect). A further point is that my paraphrase of the joke made it very unfunny and laborious: the whole point of jokes is their instantaneous effect. Anyone who tries to tell jokes will know that as soon as one has to start explaining the point of any joke, the humour is lost. The laughter is in part caused by the immediate shock effect; delay is fatal. Somehow the process of 'getting' a joke causes relief, pleasure and laughter, as if a state of tension has been instantly relieved. Freud's theories of tension and detensioning seem quite appropriate here. One might even make an analogy with sexual tension and release: the joke-teller seems to induce a state of tension in us followed by a climactic moment, when we are supposed to 'get it'.

There is still plenty of evidence that Freud's main assumption – that in jokes and dreams a conflict between censorship and desire is resolved, so that the desire is expressed in an indirect way – is both plausible and empirically well founded. The significance of applying this theory to jokes and dreams lies in the non-pathological status of these phenomena. Freud can of course go on to argue that neurotic symptoms also represent compromises between repression and expression, but he has shown with some conviction that these processes are characteristic of mental life and are not aberrations. The importance of this has already been highlighted: this model of the psyche and its processes informs us that conflict lies at the heart of our being, and that such conflicts cannot be removed, but can be mediated and expressed.

Thus *the conflict between the unconscious and the repressing force is not in itself neurotic*, but forms an integral part of human life. In dreams, jokes and neurotic symptoms, the unconscious presses upwards against the repression, and bursts forth in a disguised form. Freud states clearly that the unconscious 'has a "natural upward drive" and desires nothing better than to press forward across its settled frontiers into the ego and so to consciousness'.[13]

In the dream, the unconscious takes on a hallucinatory form, so that it seems as if the wish has been fulfilled; in a joke, there is no hallucinatory completion, but we are able to lift the inhibitions preventing us normally from expressing hostile, sexual or playful impulses and the pleasure this gives us is released in laughter; in neurosis, the conflict between unconscious and repression is expressed in the garbled form of the symptom, which also simultaneously expresses and conceals the unconscious wish.

Freud remarks in the Introductory Lectures that 'we are all ill',[14] not because we are full of unconscious conflicts, but because the primary conflict between instinctual wishes and a repressive civilization is at work in everyone. There are various means of relieving these conflicts, including dreams and jokes, but of course psychotherapy itself takes its place and attempts to bring conflicts into the open, so that the unconscious is not disguised but is laid bare. The hostile or sexual wish can be expressed openly; the pleasurable impulses, which may be normally felt to be childish, can be enjoyed in safety; one can be perhaps more open than one has ever been before in one's life.

There is also a kind of nobility to Freud's conceptions – a sense in which human beings are involved in titanic struggles of which they are not the authors. Perhaps there is a touch of tragedy here as well. One is reminded of a Greek tragedy or a tragedy by Racine – in Freud's words, we are lived by unknown forces, and our task is to discover what these forces are, before they destroy us. We cannot after all get rid of them, since they also create us.

Jokes and dreams

It is also interesting to consider ways in which jokes and dreams are not alike. If we accept that in both cases an unconscious idea is being expressed, there is a crucial distinction in that I usually know I am telling a joke, and usually I do not know I am dreaming. In other words, in the dream I am 'swallowed up' by the unconscious: the ego is in an unusually quiescent state, since I am asleep. During the telling of a joke I am fully awake, and in fact I may be in a state of mental alertness. It is interesting that some people are good at telling jokes, others are not; but it seems very odd to suggest that some people are good at dreaming while others are not – in other words, joke-telling is partly a human skill or a deliberate performance, whereas dreaming seems to be an intrinsic function of the psyche. None the less this does not mean that even a familiar joke is perfectly transparent: there may still be unconscious ideas being expressed in it. For example, the racist comedian may deny that he has aggressive or hateful feelings towards black people; indeed, we may all deny that we partly enjoy jokes out of a pleasurable sadism towards the 'victims' of the jokes. In the example cited above, how many of us dare admit that we have hidden feelings of triumph towards sick people?

Yet Freud also points out that some jokes are not predetermined, but occur spontaneously, and in such a case we have a situation which is closer to the dream-state: 'a joke has quite outstandingly the characteristic of being a notion that has occurred to us "involuntarily"'.[15] Clearly there has to be a distinction between such improvised jokes, and those situations where someone is 'telling a joke'. One can in fact memorize such jokes. The spontaneous joke seems to show an ability to think at several levels at once, for example by using puns and other plays on words.

But if one starts to examine different types of humour, a bewildering variety appears: for example, irony, sarcasm, slap-stick, stand-up comedy. There is a very physical type of humour, as found in Charlie Chaplin, and at the opposite extreme, a very cerebral kind, as found in some ironic writers such as Jonathan Swift. It is quite likely then that Freud's analysis of jokes is inadequate to a full consideration of humour and comedy, although Freud's postulate that jokes express an unconscious idea may well prove applicable to many types of humour. Sarcastic remarks are of great interest, for although there is a concealed idea – which is usually quite aggressive or cutting – both speaker and listener know about the concealment. Thus if a friend says, 'Did you have a good holiday?' and I reply: 'It was great. The hotel hadn't been built; the beach was covered in oil; and it rained every day', we both know that my sentence 'it was great' is not only false, but deliberately false. Can we speak of something unconscious here, for certainly the implied statement 'It was a horrible holiday' is not? Yet perhaps there is something else going on here: am I not being aggressive to my friend for asking the question? Am I not in fact saying, 'You're an absolute fool to be asking the question and I'm going to punish you for it'? None the less, the aggression present in sarcastic humour is pretty close to the surface, and often conveyed by tone of voice.

Why do jokes make us laugh? Often there is an incongruity or absurdity present, which seems to represent a tension between two incompatible states or situations, and the laughter seems to release the tension caused by the incongruity. Can we speak of an incongruity or absurdity in dreams? In fact, I think some dreams cause astonishment because of their bizarre or surreal quality, and there are dreams which make people laugh. Indeed, Freud makes the point that patients sometimes laugh when one makes an apposite interpretation, for the revelation of unconscious thoughts and motives seems to act almost like a joke.[16] There is also a kind of nervous laughter here, especially if one is referring to aggressive or sexual feelings in the patient. In other words, the unconscious can often strike us as comic, in part because it seems indecent or anti-social: something is uncovered which is usually covered up. In this sense, jokes seem much less mysterious than dreams, which often retain a numinous quality which is difficult to decipher. We are often aware of the point of a joke – that it is aggressive or indecent or playful, whereas the point of a dream may completely elude us.

Film and psychoanalysis

Although Freud himself seems to have been uninterested in the cinema, many commentators have noticed the similarities between film and dreams – for example, at the cinema one is in the dark, a succession of visual and auditory images are presented to us, so that we are to varying degrees taken over by them.[17] One might say that cinema is a truly 'hallucinatory' art. Of course, there are very significant differences between dreams and films. To begin with, the dream is intensely private; it is my experience, and I generally assume that 'I am the dreamer'. Cinema, by contrast, is usually a public experience – I am part of an audience; the film has been made by a group of people, so that I have no control over it. Perhaps most markedly, I usually know I am watching a film; but usually do not know that I am dreaming.

Yet as soon as one makes such distinctions, they begin to blur. For example, the idea that the dream is 'mine' begins to be eroded, for if one accepts Freud's idea that the dream contains instinctual impulses which have been repressed and are emerging in distorted form, then it is clear that the ego in some sense rejects the dream. The dream is not mine, but belongs to another – in other words, my unconscious. Perhaps like the film then, I often feel that the dream has been made by 'someone else' who is unknown to me?

Similarly, one can argue that although cinema is a collective experience it is also intensely private: as I sit in the dark watching the film, I enter into my own world. I make the film my own, give it my own significance, link it to my own life, and so on.

Do these analogies and distinctions help in any way to construct a theoretical model of film based on Freud's model of dreaming? Freud's dream theory has two important constituents: a model of dream formation and a model of dream interpretation. The first describes how the 'latent' wishes or impulses are converted into the 'manifest' images of the dream: this represents a distortion, for the latent wishes are repressed and censored, and one might say, unwelcome to the conscious mind. The model of dream interpretation shows how by means of free association, one can retrace the links between the dream image and the underlying wish or thought.

At first glance, the second model seems more adaptable to film interpretation, and may even seem intuitively appealing as a theory of how people in fact respond to films – perhaps they do go through a series of associations, memories, fantasies in connection with the film imagery? It is more difficult to see how dream formation connects with the production of a film, since the latter is so much more mechanized, overt and collective. However, one might still argue that films do contain 'latent' ideas: for example, perhaps violent films represent our own wishes to kill people, commit armed robbery, go on the rampage, go to war, and so on. Similarly, the cop film could be said to be represent two wishes: first, our own anti-social wish to commit crime, and second, our contrasting wish to control the first wish. The same kind of argument can obviously be made in relation to sexuality in the cinema – that we are watching our sexual impulses at work at a safe distance.

One of the interesting aspects of this is that increasingly in the twentieth century the actual censorship of films was relaxed, so that at the end of the century quite graphic violence and sex were found in many films. This seems to present us with an interesting dilemma in terms of Freudian theory, for we seem to be saying that repression can be mitigated or softened. However, since Freud derives the super-ego from social influences, it is reasonable to argue that as the latter change, so does the repressing force. Furthermore, the distancing effect of cinema itself constitutes a kind of repression: I am able to deny that these violent or sexual acts on screen are 'mine', just as in war the virtuous citizen may be able to deny that the various atrocities carried out by his nation's armed forces have any connection with him (while secretly he may approve of them).

The collective nature of cinema does seem crucial here, for the filmmaker is usually aiming to maximize the audience, so that if we accept that films contain underlying wishes, then these wishes belong to the mass. However, this distinction from the private dream can be shown to be partly false, since we might suppose that our dream wishes are remarkably uniform, since human beings have the same instinctual impulses. Thus arguably the film-maker is able to articulate certain moods and feelings which are extant at large in society and give them visual expression in his films.

At times modern cinema seems to take a self-conscious attitude to notions of repression, unconscious contents and dreaming. Take for example the horror film, where a series of hallucinatory images plays before us, involving actions which often have a surreal and dream-like quality. De Palma's film *Carrie* (1976) is a classic example: Carrie is a high-school student who is persecuted at home by her puritanical mother, who cannot abide any mention of sexuality, and also at school, by her cruel school-mates. The film begins brilliantly: Carrie starts her first period in the school shower and is taunted by her class-mates. At first, there are languorous images of Carrie in the shower, with a distinctly sexual and masturbatory overtone, but then images of blood trickling from her body are combined with shots of the other girls jeering at her, throwing tampons at her and so on.

This is a typically nightmarish scene in the horror film: the relations between the repressed and the repressing force are externalized and exaggerated to grotesque proportions, so that we have a cowering victim, crushed by despots. However, we become aware that Carrie has telekinetic powers: she is able to move objects at a distance. Clearly, adolescence is seen not just as a time of crisis over sexuality and identity, but as a time of burgeoning power. The repressed has the potential to revolt, and this is one of the key tensions in the horror film, for this 'revolt of the repressed' may well turn out to even more terrifying than the original persecution. In addition, female sexuality – and particularly menstruation – are seen as both very powerful and also horrifying forces.[18]

The climax of *Carrie* occurs when Carrie goes to the high school prom, is covered in pig's blood by her tormentors just as she has been crowned queen of the prom, and then unleashes a truly apocalyptic revenge on the whole school, burning it down and killing everyone inside. Carrie then goes home and kills her mother.

The question of identification is of great interest here, for the intense persecution suffered by Carrie must make the audience take her side and wish for revenge. Hence the final dénouement, as Carrie wipes everyone out, satisfies that primitive side of us that would like revenge for slights and hurts we have suffered. The director has cleverly made Carrie's suffering so intense that mass murder seems almost welcome and cathartic. In addition, the visual imagery of the film is both macabre and poetic: for example, Carrie kills her mother by telekinetically impaling her with all the knives in the kitchen. She becomes more than human, assuming a kind of archetypal quality as revenger. If her persecutors were extremely unpleasant human beings, Carrie is a demi-god unleashing thunderbolts and maledictions.

The question of identification becomes even more interesting when one considers the male audience. Do they identify with Carrie? In her book *Men, Women and Chainsaws* Carol Clover argues that identification in the cinema is extremely fluid, and permits cross-gender links to be made. One might argue, then, that Carrie is not the traditional heroine of Hollywood films, whose role was often passive; she is the demonic hero of the film.[19]

Perhaps the most interesting aspect of such films is the idea that they represent internal struggles in the psyche: the superego is portrayed as a set of monstrous figures, jeering and punishing the innocent victim. Yet the victim becomes the hero – this seems to represent the ego, which eventually triumphs over the repression, partly by harnessing the colossal forces of the unconscious. Thus part of the power of such films is that they resonate deeply with our inner conflicts and suggest wished-for if unrealistic solutions.

Spectator and image

It seems clear that the relationship between the spectator and the images on the cinema screen has an interesting parallel with the relationship between the ego and the various objects to which it is attached. For example, one can speak of the voyeuristic aspects of cinema: I sit in the dark and gaze into the private lives of the characters in the film. Feminist critics have been able to add that the male spectator takes up a traditional patriarchal role: he voyeuristically devours the image of a woman on the screen, a woman who is often the victim of violence, or who exposes her body to the viewer.

The castration complex has been adduced here, with the idea that women in films may represent images of castration, which male spectators need to gaze at repeatedly, both to get over the horror of castration and comfort themselves with the notion that they are not castrated. Here the popularity of action cinema seems relevant: its male white heroes could be said continually to demonstrate with their prowess the non-castrated nature of maleness.

However, this kind of use of psychoanalytic ideas can become rather crude and unsophisticated: as we have seen in relation to *Carrie*, some theorists have also suggested that cross-gender identification goes on in the cinema – male spectators may be identifying with female characters. The relationship between 'having' and 'being', which in Freud is related to the ego's ability to incorporate objects, thereby identifying with them, may be a very fluid one within film-watching: thus in the action cinema, it is unclear how much the male spectator identifies with the male hero and how much desires him. There certainly seems to be plenty of homoerotic material in the 'buddy' film, the western, and so on. While it may be correct to state that the female body has been the chief icon of Western cinema – particularly Hollywood – the male body is also given a considerable erotic display.

The nature of the spectator, and his or her relationship with the screen-image, has been the subject of considerable theoretical amplification by Lacanian theorists, who have focused on Lacan's concept of the Imaginary, and particularly the notion that the ego itself is formed by a series of illusory identifications.[20] This is of great interest in film theory, since in Lacanian theory one does not want to posit a pre-existent ego, which 'looks at' the screen: rather the ego founds itself in each moment by the images with which it binds itself.

This may sound totally post-Freudian: but such ideas have an undoubted provenance in Freud's speculations about the ways in which the ego loses objects but retains them inside itself, and can indeed be said to be made up of 'abandoned object-cathexes'. The notions of projection and introjection demonstrate the fluidity of the ego's image of itself, which can be made up of the images of others, and which can also be 'thrown outwards' onto others.

In addition, there may be a strongly regressive element present in the sheer size of the film-images presented to the spectator, for this may remind us of childhood, when adults no doubt seem gigantic or god-like figures, towering over us. It is often remarked that many films are not as impressive when watched on TV, since the gargantuan proportions of the cinema screen are lost. I certainly find horror films more digestible on TV, since they are less overwhelming than in the cinema.

Cinema appears as a brilliant arena, where psychoanalytic theories of the subject/object relation, the nature of the subject itself, its identifications, its acceptance of realistic and non-realistic sequences of images, its ability to glide over absurdities in time relationships and cause/effect relationships, its omnipotence (via an identification with the camera, which is able apparently to move anywhere and see anything), its narcissism (everything on the screen is presented for my delectation) can be applied with greater effect than perhaps any other art-form. This is partly because of the analogy with dreaming, but also because of the primitive 'looking' which Freud has placed at the foundation of certain psychological structures: for example, castration itself, which seems to revolve around our anxious looking for the presence or absence of a vital organ.

Cinema is the art of looking *par excellence*; it also promotes a kind of ego-surrender or self-annihilation in the presence of massive archetypal images on the screen. One can contrast one's behaviour in an art gallery: the painting may transfix one, but none the less one is free to wander backwards and forwards, to talk about the picture. In a sense, one's identity remains entirely separate from the painting in question, which remains relatively fixed as an object. In the cinema, there is a much greater assault on the spectator. Here concepts of sadism and masochism seem apposite, especially in those films, such as horror films, which almost seem to launch their images at the viewer with sadistic relish. As a spectator perhaps one is punished by such images – certainly, one may well forget oneself temporarily. Yet at the same time, one can close one's eyes or look away, thus returning to the comfort of a prior identity which will survive any such assault.

Cinema is endlessly restless, refusing to allow the viewer any point of rest or stasis: the narrative hurries on, images succeed each other almost more rapidly than one can take in. One can speak of cinema perhaps as the supreme art of the unconscious: even the most mundane film demonstrates an amazing concatenation of images, which seem quite surreal if one looks at them dispassionately. Certainly, psychoanalysis and cinema seem like bed-fellows at times: both flourished in a century which uprooted stable social conditions, promoted rootlessness and loss of identity, and delighted in the production of a bewildering array of images – in advertising, on television, at the cinema, and so on. If psychoanalysis is offered to us perhaps as the diagnosis of a profound anomie in our civilization, then cinema could be said to be the art of anomie.

12
Revisions and Criticisms

There is something ironic in speaking about revisions to Freud's ideas, since he was the greatest revisionist of all, in the sense that he was constantly re-examining key concepts in psychoanalysis. For example, when the psychoanalyst Bennett Simon attempts to summarize the concept of the Oedipus complex, he is forced to divide his discussion into six stages of development in Freud's writings.[1] The same approach is necessary in relation to other key ideas, for example, the ego and the unconscious, the instincts themselves, the nature of sexuality, femininity, and so on. To the end of his life, Freud was bringing forward new ideas which necessitated considerable adjustment to the overall schematic description of the psyche. One can cite, for example, the article on narcissism, written in 1914, which caused discomfort to other analysts, as they realized what an earthquake this concept would lead to. Ernest Jones comments: 'it gave a disagreeable jolt to the theory of instincts on which psycho-analysis had hitherto worked.'[2]

Such revisions have continued since Freud's death, so that it is true to say that many of Freud's ideas have been modified to a considerable extent, while at the same time, what might be called the core ideas – the unconscious, repression, transference, psychic determinism – may have been modified, but survive intact. There is still a recognizable body of ideas which can be termed 'psychoanalytic', and there are schools of psychotherapy which are recognizably analytically oriented, and other schools which are definitely influenced by psychoanalysis.

Let me turn then briefly to some of the key post-Freudian revisions which have been made in the psychoanalytic body of ideas.

Post-Freudian revisions

1. Energy and structure

At first glance, it would seem clear that Freud's theories of energy and pleasure have been abandoned in therapy and analysis. The idea that pleasure represents a reduction of accumulated energy seems rather nineteenth-century in its approach, both as a theory of energy and a theory of individual human beings who appear as isolated energy processing machines. The analyst W. R. D. Fairbairn argues that in this scheme the universe is conceived of as a 'conglomeration of inert, immutable and indivisible particles to which motion was imparted by a fixed quantity of energy separate from the particles themselves'.[3] Thus in Freud's theory of the instincts, the sexual drive is a form of energy separate from the ego. In other words, energy is conceived of as separate from structure.[4]

Yet in fact, one finds that an energy-oriented approach to the organism has continued in the therapeutic bodywork movement – bio-energetics, rebirthing, various styles of massage, and so on, which goes on outside the analytic therapies. Here we find close attention being paid to the flow of energy in the body, and how the individual blocks or releases this flow to go outwards, and how different parts of the body have been affected by energy structure.[5]

Similarly Freud's early notion of catharsis was picked up in the 1960s by the encounter group movement and still has some presence in Humanistic Psychology. One could also argue that Freud's sexual etiology has been partly encompassed in sex therapy. It is astonishing how many therapies look back to Freud – for example, Gestalt therapy employs the concepts of projection and internalization extensively. It is surely significant that both the founder of Gestalt and the founder of bio-energetics – Fritz Perls and Wilhelm Reich respectively – were formerly analysts. It is arguable that Freud had so many ideas about so many different things that no one school of therapy could contain them all: they have had to be distributed amonst different schools, even if these schools are often opposed to a Freudian perspective.

2. Sexual etiology

There is little doubt that in contemporary psychotherapy the importance of sexual etiology has diminished: that is, few analysts or therapists set as much store by the sexual origin of neuroses as Freud did. This is not to say that the sexual instincts have been totally wiped out: far from it. But most therapists are interested less in the erotic relationship between parents and children than in the emotional relationship, the way the child was cared for, attended to, treated as a real person, and so on.

It seems likely that Freud underestimated the effect on sexuality of emotional and relational factors. Thus, one's sexual predilections are powerfully affected by early (infantile) connections with others, and the degree to which one was met as a person. Perversion can therefore in part be defined as sex without personal contact.[6] This has considerable implications for some areas of therapy – for example, some sexual problems cannot be solved through 'technical' or behaviourial means, but through attending to the person's inability to be intimate. It seems likely that sexual opening is closely linked with emotional opening; or to put it more simply, sex connects with love.

There are innumerable examples of post-Freudian work of this nature: an excellent example can be found in a paper on exhibitionism by the psychoanalyst Christopher Lucas, in which he argues that Freud's explanation of exhibitionism as showing castration anxiety has been superseded by an object relations approach:

> There is emphasis on early pre-oedipal development and on the primary identification with the mother. If things go wrong during symbiosis and separation individuation, gender identity and masculinity are threatened. The intense affects generated threaten the integrity of the self. Perversion is an attempt to stabilise the self by sexualising the fear and rage.[7]

Particularly striking in this extract is the comment about the 'sexualization' of feelings such as anger and anxiety. One might say that there has been a kind of theoretical inversion: rather than saying, with Freud, that the sexual drive underlies many of our actions, it is possible to say that we eroticize many of our unconscious feelings, so as to avoid them.

None the less, as I indicated in Chapter 9, the instinctual emphasis found in Freud is still relevant to modern psychotherapy: one might say that the analytic therapist will tend to be more concrete, more interested in the body and more interested in the patient's personal history, than the non-analytic therapist. This, of course, has a direct bearing on the study of the transference relationship: for the analytic therapist, this will tend to focus on the ways in which the patient's emotional needs can be felt and articulated, the ways in which the patient views the therapist and treats the therapist, and so on. The analytic therapist will also be interested in the primitive aspects of the transference: Is the patient interested in the therapist's body? Do primitive needs begin to surface in fantasies and dreams? One might say that one is interested in the child hidden within the adult, with its unspoken needs and feelings, which may have never been expressed. For many patients, the adult persona conceals much more archaic material which is painful and difficult to deal with, and which often provokes feelings of fear and shame in turn. But this does not refer so much to the erotic child as the unloved child or the frightened child or the uncontained child.

Thus while it is correct to say that psychotherapy shows a markedly reduced interest in sexuality compared with Freud, none the less his stress on the instinctual forces in the psyche has left a considerable legacy.

3. Child abuse

Freud's rejection of the seduction theory – the idea that hysterics had been sexually abused as children – still causes controversy today, as some critics argue that Freud ran away from the massive amount of abuse that existed then and still exists today. In this light, Freud's attempts to locate the causes of neurosis within the psyche may seem too inward, and plays down the effect of environment, particularly of course, the role of parents. None the less, Freud's turn inwards has forced psychotherapy to take the inner world very seriously, and militates against any simplistic equation between past trauma and present neurosis. One can say that both are true: many people who come to therapy have been damaged by their treatment as children; but in addition, they treat themselves as they were treated then.

Furthermore, it is quite true that we cannot change the past, but we can make some changes to the present, that is, people's attitudes towards themselves. Perhaps, we can restore some degree of choice, so that the past does not have such an automatic effect on the present.

Curiously, Freud's treatment of the neuroses seems one of the weakest areas of his theorizing, as with the collapse of the seduction theory – which offered a clear-cut etiology for neurosis – the causation of neurosis becomes a much more shadowy area. At times, Freud almost seems to suggest that neurosis is 'organic', that is, that certain people have a 'predisposition' to return to infantile fixations.

Consideration of the case-studies shows Freud generally avoiding an 'environmental' approach in favour of the 'constitutional' theory. Thus Dora is reproached by Freud for repulsing Herr K., as she was at that stage of her sexual development at which she should have welcomed advances from an attractive man. Freud concluded that Dora was hysterical.

The same bias can be seen in the Schreber case. Schreber's psychosis is ascribed to a homosexual wish, which conflicts with his ego. However, later investigators have pointed out how many of Schreber's delusions have a close resemblance to the treatment Schreber received from his father, a well-known educationalist, who developed mechanical devices to correct children's posture, and seems to have taken a very severe and harsh attitude to his own children. Again, the environmental factors, particularly in early childhood, are neglected in Freud's account.[8]

This is also seen in the Little Hans case, which Freud makes strenuous efforts to fit into the Oedipal mould. However, there is plenty of evidence in the text as given by Freud that Hans has been treated very harshly by his parents – his mother threatened to leave him, threatened him with castration, his father objected to Hans cuddling his mother in bed, there was constant friction between his parents – Freud's picture of an idyllic family is belied by this evidence, and leads one to suggest in part that Hans's neurotic symptoms are quite understandable, given the context in which he lived. However, Freud largely ignored this, as he ignored the evidence that Hans was more afraid of his mother than of his father.

Freud did pay attention to the environment in his overall thesis concerning the conflicts between human civilization and sexual desire: that the one was inimical to the other, and inevitably leads to widespread neurosis, caused by sexual frustration. So in a sense there is a wider environmental factor at work in the neurosis: the repression of sexual desire in Western culture. However, this ignores the individual's own environment, and particularly the role of parents and other family members. Certainly contemporary psychotherapy, under the influence of object relations theory, places a considerable importance on the early years of infancy and the care that was given to the infant – or lack of it. However, arguably this trend has gone too far, and has tended to ignore the self-damaging aspects of neurosis, which are after all the prime material which therapy can hope to rectify.

4. Relatedness

I have outlined in Chapter 7 the ways in which Freud's drive theory gradually became adapted to a more 'object'-relational approach, and post-Freudian analytic thought can be said to have continued this trend, so much so that it is possible to argue that Freud's pleasure principle has been replaced by a new 'relatedness principle'. In other words, for many post-Freudian theorists psychic energy is not directed towards reducing unpleasurable tension but towards having contact with other people. In

Fairbairn's words: 'it is not the libidinal attitude which determines the object-relationship, but the object-relationship which determines the libidinal attitude.'[9] In fact, one can say that people will put up with unpleasurable contact as long as it is contact and it is familiar: this is the repetition compulsion forcing us into old patterns of relationship. Indeed, it strikes me that many people's relationships are not all that pleasurable!

This also means that the drive as such diminishes in importance, or that the drive is considered to be intrinsically object-seeking, rather than being, as in Freud's formulations, objectless. In this light, Freud's conception of the human infant seems a rather autistic one, and indeed arguably his conception of the human being is somewhat autistic. Later analytic theory can therefore be seen as more socialized, in that the individual is seen as implicitly bound up with and emerging from social ties, or even that the individual cannot be conceived of in isolation. Rather than saying with Freud that our drives lead us in the end to others, it can be said that our relations with others create certain needs in us which remain in place for the rest of our life. In this light, neurosis can be defined as the perpetuation of a self-defeating need: for example, I need to keep trying to get close to someone who doesn't want to be close. Can therapy, as a new kind of relationship, help me first to notice that this is a basic pattern of mine, and second, to establish an alternative way of relating to someone who can tolerate intimacy? Of course, therapy doesn't 'cause' this change: that is the patient's choice and act. What therapy can do is elucidate the choices that are available and also bring to light how the patient's sense of choice had been blocked originally.

This clearly marks a different approach to analysis or therapy: for in the 'relational' approach the relationship between analyst and patient might well be considered to be the main agent of change, rather than the insightful interpretations provided by the analyst. To put it another way, patients can be said to be looking for relationship, when they first come to therapy, no doubt because early relationships in their life have failed to provide them with some vital element, such as containment, concern, reflecting back, and so on. In this context, insightful interpretations work only in so far as they are part of the relationship, not as isolated acts of intellectual perspicacity.

5. Fantasy

In the main, Freud sees fantasy as the result of frustration, but in later formulations, for example in Melanie Klein, fantasy – or in Klein's terminology, 'phantasy' – comes to be seen as one of the core ingredients of mental life. In other words, the psyche is a fantasizing organ; it doesn't create fantasies because reality is disappointing, but creates them all the time. We don't fantasize because we are unhappy; we are just as likely to do it when we are happy and fulfilled.

This offers some interesting links with creativity, which can in this context be seen as a primary function of the human mind. Rather than seeing creative acts as sublimated sexual urges, one can see creativity as a means of creating meaning, and that without that, human existence can come to seem empty and sterile.

The notions of the 'object' and of fantasy life have an interesting intersection here, for in the postwar development of analytic thought the notion of 'internal objects' becomes important. Clearly this idea is not new, for Freud's super-ego can be classed as an internal object (as indeed can the ego itself), but later theorists would considerably enlarge the concept so that the external world could be paralleled by a rich internal world, peopled in part by figures derived from outside, but having a life of their own. Thus one can speak of the internalized family, the inner critic, the lover, the demonic foe, and so on, as well as sub-human internal objects, such as breasts, penises, animals, fragments of objects, and so on.

This represents a considerable enrichment of the inner world, and can indeed achieve a theoretical primacy, in that some analytic therapists almost state that our key relationships are with inner figures, and that external relationships are reflections of these. This seems a rather frightening picture of human life, for it is almost solipsistic. I fall in love with one person in order to mirror one inner object; and come to hate another person in order to represent another. Yet the notion of an inner world peopled with such objects has great theoretical power: for example, it explains projection and introjection very elegantly. These ideas also bring about some surprising rapprochements: for example, Klein's theories often seem to run in parallel with Jung's – in both, the unconscious is considerably enriched and achieves an almost mythic or mythopoetic quality.

However, a compromise between inner-directed and outer-directed theory is possible. This would argue that one of the principal human responsibilities is to acknowledge the existence of an objective reality and to form satisfactory relationships with it and the people in it. In this light, those people who cling too much to their inner world and impose its order on the outer world can be said to be too introverted; just as perhaps those who deny the existence of an inner world at all can be said to be too extroverted. In psychotherapy one meets both kinds of people: the first deny the existence of the therapist; the second refuse to reflect on their own existence.

6. Language

In chapter 6 I made some brief remarks about the remarkable affinity between psychoanalysis and literature, and suggested that Freud had underlined the importance of story-telling in the therapeutic project. The rise of Lacanian psychoanalysis has considerably deepened and elaborated these ideas, so much so that for this school analysis itself might be described as a purely metacommunicative event. This not only relates to the conversations between analyst and patient, but also to the 'speech' of the unconscious itself, or the 'conversations' between different elements of the psyche. In such a model language achieves a tremendous importance: for out of speech and language the human self is created; knowledge itself can be conceived of only as a form of language; or most extremely, reality is a metalinguistic term. These ideas are closely connected with postmodernism, for now the analytic task is not to 'find the truth' about someone's life, or even to allow them to 'speak the unspeakable', but to come to the realization that the speaker was always defined by speech itself and cannot jump out of speech into some extra-linguistic Paradise. In other words, my desire is always circumscribed by the language of desire and cannot therefore ever truly fix on its object and feel satisfied – for we can never fill the lack created by our existence as figments of speech and language, nor find the object which is only another figment. In this sense, alienation is built into our existence as separate beings who speak: our speech attempts to cross the space between us, but how can it do so when I am always left with my irredeemable loneliness, always looking for a listener who will take this unbearable weight of words from me? In the most stark formulation, the ego is created out of dissatisfaction and can therefore never resolve it.

One might say that such ideas mark a fundamental divergence from Freud, yet there is a recognizable continuity as well. Freud also suggests that sexual desire is a kind of closed loop, which fixes on an object almost as a by-product, and therefore never finds resolution in the object. In desperation the ego takes the object into itself in order to achieve a perfect merger only to find that 'an object loss is turned into an ego loss'. The attempted merger has produced an horrific result: my own identity is undone by your absence.

Perhaps the 'linguistic turn' makes therapy too cerebral and too abstract. It certainly seems to take us away from Freud's stress on the instinctual side of life. Perhaps one of the sharpest criticisms of Lacanian analysis is that it neglects the body and the 'animal aspect of ourselves' which I referred to in chapter 9. In this sense, Lacan has bowdlerized Freud.

At the same time, the Lacanian emphasis on language is valuable in psychotherapy, for as a therapist or as a patient one is always balancing between the need to speak, which seems to offer some relief, and the realization that one can never speak the truth, which is always tantalizing us. This is probably part of the pessimism in Freud, and also throws into relief those critics of Freud, who have for example dug up old patients, such as the Wolf Man, and cry in triumph: 'But he is still neurotic!' Alternatively, one can find someone who has done analysis for twenty years and ask, 'What good has it done him?' Such derision misses the point: one might as well say that he has lived for twenty years, and what good has it done him.

Is the point of psychoanalysis to improve people's lives? I would say that misses the point as well, which is to find out first what your dissatisfaction is, for it is very likely that that dissatisfaction exists *sui generis*. Therefore I cannot improve your life, or even help you improve it – for you will be dissatisfied with that! In such ways, one can perhaps inch closer to the agonizing point of creation, whereby I have constructed my own dissatisfaction with life, in order to say of the world: 'I have made this'. This is the god-like omnipotence which haunts all human beings – and how unwilling we are to deconstruct such edifices, no matter how self-tormenting they are, for they give us the satisfaction of existing as selves and potent creators.

A multiple shift

It is clear that a multiple shift has occurred in psychoanalytic thought. It can be broken down into constituents: from sexuality to relationship; from drive to object; from internal to environmental etiology; from Oedipal to pre-Oedipal; from the paternal to the maternal emphasis. These shifts are often subsumed under the school of 'object relations' psychology, which first developed in Britain; but they are also characteristic of a number of American analysts, such as Kohut and Margaret Mahler. There is also the separate shift towards a discourse-related theory, so that a concern with historical 'events' or even inner objects has been partly superseded by a focus on our description of these things or, more pertinently, our inability to describe them.

No doubt the detractors of Freud are able at this point to throw their hands in the air and declare with glee that Freud has been routed; some of his most cherished ideas have been overthrown. However, this would be a spectacularly shallow judgement, rather akin to arguing that developments in Einsteinian physics demonstrate Newton's wrong turnings! This would be a bizarre view of scientific development, and indeed of the history of ideas in general – that a pioneer's ideas are invalidated by subsequent developments. On the contrary, it is preferable to say that in all disciplines, progress occurs through mistakes, or in the words of the American psychiatrist Herbert Peiser, 'psychoanalysis has moved forward over the graves of bad ideas'.[10]

Second, such a rejection of Freud would also ignore the fact that he anticipated many later developments in psychoanalysis. He seems to have had an uncanny ability to uncover ideas which would be developed more fully by later analysts. Thus the whole notion of object relations is surely implicit in Freud's development of the Oedipal complex, which focuses on the relationships between the infant and its parents. Similarly, the shift from the drive to the object is anticipated in Freud's later work on mourning, narcissism and other areas, wherein he argues that the ego is deeply implicated in its relations with an object, or even, that the ego is made up of abandoned relations with objects. The pre-Oedipal shift is also anticipated in Freud's late writings on femininity, where we see him discussing the early relationships between mother and female infant.

The multiple shift I have referred to can be described as a dual one: a shift from 'internal' to 'environmental' emphasis, and a shift from phallocentric to matricentric psychology. The first shift reverses the one that Freud made in the 1890s, when he abandoned the 'seduction theory'. However, object relations theory is less interested in the possibility of sexual abuse than in the emotional deprivation or emotional intrusiveness suffered by infants, particularly in their relationship to their mother. It is clear that the alternation between intra-psychic relations and external relations with others forms a key tension in psychoanalytic thought: that tension exists clearly enough in Freud, and its subsequent evolution in psychoanalysis is not surprising.

The shift towards mother/infant relations also seems inevitable in retrospect. Freud's leaning towards the paternal influence was so predominant, insistent even, that a reversal of it might be predicted and began to occur during his lifetime.

Another interesting development in psychological thought has been a growing rapprochement between psychoanalysis and Jungian psychology. This can be seen going on on both sides: a number of Jungians are interested in developments in psychoanalysis, and also find much of value in Freud's writings. Within psychoanalysis, the old hostility to Jung has abated amongst some analysts. One of the interesting areas of rapprochement concerns the notion of the 'self', which has been developed by analysts such as Kohut and Winnicott. Some Jungian analysts are able to bring these psychoanalysis developments into relationships with Jung's ideas about the Self, but at the same time it is arguable again that the concept of the self was anticipated in Freud, who often uses the notion of the ego to refer to a self-like phenomenon.

One might argue that if Freud could return, he would be appalled at the changes that have occurred in psychoanalysis. No doubt this is often true of intellectual pioneers, who become highly jealous of their own formulations. But what is unusual about Freud is his never-ending intellectual restlessness: he himself was able to revise his own ideas frequently. He was by no means a conservative thinker and was not afraid to change his mind.

Freud and Jung

Some critics of Freud have poured scorn on the various splits that have occurred within psychoanalysis and within psychotherapy as a whole. How can there be a canonical set of truths about the psyche, if the several hundred schools of therapy cannot agree amongst themselves about such truths? To my mind, this attitude betrays a naive view of the psyche and theories about it, and indeed a naive view of the general history of ideas. As far as I can see, modern astrophysics contains a number of theories about the Big Bang, the nature of the universe, and so on. Does this mean that physics is a non-science and is not intellectually viable? One might suggest the opposite: that physics is pushing back the frontiers in exciting ways and is peering as much into the unknown as the known.

In relation to psychotherapy, I would suggest that the psyche is so complex and fluid a phenomenon that one single set of hypotheses about it cannot capture its essence or its living manifestations. Let me give a personal example: in my lifetime, I have done three bouts of therapy, from three different schools – Humanistic, Jungian and Freudian. It would be bizarre to say that any one of those was 'incorrect' while another was 'correct': rather, at different periods of my life I needed a different approach. Furthermore, in some ultimate manner which I find very difficult to express, these three different outlooks on the psyche (and on life) do not contradict each other.

In this context, the Freud/Jung split bears closer scrutiny, for it is the most important split in the history of psychotherapy, and around it constellate a whole range of ideas about the psyche, about human existence and about therapy itself. Freud and Jung are the two founding fathers of modern psychotherapy. Their mutual fascination and then repulsion form one of the great tragic themes in modern thought, yet the split between them can be seen ultimately as necessary for the development of both sets of ideas. Furthermore, postwar psychotherapy has seen many movements towards reintegration and reconciliation between the two wings – for example, the so-called 'London' school of Jungian analysis has integrated many Freudian ideas; and certain psychoanalysts such as Kohut have incorporated a notion of the 'self' which appears to borrow much from Jung.[11] So although at times Freud and Jung seem remarkably distinct in their approach to the psyche and to the treatment of neurosis and psychosis, there are also bridges between the two which are being exploited today.

But let us begin with the differences. Early on in their relationship Jung wrote to Freud that as well as a 'psychoanalysis' he saw the need for a 'psychosynthesis'.[12] This did not meet with Freud's approval, and one can see in this apparently terminological quibble an important harbinger of the coming split. For Jung was already seeing neurosis as a forward-looking phenomenon – what he later called an unfulfilled life-task – whereas Freud was mostly concerned with the roots of neurosis in the past. In his case-study on the Wolf Man, Freud expressed his scorn about the Jungian notion of the life-task – how can a five-year-old have such ambitions?

> The study of children's neuroses exposes the complete inadequacy of these shallow or high-handed attempts at re- interpretation. It shows the predominant part that is played in the formation of neuroses by those libidinal motive forces which are so eagerly disavowed, and reveals the absence of any aspirations towards remote cultural aims, of which the child still knows nothing, and which cannot therefore be of any significance for him.[13]

The reference here to 'remote cultural aims' is undoubtedly a dig at Jung's notion of the teleological function of neurosis, pointing forwards to some goal in life which remains unfinished. These disagreements point to a radical differentiation in therapeutic technique. For Freud, the task is to uncover the unconscious and infantile roots of the neurosis; for Jung, to uncover the task which is yet to be accomplished and for which the neurotic symptoms act both as camouflage and emblem.

We can see also a difference in attitude to life: Freud is more concrete and practical; Jung more metaphysical and spiritual. Thus Freud's critics – including Jung – have often accused him of being reductive – perhaps a strange criticism, since all psychological procedures, including Jung's, are in the last analysis reductive, in the sense that they take the appearance of phenomena and give them an underlying reading.

I can illustrate these points with a concrete example. A patient of mine had a startling and beautiful dream in which he went on pilgrimage to Mecca (he is not a Muslim). When he arrived there, he made his way to the huge black rock at the centre of the site. Here he joined in the vast throngs who wheel around the rock in concentric circles. He described the ecstatic feelings as he joined in this mass worship.

I have presented this dream in several supervision groups and seminars, and it has been fascinating to hear the different reactions to it. Several Freudian or post-Freudian therapists suggested that the black rock represented the patient's mother, or even her breast or nipple; Jungian therapists that it represented the Self, around which everything in life revolves. The image of the crowds around the rock also reminds Jungians of the mandala – the circular symbol which Jung saw as an image of integration.

It strikes me that both interpretations are 'correct', and it would be absurd to say that one is 'better' than the other. Furthermore, different people at different periods in their lives might find one or the other interpretation valuable. Indeed, I have found with my own dreams that both quasi-Freudian and quasi-Jungian ideas about them occur to me at different times.

It is interesting that one of the patient's own readings of the Mecca dream was quite simply his growing spiritual life and his interest in religion and God. This can be termed a rather 'transparent' interpretation, but it is none the worse for that, although without doubt Freud would have been critical of it.

Furthermore, we can argue that the two sides are connected. In the above example, the notion of 'mother' and the notion of 'Self' could be said to be indelibly joined, since it is first through the relationship with one's mother that one begins to develop one's first sense of self and one's first apprehension that we are all joined together by having a common 'Self'.

Other differences are apparent in this example: Freud looks for a concrete, physical and sexual root to the dream-image; Jung is much less tied to the earth and sees such imagery as revelations of the soul's aspirations. One might say that for Jung, therapy is 'soul-work', for Freud, 'ego-work'.

Accordingly, there are two quite distinct attitudes to the unconscious. Freud sees it as infantile and potentially dangerous; Jung sees it as non-infantile, the source of creativity, the place of the soul, and also potentially dangerous. Whereas for Freud, the unconscious contains the repressed desires from infancy, for Jung it contains the desires for individuation which lead us to true adulthood. Hence a 'Freudian' therapy will tend to be much more regressive and concrete than a Jungian one.

Polarities

One can posit a set of polarities which distinguish Freud and Jung, although as already mentioned, there has been a considerable rapprochement between the two sides in the last two or three decades.

1. Instinct and psyche

For Freud, the instincts are biological forces which influence the psyche and produce the 'drives', which are psychic driving forces, in particular the sexual drive. Hence the Freudian theory of the psyche is a dualist one: body acts upon the mind. Much modern neurosis, Freud believes, stems from our inadequate attempts to deal with such primitive instinctual demands, to which modern civilization has generally been hostile.

For Jung, the psyche is a much more self-determining organ. It has its own processes and is not determined by the body's needs. Rather, Jung sees the need for 'individuation' – that is, the self-realization or fulfilment of the individual self – as the main driving force in the psyche.

There is a statement in one of Jung's letters which outlines the distinction between the two sides very eloquently (Jung is discussing the use of the term 'castration complex', which of course is a key concept in Freud):

> I regard this term not only as an aesthetic mistake but also as an erroneous overvaluation of sexual symbolisms. This complex actually has to do with the archetype of sacrifice, a far more comprehensive term and one which takes account of the fact that for primitives sex does not have anything like the significance it does for us. In primitive psychology one must always bear in mind that the search for food, or hunger, often plays a decisive role. Thus the symbols of

> sacrifice are not just castrations or derivates of the same, as is especially obvious when you consider the taboos, all of which have a sacrificial meaning. The tabooing of words or syllables, for instance, can only be derived from castration by sheer force. Rather we must look at actual or alleged castration in the light of the archetype of sacrifice, which would make all these manifold forms far easier to understand in an unobjectionable way. The term 'castration complex' is much too concretistic for my taste and too one-sided, although there are plenty of phenomena to which it proves perfectly applicable. But *I would have avoided everything that gives the appearance of deriving psychic events from a specific instinct. We must put the essence of the psyche at the beginning as a phenomenon sui generis and understand the instincts as being in a special relationship to it.* If we don't do this, all psychic differentiation is at bottom 'nothing but'. (added emphasis)[14]

This gives a very precise outline of the some of the key distinctions between Freud and Jung. Jung argues that terms such as 'castration complex' exaggerate the importance of sexuality, and crucially, obliterate the connection with deeper psychic structures – the archetype – in this case, that of sacrifice. Jung uses the word 'concretistic', which is a very significant term. He shies away from the instincts defined as primitive concrete demands on the organism and prefers the more metaphysical notion of the archetype.

This argument has a remarkable similarity to the distinctions between Hegel and Marx. Where Hegel posited abstract universals as the determining cause of history – for example, the idea of the state – Marx inverted this, and argued that the concrete or material processes of history gave rise to human concept such as 'state'. In other words, Hegel propounded a variety of idealism, and Marx reversed the equation to produce his own brand of materialism.[15]

One can say, therefore, that Jung is much more 'Hegelian' than Freud, particularly in his positing of the psyche as a 'phenomenon *sui generis*', not derivable from other phenomena. Jung's phrase 'nothing but' is rather scornful and was used in psychological arguments of the period to denote a simplistic form of reductionism – although of course, as I have pointed out, to relate castration to the 'archetype of sacrifice' is only another form of reductionism!

This discussion also makes it clear that many of the arguments concerning the respective merits of Freud and Jung can be attributed to the personalities of the disputants. Some people are naturally attracted to the more metaphysical speculations of Hegel, and others to the more earthy theories of Marx, and the same is true of Freud/Jung. We might say that Freud rests firmly on the earth, and is interested in heaven only in so far as he sees it as a reflection (or distortion) of earthly desires; whereas Jung accepts the existence of both heaven and earth and is fascinated in the relationship between them.

2. Past and future

To put it in simple terms, Freud looks back at the origins of neurosis, whereas Jung looks to the 'life-task' of which the neurosis is a sign. Even more starkly, we could say that Freud's project is reconstructive, Jung's teleological. The Freudian task is to remember, the Jungian task to uncover the drive to individual fulfilment.

At first, this distinction had very direct consequences for psychotherapy: whereas Freudian analysis and therapy focused on infantile developmental aspects, Jungian analysis was less concerned with this. Similarly, the Freudians traditionally have been more concerned with the relationship between therapist and patient as a prime exemplar of the patient's neurotic tendencies, whereas Jungians were more concerned with the imaginative life of the patient, especially in the shape of dreams, fantasies, creative work, and so on. However, these distinctions have been eroded since the 1970s – for example, the 'London' school of Jungian psychology has incorporated developmental psychology into its theoretical schema.[16]

None the less, these traditional distinctions still seem to hold. I recall talking about Oliver Cromwell with a group of therapists, and I was very struck by the difference between Freudians and Jungians: the former were very interested in Cromwell's relationship with his father (which led him to cut off the king's head), the Jungians with the mythological meanings of regicide. Certainly, if we go back in time and present this example to Freud and Jung, there is little doubt as to the very different responses of the two men.

The temporal distinction between past and future can also be related to that between personal and archetypal. For Freud, the past is a personal construction which shapes us today; for Jung, the archetype is an impersonal collective structure which gives us our destiny. Here the distinctions become quite glaring: both agree that we are lived by the unconscious, but for Freud that is a personal unconscious, for Jung a collective one.

3. Individual and collective

The concept of the collective unconscious is probably one of the most well-known features of Jung's psychology and provides a very sharp distinguishing trait from Freud. It can be seen at work in the argument over incest, which was one of the disagreements precipitating the final break. For Freud, the incest taboo is a barrier against genuine desire between parent and child. In this sense, incest is a concrete reality, always pressing itself against the taboo. However, for Jung the theme of incest is a much more mythological one, as he says in a letter to Freud:

> In my opinion the incest barrier can be no more explained by reduction to the possibility of real incest than the animal cult can be explained by reduction to real bestiality. The animal cult is explained by an infinitely long psychological development which is of paramount importance and not by primitive bestial tendencies . . . the incest taboo is the symbol or vehicle of a far wider and special meaning which has as little to do with real incest as hysteria with the sexual trauma.[17]

In effect, this letter, written in 1912, signifies an irrevocable movement away from Freud's position, which Freud was quick to appreciate, for Jung had turned the Freudian position upside down. Whereas Freud argued that the incest taboo – and many other sociological phenomena – comes into being as a response to real instinctual desires (the wish to have sex with one's parents), Jung was in effect arguing that incest has a wider and deeper symbolic significance, and that actual incest is the physical realization of this. One might make this distinction about sex in general: whereas Freud might argue that spirituality and religion are 'spiritualized' attempts to dilute or avoid sexual desire, Jung could argue within his own terms that sexual intimacy is a spiritual link or marks a bond between two souls. Another example of this inverse relationship can be seen in relation to religion. Whereas Freud argues that the notion of God represents a projection of infantile feelings about one's father, Jung argues that the infant projects onto his father archetypal and pre-existing images about God or the Self.[18]

To put it most bluntly, for Freud the archetype is a projection of the instinct; for Jung, the instinct is an expression of the archetype.

4. Rationalism and Romanticism

I have already discussed the combination in Freud of Enlightenment rationalism and German Romanticism – a combination which has provoked great hostility from both camps. Those who favour the rational/scientific world-view have criticized Freud for adopting 'subjective' and 'irrational' perspectives on psychology; those who favour the creative/imaginative side have criticized him for being too rational and too much concerned with understanding mental phenomena.

This polarity provides an interesting perspective on the Freud/Jung split, for Freud is aghast at Jung's exploration of mythology, mysticism, the occult – the 'black mud' which Freud seems to be both threatened and horrified by. One of Freud's tasks is to reduce such phenomena to rational principles, in particular infantile experience. For example, one can sense his pleasure as he informs Jung he has 'solved' the problem of the many myths of twins found in different cultures – that it relates to the placenta in the womb, conceived of as a 'lost' twin.[19]

One might say, therefore, that Jung went too far into the murky realms of Romanticism for Freud, and furthermore, Jung did not hasten to derive such phenomena from biological foundations, but argued that they existed in their own right. In particular, his notion of the archetype argues that the human mind is constructed in such a way that it spontaneously constructs mythical systems as reflections of itself. Thus one can argue that the relationship between the Virgin Mary and the Divine Child relates to the relationship between the unconscious and the ego which comes to life, in order to die again. In this sense, Jung's psychology is no less 'reductive' than Freud's, but it does grant the psyche its own order, whereas Freud tends to see psychic structure as emanations of instinctual drives. Jung almost inverts this, arguing as he does that the instinct flows from the archetype.

Jung can be said, therefore, to be both a Romantic and idealist; whereas Freud is a Romantic materialist. Of course, these labels are very crude and often misleading, but they do point to crucial distinctions between the two figures.

One might say that Jung's ideas are attractive to those people who need to explore the imaginative powers of the mind or need to escape from too mundane or 'earthly' existence. But for intellectuals and others who are oriented to the mind, Jungian thought can prove too heady I believe, and here Freudian therapy or analysis, with its emphasis on the instinctual and primitive aspects of our desires, is a healthy corrective.

13
Conclusions

I began this book by speaking of Freud as an Enlightenment rationalist, perhaps the last great exponent of such a mode of thought, and as a modernist. I have finished by describing him as a Romantic and a materialist. This is a pretty heady combination of characteristics to ascribe to anyone! Yet perhaps this gives us a clue to Freud's wide-ranging influence, which continued to the end of the twentieth century, and shows no sign of abating. Freud was not a narrow specialist, interested only in the technical causes of neurosis. His interests are remarkably catholic, ranging from the minutiae of psychological mechanisms to literature, history, human sexuality, anthropology, religion, and so on. We could say he was a great European thinker, bringing together many of the influences that have fertilized that continent's thought for centuries, including Judaism, empirical scientific studies, a Romantic fascination with the individual and a fierce anti-Christian polemic that is crucial to his psychological stance, which rejects overly ethical considerations of sexual behaviour.

Freudian thought has come in for heavy criticism from postmodernists for its grandiose claims, yet this is part of the appeal of psychoanalysis: it has a grandeur and nobility of thought and aspiration, that may seem redolent of nineteenth-century thought, somewhat reminiscent of Marx's grand sweep, but which still remains attractive to some today. Yet at the same time, Freud seems to point forward to some of the ideas found in postmodernism – the critique of moral schemes, the fragmentation of the self, the impossibility of knowing the objective truth or an objective past.

Above all, psychoanalysis as a practice is a fiercely intense and private experience for both analyst and patient, and marks both a celebration and a constant questioning of human subjectivity. In the end, it not only puts the question 'What is your story?', but also the more hazardous, 'Who is the story-teller?' People can eventually face the awful question as to whether they exist at all, and if they do, what stability or value their existence has, how much is it dependent on others' judgements, how much they are still living out their parents' fantasies, to what extent their life is run by unconscious fantasies, and so on. Of course, we are all inauthentic in varying degrees. Freud argues gloomily that civilization demands that sacrifice from us, if we are to live in community; others might dispute that and argue instead that industrialism and capitalism have caused this fundamental alienation. But the psychoanalytic procedure provides a context in which such alienation can be laid bare and partially rectified. Indeed, to be able to make the statement 'I am being inauthentic', strikes me as a considerable blow for authenticity!

The only comparison that I can find for psychoanalysis in human experience is Zen meditation, which also examines the nature of identity and selfhood in the most unrelenting, one might even say ruthless, manner. Truly, an intense analysis or psychotherapy is a formidable experience, which places one in front of that most unflattering of all mirrors: another human being.

Freud's conception of the unconscious made an indelible mark on the twentieth century: it struck a chord in many thinkers, artists, writers, film-makers. It is at once a Romantic assertion and yet also a cerebral one: it describes the foundation of human existence in terms of the primitive and the archaic, yet it also prizes our unravelling of its twists and turns, and our partial understanding of it.

It is clear that Freud lost his therapeutic zeal as he got older and more experienced; at times he verged on the edge of pessimism – that therapists are not in the business of 'curing' people, but work to earn money, and perhaps to help their patients understand their own peculiarities a little better, if they so wish. Yet behind that modest aim what a burning ambition can be felt in Freud's writings; what a fierce drive to describe and explain those puzzling messages from the unconscious. In a typically rhetorical passage, Freud describes how an obsessional structure which, he says, 'in waking life is known only in a truncated and distorted form, like a mutilated telegraph message, may have its actual text brought to light in a dream'.[1] In the same section of the Rat Man case, Freud observes that during an analysis the patient's disease 'speaks more plainly than before'. Those phrases are very Freudian somehow: on the one hand, 'a mutilated telegraph message', on the other hand, 'its actual text', which 'speaks plainly', and they have of course sparked great interest amongst contemporary students of discourse.

Thus for Freud, the unconscious does speak to us, but in a garbled form. Our task is to listen patiently to these messages and learn to decode them. It is evident that Freud was fascinated by these processes: the process of distortion and mutilation, and the converse process of elucidation and making clear. One voice wishes to speak to us; yet another sets itself against too plain speaking and brings in an obfuscation and a corruption which defies our understanding. Surely for Freud, the unconscious continues to fascinate precisely because it speaks in a mutilated form – at times, his efforts to decode it seem like sophisticated puzzle-solving; yet at its best, it forms part of a grandiose plan – to comprehend the Word which is our beginning and which we can no longer hear clearly. Lacan describes this in his enigmatic way: 'One began only to repeat after Freud the word of his discovery: *it speaks*, and no doubt, where it is least expected, namely, where there is pain.'[2] This strikes me as a brilliant distillation of Freud's discovery: that 'it' speaks, or even, in Freud's formulation, that it lives our lives, often unknown to us.

Freud dared to take on the unconscious. He dared to smoke the dragon out of its lair, not to kill it as St George did but to bring it into the daylight. He said to us that we don't have to be the victim of the unconscious, or be over-identified with it, or project it onto the outside world. We can become a little more separate from it, so that we can have a relationship with it.

This is why the details of Freud's theories can be endlessly criticized while at the same time the main thrust of his works stands as a permanent discovery, a conquest of the darkness and the invisible forces inside us. Even those ideas – such as the death instinct – which seem to show Freud over-reaching himself, none the less cause one to marvel at the grandeur of the conception.

Applied psychoanalysis

Why has psychoanalysis been used in so many other disciplines? In the first place, it is the most systematic theory of human psychology that is extant – probably its only serious competitor is Jungian psychology.

Second, its postulate of the ego/unconscious divide offers theorists and researchers in other disciplines a very sharp tool with which to analyse texts, behaviours, identities, and so on.

Third, one can point to Freud's dialectical model of the psyche: everything contains its opposite; A coexists with A; A turns into A, and back again; the notions of projection and introjection produce a very subtle instrument for examining the ways in which phenomena contain each other. This may seem a rather technical approach to Freud, but it proves invaluable in certain structural types of analysis, for example, in literature or cinema.

Fourth, one can point to the 'failure of identity' which sits at the heart of Freudian thought. This is very attractive to a contemporary or even postmodern critic or writer, for it points to the fractured nature of modern identity. For example, in gender studies a grounding in psychoanalytic thought enables us to say that no one entirely becomes a man or a woman, but achieves a partial approximation to those images, and that there will be many strange transitional phenomena on the boundaries, where for example a man longs to be a woman and vice versa.

Fifth, the notion of the unconscious as an irrational and primitive organ is welcome to those theorists who wish to puncture any claims to hegemony which rationalism might still be foolish enough to claim. For example, in the study of popular culture, it is clear enough that one of its driving forces is 'bad taste'. But why should this be so? In psychoanalytic terms, bad taste signifies those desires which are repressed, but which still force their way through into some kind of representation.

Sixth, psychoanalysis is developmental: it seeks to explain our present identity through shaping influences in the past; yet at the same time, the core of those influences – in the Oedipus complex – grounds each individual, and each family, in a universal framework. These ideas have been considerably adapted, for example in feminism, towards a more socio-political grasp of patriarchal culture, yet they prove valuable in bringing together individual psychology and collective sociological structures.

Thus Freud offered in his overall model of psychic development a series of observations with different focal lengths: first, the individual psyche with its fantastic internal dynamism; then the individual placed within a family nexus which prohibits certain desires and encourages others, and gives shape to the emerging identity of the infant; then the family placed within a civilization militantly opposed to pleasure, and reinforcing those critical and repressive voices. Although many of the details of this model can be, and have been, fiercely criticized, for their excessive reliance on anatomical distinctions or their masculinist bias, and so on, the overall schema of psyche–family–culture, wherein the family is seen as the conduit for various types of information, still represents one of the most elegant models of human psychology ever constructed. Furthermore, audaciously enough, Freud offered us not simply a descriptive model of the psyche but an explanatory one as well.

Which Freud?

At the beginning of chapter 6 I referred briefly to the different ways in which one might approach Freud. Certainly, in relation to psychoanalysis as a whole, there is a fundamental division between an intellectual approach and a personal approach. Someone who has encountered Freud's ideas as part of an educational project will have a very different sense of Freud from someone who has done an analytic therapy or an analysis. We might say that the first person will find psychoanalytic ideas interesting or uninteresting; the second person will probably have felt tortured by them, but hopefully in the end redeemed by them. A lengthy in-depth analysis is a journey to hell in some ways. I don't think that is an exaggeration, for it is a journey into one's own unconscious where the forces of darkness have gathered. Some of the ideas which Freud advanced, such as the infantile unconscious, may achieve an almost unbearable poignancy; the transference may come to dominate one's life; the sense of an 'it' directing one's life may feel terrifying; one's sense of guilt may come to seem outlandish. This may seem a gloomy or lurid portrait of analysis or therapy, yet I think for many people, it is like that. Of course, it also offers intimacy, understanding, love. Yet these aspects of relationship in themselves can prove very painful and difficult to take in.

There is a fundamental paradox here: Freud's ideas have had enormous appeal to many intellectuals in different disciplines and have considerably fertilized those disciplines, yet the practical therapeutic application of them involves both therapist and patient in hard, unrelenting work. I think this is part of Freud's appeal. He looked into the jaws of hell and came back and gave us various reports, couched admittedly in rather dry and ironic language. Yet this is a man who had seen death and pain and the agony of non-being which afflicts so many people in the West – a loss of soul, to use that seemingly unFreudian Freudian word. It is not surprising that his language is dry and ironic: this is a necessary defence against so much human pain and longing. How can one deal with this? How can one not? The fact that we can make this journey and return safely is in part owing to Freud's discoveries and work.

Notes

1 Introduction

1. J. Lacan, 'The Agency of the Letter in the Unconscious or Reason since Freud', in *Ecrits: A Selection* (London: Routledge, 1989), p. 172.
2. S. Freud, 'The Unconscious' in *On Metapsychology: The Theory of Psychoanalysis* (PFL Vol. 11) (Harmondsworth: Penguin, 1991), p. 191; and *Beyond the Pleasure Principle*, in *On Metapsychology*, pp. 299–300.
3. See H. F. Ellenberger, *The Discovery of the Unconscious: The History and Evolution of Dynamic Psychiatry* (London: Fontana, 1994).
4. S. Freud, *An Outline of Psychoanalysis* in *Historical and Expository Works on Psychoanalysis* (PFL Vol. 15) (Harmondsworth: Penguin, 1993), pp. 438–40.
5. S. Freud, *The Ego and the Id*, in *On Metapsychology*, p. 362.
6. See, for example, Jeffrey Masson, *The Assault on Truth: Freud and Child Sexual Abuse* (London: Fontana, 1992); F. Crews, *The Memory Wars: Freudian Science in Dispute* (New York: New York Review, 1995); F. Crews, *Unauthorized Freud: Doubters Confront a Legend* (Harmondsworth: Viking, 1998); A. Grünbaum, *The Foundations of Psychoanalysis: A Philosophical Critique* (Berkeley: University of California Press, 1984); Richard Webster, *Why Freud Was Wrong: Sin, Science and Psychoanalysis* (London: Fontana, 1996).
7. Freud, *The Ego and the Id*, pp. 393–4.
8. S. Freud, *Civilization and its Discontents*, in *Civilization, Society and Religion*, (PFL, Vol. 12) (Harmondsworth: Penguin, 1991) p. 303.
9. See Webster, *Why Freud Was Wrong*, pp. 299–510.
10. C. G. Jung, 'Diagnosing the Dictators', in W. McGuire and R. F. C. Hull (eds), *C. G. Jung Speaking* (London: Picador, 1980) pp. 123–40.
11. Freud, *The Ego and the Id*, pp. 390–401; S. Freud, 'The Economic Problem in Masochism', in *On Metapsychology*, pp. 413–26; S. Freud, 'A Disturbance of Memory upon the Acropolis', in *On Metapsychology*, pp. 447–56.
12. S. Freud, 'Mourning and Melancholia', in *On Metapsychology*, pp. 251–68.

2 Freud, modernism and postmodernism

1. T. S. Eliot, 'The Metaphysical Poets', in *Selected Prose*, ed. John Hayward (London: Penguin, 1953) p. 117.
2. C. McGinn, *The Character of Mind: An Introduction to the Philosophy of Mind* (Oxford: Oxford University Press, 1997) Chapter 2.
3. S. Freud, *An Autobiographical Study*, in *Historical and Expository Works on Psychoanalysis*, p. 242.
4. See I. Marshall and D. Zohard, *Who's Afraid of Schroedinger's Cat?* (London: Bloomsbury, 1997).
5. Peter Nicholls, *Modernisms: A Literary Guide* (Basingstoke: Macmillan, 1995) p. 18.

6. Patricia Waugh, 'Stalemates? Feminists, Postmodernists and Unfinished Issues in Modern Aesthetics', in P. Rice and P. Waugh (eds) *Modern Literary Theory: A Reader* (London: Arnold, 1996) p. 326.
7. S. Freud, *Introductory Lectures on Psychoanalysis* (PFL Vol. 1) (Harmondsworth: Penguin, 1991) p. 326.
8. Ibid., p. 326.
9. S. Freud, *New Introductory Lectures on Psychoanalysis* (PFL Vol. 2) (Harmondsworth: Penguin, 1991), pp. 195 ff.
10. Masud R. Khan, 'Freud and the Crises of Psychotherapeutic Responsibility', in *Hidden Selves: Between Theory and Practice in Psychoanalysis* (London: Karnac, 1989) p. 11.
11. Ibid., p. 29.
12. Masud R. Khan, 'Montaigne, Rousseau and Freud', in *The Privacy of the Self: Papers on Psychoanalytic Theory and Technique* (London: Hogarth, 1986) p. 111.
13. Freud, *Introductory Lectures on Psychoanalysis*, p. 53.
14. S. Freud, *The Interpretation of Dreams* (PFL Vol. 4) (Harmondsworth: Penguin, 1991), p. 769.
15. Freud, *Introductory Lectures on Psychoanalysis*, p. 112.
16. Freud, *The Interpretation of Dreams*, p. 705.
17. Freud, *Civilization and its Discontents*, p. 292.
18. J. Lacan, 'The Function and Field of Speech and Language in Psychoanalysis', in *Ecrits: A Selection* (London: Routledge, 1989), p. 42.
19. Freud, *Introductory Lectures on Psychoanalysis*, p. 130.
20. Joseph-Emile Muller and Frank Elgar, *A Century of Modern Painting* (London: Thames and Hudson, 1972), p. 75.
21. Freud, *An Autobiographical Study*, p. 214.
22. Freud, *The Ego and the Id*.
23. Freud, *New Introductory Lectures on Psychoanalysis*, pp. 187–8.
24. Ian Parker, 'Postmodernism and its Discontents: Therapeutic Discourse', *British Journal of Psychotherapy*, 12:4 (1996) p. 448.
25. J. Lacan, 'The Function and Field of Speech and Language in Psychoanalysis', in *Ecrits*, pp. 30–113.
26. J. Breuer and S. Freud, *Studies on Hysteria* (PFL Vol. 3) (Penguin: Harmondsworth, 1991), pp. 289, 346, 376.
27. S. Freud, 'Observations on Transference Love', in J. Strachey (ed.), *The Standard Edition of the Complete Psychological Works of Sigmund Freud*, Vol. 12 (London: Hogarth, 1986) pp. 162 and 168.
28. S. Freud, 'Analysis of a Phobia in a Five-Year-Old Boy ("Little Hans")', in *Case Histories I* (PFL, Vol. 8) (Harmondsworth: Penguin, 1990) p. 301.
29. Lawrence Cahoone, 'Introduction', *From Modernism to Postmodernism* (Cambridge, Mass., Basil Blackwell, 1996) pp. 14–16.
30. E. Grosz, *Jacques Lacan: A Feminist Introduction* (London: Routledge, 1990) pp. 35 and 80.
31. Freud, *Civilization and its Discontents*, pp. 263–73.
32. Ibid., p. 305.
33. See Lis Moller, *The Freudian Reading: Analytical and Fictional Constructions* (Philadelphia: University of Pennsylvania Press, 1991).

34. S. M. Gilbert and S. Gubar, *The Madwoman in the Attic: The Woman Writer and the Nineteenth-Century Literary Imagination* (New Haven: Yale University Press, 1984) pp. 336–71.
35. See E. A. Kaplan, *Psychoanalysis and Cinema* (New York: Routledge, 1990).

3 Truth, knowledge and subjectivity

1. S. Freud, 'Notes upon a Case of Obsessional Neurosis', in *Case Histories II* (PFL Vol. 9) (Harmondsworth: Penguin, 1991), p. 57.
2. S. Freud, *An Autobiographical Study*, in *Historical and Expository Works on Psychoanalysis*, pp. 217–18.
3. Jeffrey Masson, *The Assault on Truth: Freud and Child Sexual Abuse* (London: Fontana, 1992) p. 11.
4. S. Freud, 'Neurosis and Psychosis', in *On Psychopathology* (PFL Vol. 10) (Harmondsworth: Penguin, 1993) pp. 213–14.
5. S. Freud, 'Fragment of an Analysis of a Case of Hysteria ("Dora")', in *Case Histories I*, p. 59.
6. Michel Foucault, *The History of Sexuality: An Introduction* (Harmondsworth: Penguin, 1990) pp. 53–4.
7. S. Freud, 'Notes upon a Case of Obsessional Neurosis', in *Case Histories II*, p. 103.
8. Karl Marx, 'Concerning Feuerbach', in *Early Writings* (Harmondsworth: Penguin, 1981) p. 423.
9. S. Freud, *New Introductory Lectures on Psychoanalysis*, pp. 105–7.
10. Freud, *The Ego and the Id*, p. 364.
11. Ibid., p. 376.
12. James Grotstein, 'Bion, The Pariah of "O"', *British Journal of Psychotherapy* (1997) 14:1, pp. 77–90.
13. B. Bettelheim, *Freud and Man's Soul* (New York: Knopf, 1983).
14. Richard Webster, *Why Freud Was Wrong: Sin, Science and Psychoanalysis* (London: Fontana, 1996), pp. 467–9.
15. C. Sheridan and S. Radmacher, *Health Psychology: Challenging the Biomedical Model* (New York: Wiley, 1992).
16. See David Smith, 'On the Eve of a Revolution: Freud's Concepts of Consciousness and Unconsciousness in "Studies in Hysteria" and "The Project for a Scientific Psychology"', *British Journal of Psychotherapy* (1992) 9:2, pp. 150–6.
17. Stephen Frosh, *For and Against Psychoanalysis* (London: Routledge, 1997) p. 40.
18. Ibid., pp. 35–8 and 234–5.
19. See Colin McGinn, *The Character of Mind* (Oxford: Oxford University Press, 1997), pp. 107–16.
20. See Donna Haraway, *Primate Visions: Gender, Race and Nature in the World of Modern Science* (New York: Routledge, 1989).
21. See Paul Kline, *Psychology and Freudian Theory: An Introduction* (London: Routledge, 1995).
22. F. Crews, *The Memory Wars* (New York: New York Review, 1995), p. 36.
23. Freud, *The Ego and the Id*, pp. 355–6.

4 The unconscious

1. H. F. Ellenberger, *The Discovery of the Unconscious* (London: Fontana, 1994), pp. 271–8.
2. Freud, *Introductory Lectures on Psychoanalysis*, p. 250.
3. Freud, *New Introductory Lectures on Psychoanalysis*, p. 106.
4. Freud, *Introductory Lectures on Psychoanalysis*, p. 130.
5. Freud, *Civilization and its Discontents*, p. 305.
6. See P. Polledri, 'Forensic Psychotherapy with a Potential Serial Killer', in *British Journal of Psychotherapy* (1997) 13: 4, pp. 473–88.
7. S. Freud, 'The Unconscious', in *On Metapsychology*, p. 168.
8. Ibid., p. 168.
9. S. Freud, 'Notes upon a Case of Obsessional Neurosis', in *Case Studies II*, p. 66.
10. Freud, *An Autobiographical Study*, p. 245.
11. H. F. Searles, 'The Schizophrenic's Vulnerability to the Therapist's Unconscious Processes', in *Collected Papers on Schizophrenia and Related Subjects* (London: Maresfield, 1986) pp. 192–215.
12. Freud, *Introductory Lectures on Psychoanalysis*, p. 256.
13. James S. Grotstein, 'Reflections on a Century of Freud: Some Paths Not Chosen', *British Journal of Psychotherapy*, (1992) 9:2, pp. 181–7.
14. Freud, *New Introductory Lectures*, pp. 105–7.
15. Freud, *Introductory Lectures on Psychoanalysis*, p. 453.
16. Freud, *Civilization and its Discontents*, p. 295.
17. Ibid., p. 306.
18. See T. E. Hays and P. H. Hays, 'Opposition and Complementarity of the Sexes in Ndumba Initiation', in Gilbert Herdt (ed.), *Rituals of Manhood: Male Initiation in Papua New Guinea*, (Berkeley: University of California, 1982).
19. Freud, *Case Histories I*, p. 301.
20. Freud, *Civilization and its Discontents*, p. 85.
21. H. F. Searles, 'Positive Feelings in the Relationship between the Schizophrenic and his Mother', in *Collected Papers*, p. 216.
22. Freud, *An Outline of Psychoanalysis*, pp. 392 and 404–7.
23. Ibid., p. 437.
24. Freud, *The Ego and the Id*, p. 355.
25. Ibid., p. 356.
26. Ibid., p. 363.
27. Freud, *Beyond the Pleasure Principle*, p. 311.
28. Ibid., p. 327.
29. Ibid., pp. 311–12.

5 Forgetting, repeating and remembering

1. Freud, *Introductory Lectures on Psychoanalysis*, p. 507.
2. S. Freud, 'Observations on Transference Love', in *Standard Edition*, Vol. 12, p. 166.
3. See S. Freud, 'Remembering, Repeating and Working-through' in *Standard Edition*, Vol. 12, pp. 147–56.

4. J. Lacan, 'The Function and Field of Speech and Language in Psychoanalysis', in *Ecrits: A Selection* (London: Routledge, 1989) p. 52.
5. S. Freud, *Beyond the Pleasure Principle*, in *On Metapsychology*, p. 311.
6. S. Freud, 'Remembering, Repeating and Working-through', in *Standard Edition*, Vol. 12, p. 149.
7. Christopher Bollas, *The Shadow of the Object: Psychoanalysis of the Unthought Known* (London: Free Association, 1987).
8. On castration, see Freud, 'Some Psychical Consequences of the Anatomical Differences between the Sexes'; on the primal scene, see S. Freud, 'From the History of an Infantile Neurosis (the "Wolf Man")', in *Case Histories II*, pp. 281–95.
9. J. M. Masson (ed.) *The Complete Letters of Sigmund Freud to Wilhelm Fliess 1887–1904* (Cambridge, Mass.: The Belknap Press, 1985) p. 207.
10. For a fuller discussion, see R. Shafer, *Retelling a Life: Narration and Dialogue in Psychoanalysis* (New York: Basic Books, 1992).
11. Freud, *The Interpretation of Dreams*, p. 705.

6 Story-telling

1. See R. Shafer, *Retelling a Life: Narration and Dialogue in Psychoanalysis* (New York: Basic Books, 1992).
2. S. Freud, 'Fragment of an Analysis of a Case of Hysteria ("Dora")' in *Case Histories I*, p. 45.
3. Ibid., p. 47.
4. S. Freud, 'Notes upon a Case of Obsessional Neurosis', in *Case Histories II*, pp. 50 and 53.
5. Ibid., p. 90.
6. Ibid., p. 97.
7. Freud, 'Fragment of an Analysis of a Case of Hysteria ("Dora")', p. 93.
8. S. Freud, 'Remembering, Repeating and Working-through', in *Standard Edition*, Vol. 12, p. 147.
9. S. Freud, 'From the History of an Infantile Neurosis', *Case Histories II*, p. 285.
10. Freud, 'Notes upon a Case of Obsessional Neurosis', p. 87.
11. See Lionel Trilling, 'Freud and Literature', in D. Lodge (ed.) *Twentieth Century Literary Criticism* (London: Longman, 1972) pp. 276–90.
12. Terry Eagleton, *Literary Theory: An Introduction* (Oxford: Blackwell, 1996), pp. 64–78.
13. A. C. Bradley, *Shakespearean Tragedy* (London: Macmillan, 1904); compare J. Dollimore and A. Sinfield (eds) *Political Shakespeare: Essays in Cultural Materialism* (Manchester: Manchester University Press, 1994).
14. S. Freud, 'The Unconscious', in *On Metapsychology*, pp. 206–10.

7 Instincts and environment

1. See J. R. Greenberg and S. A. Mitchell, *Object Relations in Psychoanalytic Theory* (Cambridge, Mass.: Harvard University Press, 1983).
2. Freud, *Introductory Lectures on Psychoanalysis*, pp. 355–6.
3. S. Freud, *The Ego and the Id*, p. 374.

4. Masud R. Khan, 'Montaigne, Rousseau and Freud', in *The Privacy of the Self* (London: Hogarth, 1986).
5. See L. Appignanesi and J. Forrester, *Freud's Women* (London: Weidenfeld & Nicolson, 1992), pp. 240–71.
6. Ibid., pp. 387–91.
7. S. Freud, 'Instincts and their Vicissitudes', in *On Metapsychology*, p. 116.
8. Freud, *Introductory Lectures on Psychoanalysis*, p. 407.
9. S. Freud, *Inhibitions, Symptoms and Anxiety*, in *On Psychopathology*, p. 294.
10. John Bowlby, *Attachment and Loss*, Volume 2, *Attachment* (Harmondsworth: Penguin, 1978), p. 104.
11. M. Brook and T. Birkhead (eds) *The Cambridge Encyclopedia of Ornithology* (Cambridge: Cambridge University Press, 1991), pp. 249–50.
12. An example found in John Bowlby, *Attachment and Loss*, Volume 1, *Separation: Anxiety and Anger* (Harmondsworth: Penguin, 1978), pp. 40–1.
13. M. Balint, 'Changing Therapeutical Aims and Techniques in Psychoanalysis', in *Primary Love and Psycho-analytic Technique* (London: Maresfield, 1985), p. 227.
14. Freud, *New Introductory Lectures in Psychoanalysis*, p. 108.
15. S. Freud, 'Neurosis and Psychosis', in *On Psychopathology*, p. 214.
16. Freud, *Introductory Lectures in Psychoanalysis*, p. 393.
17. Lou Andreas-Salomé, *The Freud Journal* (London: Quartet, 1987) pp. 91–2.
18. Freud, *Introductory Lectures in Psychoanalysis*, pp. 398–9.
19. Ibid., pp. 355–6.
20. Ibid., p. 380.
21. Freud, 'Instincts and their Vicissitudes', p. 119.
22. Freud, *The Ego and the Id*, p. 367.
23. Ibid., p. 374.
24. Ibid., pp. 368–9.
25. Ibid., p. 369.
26. Greenberg and Mitchell, *Object Relations in Psychoanalytic Theory*, pp. 400–1.
27. Ibid., p. 402.
28. Ibid., p. 407.
29. A. Piontelli, 'Pre-natal Life and Birth as Reflected in the Analysis of a Two-year old Psychotic Girl', *International Review of Psycho-analysis* (1988) 15, pp. 73–81.
30. C. Shelley, *Contemporary Perspectives on Psychotherapy and Homosexualities* (London: Free Association, 1998).

8 Dialectics in the psyche

1. S. Freud, 'A Disturbance of Memory upon the Acropolis', in *On Metapsychology*, p. 450.
2. S. Freud, 'Mourning and Melancholia', in *On Metapsychology*, pp. 252–3.
3. Ibid., p. 258.
4. Ibid., p. 257.
5. See M. Klein, *Envy and Gratitude*, in *Envy and Gratitude and Other Works 1946–63* (London: Virago, 1988) pp. 176–235.
6. Freud, 'Mourning and Melancholia', p. 260.

7. Ibid., pp. 260–1.
8. Freud, *Civilization and its Discontents*, p. 322.
9. Freud, 'Mourning and Melancholia', p. 253.
10. Ibid., p. 261.
11. See D. W. Winnicott, 'The Theory of the Parent–Infant Relationship', in *The Maturational Processes and the Facilitating Environment: Studies in the Theory of Emotional Development*, (London: Karnac, 1990) pp. 37–55; D. W. Winnicott, 'Mirror-role of Mother and Family in Child Development', in *Playing and Reality* (Harmondsworth: Penguin, 1985) pp. 130–8.
12. P. Polledri, 'Forensic Psychotherapy with a Potential Serial Killer'.
13. S. Freud, 'The Dynamics of Transference', in *Standard Edition* Vol. 12, p. 108.
14. Freud, *Introductory Lectures on Psychoanalysis*, p. 331.
15. Ibid., p. 332.
16. S. Freud, 'Observations on Transference-Love', *Standard Edition* Vol. 12, pp. 165–6, 169–71.

9 Contradictions in sexuality

1. M. Foucault, *The History of Sexuality*, Vol. I, *An Introduction* (Harmondsworth: Penguin, 1990), p. 7.
2. Ibid., p. 159.
3. S. Freud, *Introductory Lectures on Psychoanalysis*, p. 341.
4. Ibid., p. 401.
5. Freud, *An Outline of Psychoanalysis*, p. 433.
6. Freud, *Civilization and its Discontents*, p. 263.
7. Ibid., pp. 263–4.
8. M. Foucault, *The History of Sexuality*, Vol. I, *An Introduction*, p. 69.
9. Ibid., p. 12.
10. Ibid., p. 105.
11. Ibid., p. 63.
12. Freud, *Three Essays on the Theory of Sexuality*, pp. 131–3.
13. S. Freud, '"Civilized" Sexual Morality and Modern Nervous Illness', in *Civilization, Society and Religion*, p. 43.
14. See Chris Knight, *Blood Relations: Menstruation and the Origin of Culture* (New Haven: Yale University Press, 1991).
15. K. Lewes, *The Psychoanalytic Theory of Male Homosexuality* (London: Quartet, 1989).
16. S. Freud, 'The Sexual Enlightenment of Children', in *On Sexuality*, p. 178.
17. S. Freud, '"Civilized" Sexual Morality and Modern Nervous Illness', in *Civilization, Society and Religion*, p. 47.
18. J. Lacan, *Ecrits: A Selection* (London: Routledge, 1989), p. 42.
19. J. Lacan, 'God and the *Jouissance* of The Woman', in J. Mitchell and J. Rose (eds), *Feminine Sexuality: Jacques Lacan and the école freudienne* (Basingstoke: Macmillan, 1982) p. 143; 'Seminar of 21 January 1975', in *Feminine Sexuality*, p. 170.
20. J. Brenkman, *Straight Male Modern: A Cultural Critique of Psychoanalysis* (New York: Routledge, 1993).
21. P. Gay, *Freud: A Life for our Time* (London: Papermac, 1995) pp. 470–87.

22. S. Freud, *Beyond the Pleasure Principle*, in *On Metapsychology*, pp. 324–5.
23. S. Freud, *The Ego and the Id*, p. 386.
24. J. Rose, 'Femininity and its Discontents', in *Sexuality in the Field of Vision* (London: Verso, 1991), p. 91.
25. R. Horrocks, *Masculinity in Crisis: Myths, Fantasies and Realities* (Basingstoke: Macmillan, 1994).
26. Rose, 'Femininity and its Discontents', p. 90.
27. Ibid., p. 93.

10 Femininity, feminism and psychoanalysis

1. See R. Horrocks, *Male Myths and Icons: Masculinity in Popular Culture* (Basingstoke: Macmillan, 1995) pp. 101–25.
2. See D. Gilmore, *Manhood in the Making: Cultural Concepts of Masculinity* (New Haven: Yale University Press, 1990) pp. 26–9, 93–8.
3. Ibid., pp. 30–55.
4. Freud, *Three Essays on the Theory of Sexuality.*
5. Freud, *An Outline of Psychoanalysis*, p. 386.
6. Freud, *New Introductory Lectures on Psychoanalysis*, p. 151.
7. Freud, *Introductory Lectures on Psychoanalysis*, p. 360.
8. S. Freud, 'On the Sexual Theories of Children', in *On Sexuality.*
9. Ibid., p. 195.
10. Karen Horney, 'The Dread of Woman', in *Feminine Psychology* (New York: W. W. Norton, 1973) p. 144.
11. Freud, *New Introductory Lectures on Psychoanalysis*, p. 160.
12. S. Freud, 'Female Sexuality', in *On Sexuality*, pp. 383–7.
13. S. Freud, 'The History of the Psychoanalytic Movement', in *Historical and Expository Works on Psychoanalysis*, pp. 115–16.
14. S. Freud, 'Some Psychical Consequences of the Anatomical Distinction Between the Sexes', in *On Sexuality*, p. 337.
15. Freud, 'Female Sexuality', p. 391.
16. Freud, *New Introductory Lectures on Psychoanalysis*, p. 149.
17. Ibid., p. 166.
18. Freud, 'Female Sexuality', p. 373.
19. S. Freud, 'Analysis of a Phobia in a Five-Year-Old Boy ("Little Hans")', *Case Studies I*, p. 182.
20. Ibid., p. 256.
21. Ibid., p. 254.
22. Ibid., p. 252n.
23. See M. Sprengnether, *The Spectral Mother: Freud, Feminism and Psychoanalysis* (Ithaca, NY: Cornell University Press, 1990) pp. 55–63.
24. Freud, 'Analysis of a Phobia in a Five-Year-Old Boy ("Little Hans")', pp. 229, 250, 284–6.
25. Freud, 'The History of the Psychoanalytic Movement', p. 115.
26. Gay, *Freud: A Life for our Time* (London: Papermac, 1995), p. 236.
27. Freud, 'Analysis of a Phobia in a Five-Year-Old Boy ("Little Hans")', p. 299.
28. See L. Hudson and B. Jacot, *The Way Men Think: Intellect, Intimacy and the Erotic Imagination* (New Haven: Yale University Press, 1991).

29. J. Mitchell, *Psychoanalysis and Feminism* (Harmondsworth: Penguin, 1990), p. xv.
30. K. Horney, 'The Flight from Womanhood', in *Feminine Psychology*, pp. 60–2.
31. Simone de Beauvoir, *The Second Sex* (Harmondsworth: Penguin, 1972) p. 82.
32. Eva Figes, *Patriarchal Attitudes* (London: Faber & Faber, 1970) p. 148.
33. Freud, *Introductory Lectures on Psychoanalysis*, p. 112.
34. But see L. Segal, *Slow Motion: Changing Masculinities, Changing Men* (London: Virago, 1990).

11 Dreams, jokes and films

1. S. Freud, 'A Note on the Unconscious in Psychoanalysis', in *On Metapsychology*, p. 55
2. Freud, *New Introductory Lectures on Psychoanalysis*, p. 43.
3. Ibid., p. 47
4. Freud, 'A Note on the Unconscious in Psychoanalysis', pp. 55–6.
5. Freud, *The Interpretation of Dreams*, p. 714.
6. Freud, *New Introductory Lectures on Psychoanalysis*, p. 39.
7. Freud, *Introductory Lectures on Psychoanalysis*, p. 238.
8. Freud, *The Interpretation of Dreams*, p. 748.
9. C. G. Jung, *Two Essays on Analytical Psychology*, in H. Read, M. Fordham and G. Adler (eds) *The Collected Works of C. G. Jung*, Volume 7 (London: Routledge & Kegan Paul, 1977) pp. 63–111.
10. S. Freud, *Jokes and their Relation to the Unconscious* (PFL Vol. 6) (Harmondsworth: Penguin, 1991) p. 140.
11. Ibid., p. 222.
12. Ibid., pp. 227–8.
13. Freud, *An Outline of Psychoanalysis*, p. 413.
14. Freud, *Introductory Lectures on Psychoanalysis*, p. 404.
15. Freud, *Jokes and their Relation to the Unconscious*, p. 224.
16. Ibid., p. 228n
17. The literature on psychoanalysis and cinema is vast: I have used C. Metz, *Psychoanalysis and Cinema: The Imaginary Signifier* (London: Macmillan, 1983); E. A. Kaplan (ed.) *Psychoanalysis and Cinema* (New York: Routledge, 1990); Y. Tasker. *Spectacular Bodies: Gender, Genre and the Action Cinema* (London: Routledge, 1993); Tania Modleski, *The Women who Knew Too Much: Hitchcock and Feminist Film Theory* (New York: Methuen, 1988); C. Penley (ed.) *Feminism and Film Theory* (New York: Routledge, 1988); B. Creed, *The Monstrous-Feminine: Film, Feminism and Psychoanalysis* (London: Routledge, 1993); S. Cohan and I. R. Hark (eds) *Screening the Male: Exploring Masculinities in the Hollywood Cinema* (London: Routledge, 1993); C. Clover, *Men, Women and Chainsaws: Gender in Modern Horror Film* (London: BFI, 1992); J. Rose, *Sexuality in the Field of Vision*; V. Lebeau, *Lost Angels: Psychoanalysis and Cinema* (London: Routledge, 1995).
18. See B. Creed, *The Monstrous-Feminine*, pp. 73–83.
19. Carol Clover, *Men, Women and Chainsaws*, pp. 3–5.
20. J. Rose, 'The Imaginary' in *Sexuality in the Field of Vision* (London: Verso, 1991).

12 Revisions and criticisms

1. B. Simon and R. B. Blass, 'The Development and Vicissitudes of Freud's Ideas on the Oedipus Complex', in J. Neu (ed.) *The Cambridge Companion to Freud* (Cambridge University Press, 1991) pp. 161–74.
2. Ernest Jones, 'Psycho-analysis and the Instincts', in *Papers on Psycho-analysis* (London: Karnac, 1977) p. 139.
3. W. R. D. Fairbairn, 'Endopsychic Structure Considered in Terms of Object-relationships', in *An Object-relations Theory of the Personality* (New York: Basic Books, 1952) p. 127.
4. See J. R. Greenberg and S. A. Mitchell, *Object Relations in Psychoanalytic Theory* (Cambridge, Mass: Harvard University Press, 1983), pp. 154–5.
5. A. Lowen, *Bioenergetics* (Harmondsworth: Penguin, 1978).
6. See Masud R. Khan, 'Intimacy, Complicity and Mutuality in Perversion', in *Alienation in Perversion* (London: Maresfield, 1989) pp. 18–30.
7. Christopher Lucas, 'Exhibitionism', *British Journal of Psychotherapy* (1990) 7:1, p. 19.
8. S. Freud, 'Psychoanalytic Notes on an Autobiographical Account of a Case of Paranoia (Dementia Paranoides)', in *Case Histories II*, pp. 131–223; L. Breger, *Freud's Unfinished Journey: Conventional and Critical Perspectives in Psychoanalytic Theory* (London: Routledge & Kegan Paul, 1981) Chapter 5.
9. W. R. D. Fairbairn, *Psychoanalytic Studies of the Personality* (London: Routledge & Kegan Paul, 1952) p. 34.
10. F. Crews, *The Memory Wars* (New York: New York Review, 1995), p. 93.
11. K. Lambert, *Analysis, Repair and Individuation* (London: Academic Press, 1981).
12. W. McGuire (ed.) *The Freud/Jung Letters: the Correspondence between Sigmund Freud and C. G. Jung* (London: Hogarth, 1974), p. 216.
13. S. Freud, 'From the History of an Infantile Neurosis', in *Case Histories II*, p. 236.
14. G. Adler (ed.) *C. G. Jung: Letters* (London: Routledge & Kegan Paul, 1973), p. 467.
15. K. Marx, 'Critique of Hegel's Doctrine of the State', in *Early Writings* (Harmondsworth: Penguin, 1974), pp. 57–198.
16. Lambert, *Analysis, Repair and Individuation*, pp. 106–32.
16. McGuire (ed.) *The Freud/Jung Letters*, p. 506.
18. C. G. Jung, 'The Psychology of the Unconscious', in *Two Essays on Analytical Psychology*, pp. 88ff.
19. McGuire (ed.) *The Freud/Jung Letters*, p. 449.

13 Conclusions

1. S. Freud, 'Notes upon a Case of Obsessional Neurosis', in *Case Histories II*, p. 103.
2. J. Lacan, *Ecrits: A Selection* (London: Routledge, 1989) p. 125.

Index